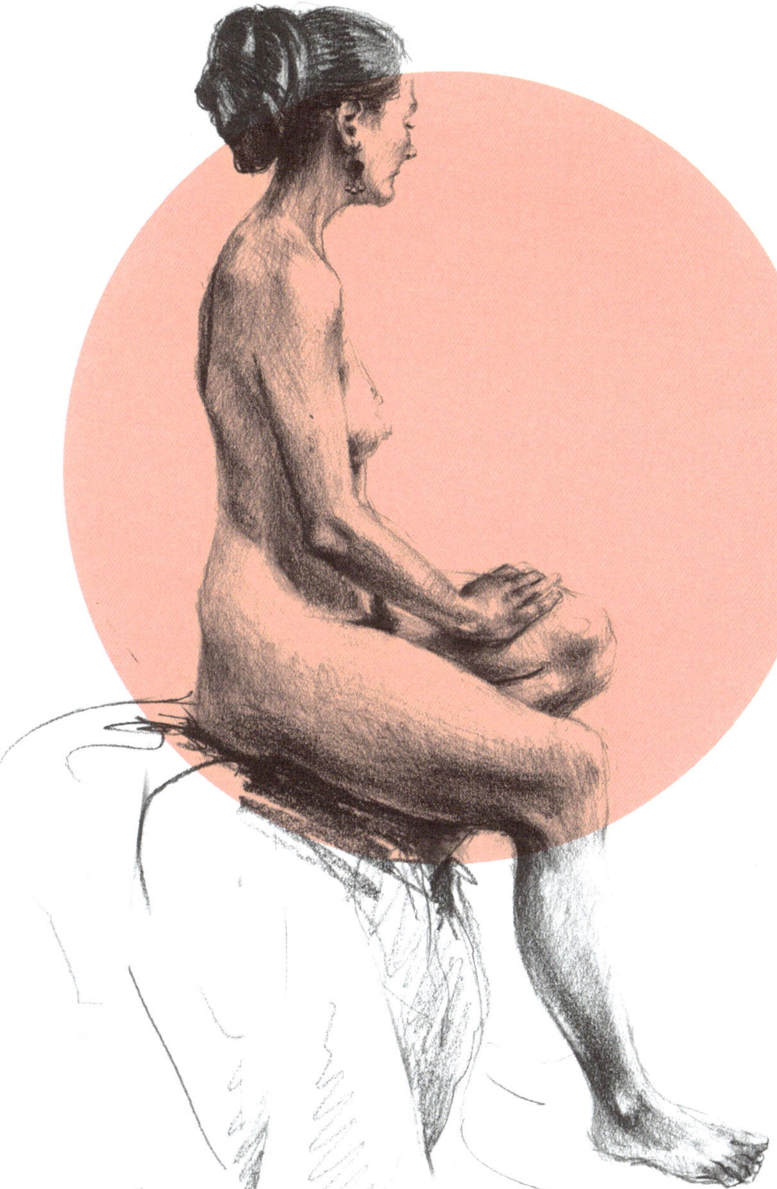

Sketch Club

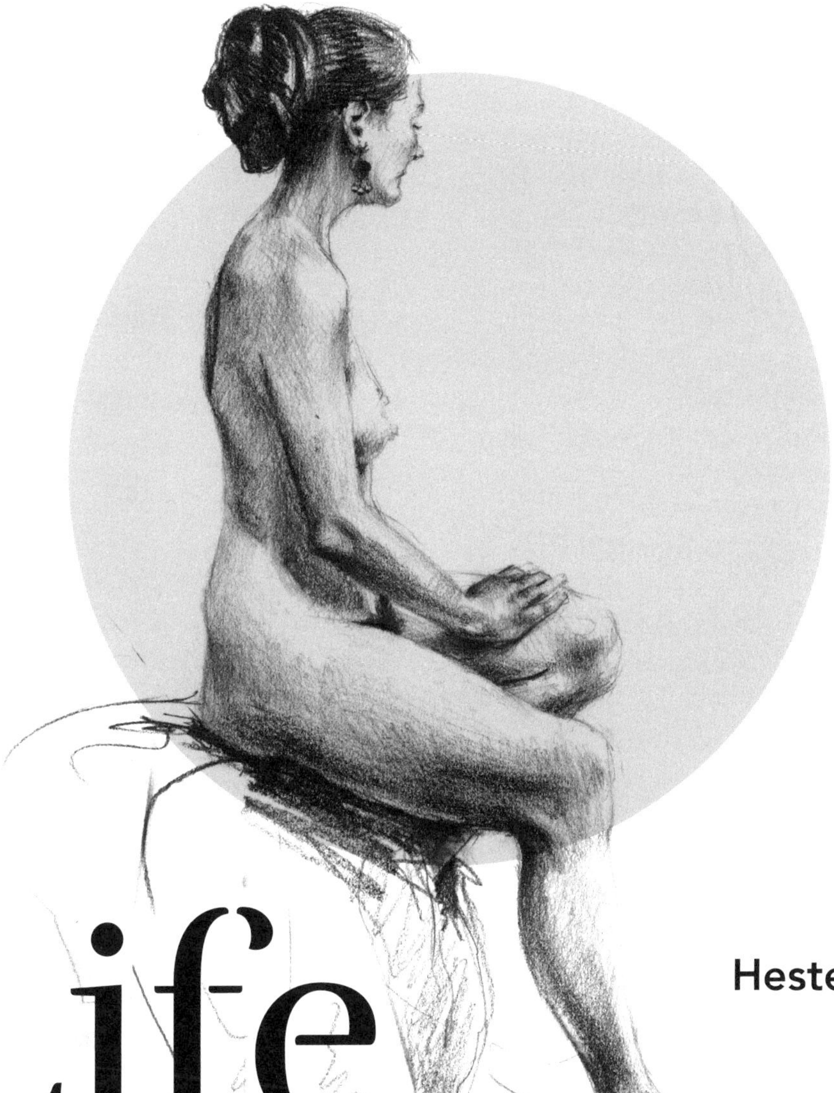

Life Drawing

Hester Berry

ilex

An Hachette UK Company
www.hachette.co.uk

First published in Great Britain in 2019 by
ILEX, an imprint of Octopus Publishing Group Ltd
Octopus Publishing Group
Carmelite House
50 Victoria Embankment
London, EC4Y 0DZ
www.octopusbooks.co.uk

Distributed in the US by Hachette Book Group,
1290 Avenue of the Americas, 4th and 5th Floors,
New York, NY 10104
Distributed in Canada by Canadian Manda Group,
664 Annette St., Toronto, Ontario, Canada M6S 2C8

Publisher: Alison Starling
Editorial Director: Zena Alkayat
Commissioning Editor: Zara Anvari
Managing Editor: Rachel Silverlight
Project Editor: Ellie Wilson
Junior Editor: Ellie Corbett
Art Director: Ben Gardiner
Production Manager: Caroline Alberti
Design: JC Lanaway

Ilex is proud to partner with Tate; supporting the gallery in its mission to promote public understanding and enjoyment of British, modern and contemporary art.

ISBN 978-1-78157-654-0

A CIP catalogue record for this book is available from the British Library

Printed and bound in China

10 9 8 7 6 5 4 3 2 1

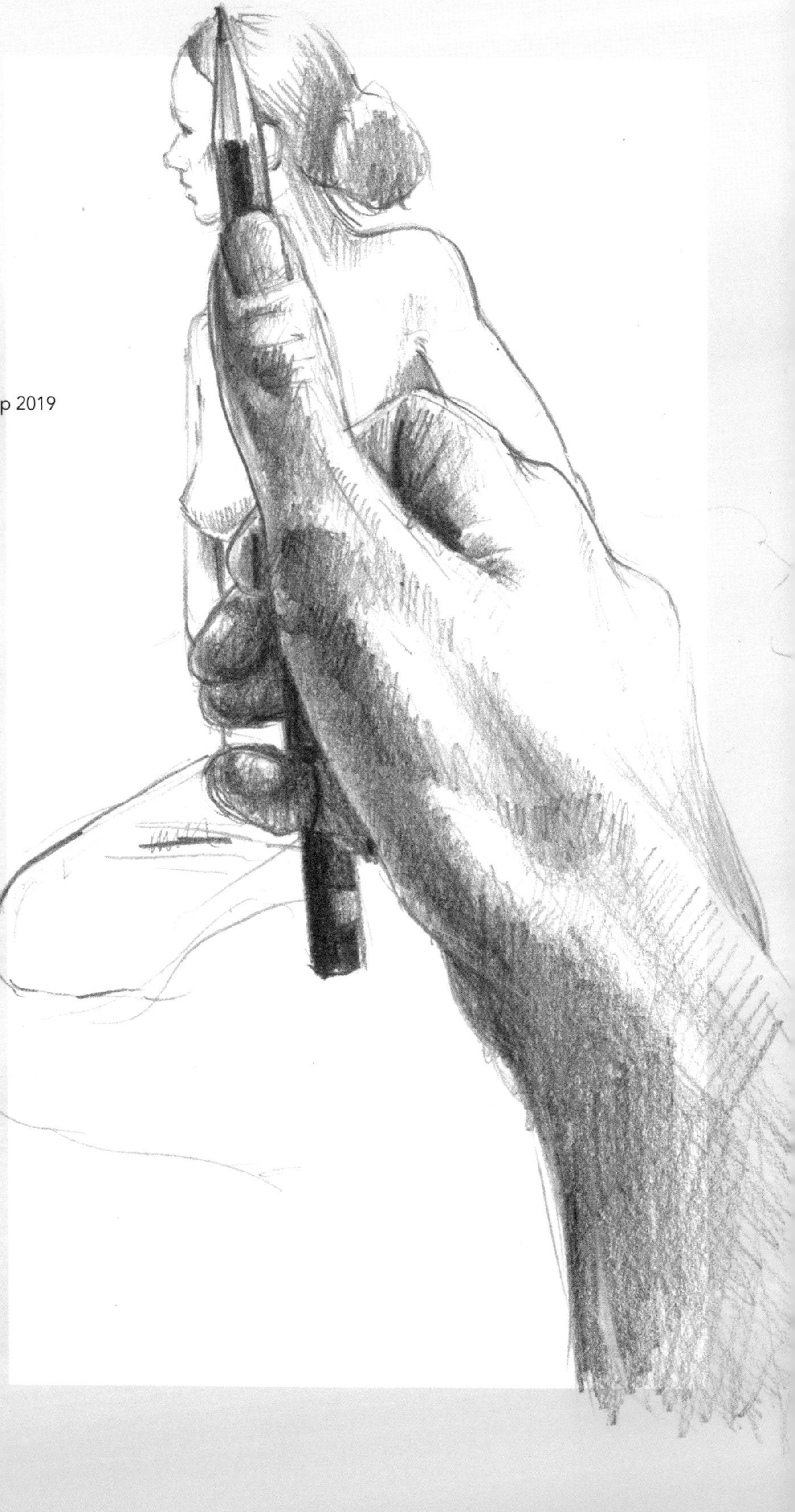

Contents

Each topic covered includes one or two exercises for you to practise

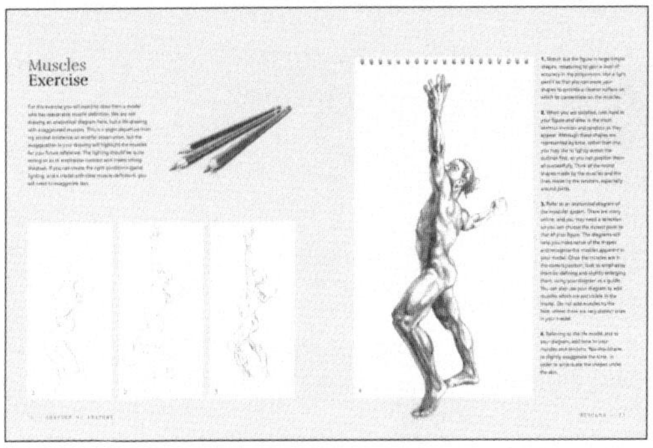

Introduction

We draw the human figure because it is a subject we can all relate to and engage with – it's a pleasing subject which serves as an outlet for our creativity and self-expression. Although it is such a familiar image, each body is unique and enormously varied, and so each and every model and each and every pose is a revelation and a challenge. It is thus impossible to learn formulae and rules for drawing the figure – it is necessary to approach each drawing anew, seeing the figure as if for the first time, making no assumptions about anything in front of us.

The figure is an unforgiving subject – it allows no room for error in the way a landscape or an abstract work does. As the human figure has relatively familiar and reliable proportions, if something in a drawing is out of proportion or too dark, it is immediately obvious to the viewer. Because of this, it is an ideal subject to choose to practise draughtsmanship and measure improvement.

This book encourages the drawer to look objectively at the model, bringing no preconceptions about what a human figure should look like. I believe that the only ways to improve are through lots of practise and, above all, strict observation. I will often talk about seeing the figure as a collection of shapes instead of as a human being. I find that this deliberate dissociation and disengagement allows for a clearer mind and sharper visual perception, which assists accuracy. This detachment often ends up yielding a more human and sensitive picture of the model; the unintentional by-product of accuracy and adherence to truth is frequently a suggestion of personality, mood and other abstract notions and deeper meanings. A very subtle visible feature, such as the slight curl of a lip, the direction of gaze or tension in the hand may transmit something that we as the artist could not describe on purpose – we describe the physical suggestion or manifestation of the abstract notion, rather than seeking to portray the abstract itself.

This book goes through techniques and elements of life drawing in a similar order to the one with which I would approach any single drawing. That is, starting with quick marks and basic shapes, measuring and consolidating those shapes, building up tone while thinking about the structures under the skin, adding finishing touches such as hair and wrinkles, and then carefully checking for mistakes and opportunities to improve and develop. However, readers should feel free to skip through to suit their needs – it is not always necessary to read one part before moving on to the next. Where I think it is helpful, I have included references to previous exercises.

Nothing in this book is a hard and fast rule – drawers should experiment and make up their own minds about the techniques and processes that suit them. There will always be alternative approaches to those I describe. I have chosen to explain how I personally work and have included things that I have found helpful in contributing to my artistic development. The processes I use have served me well, and I hope some of them prove useful for you in your artistic development.

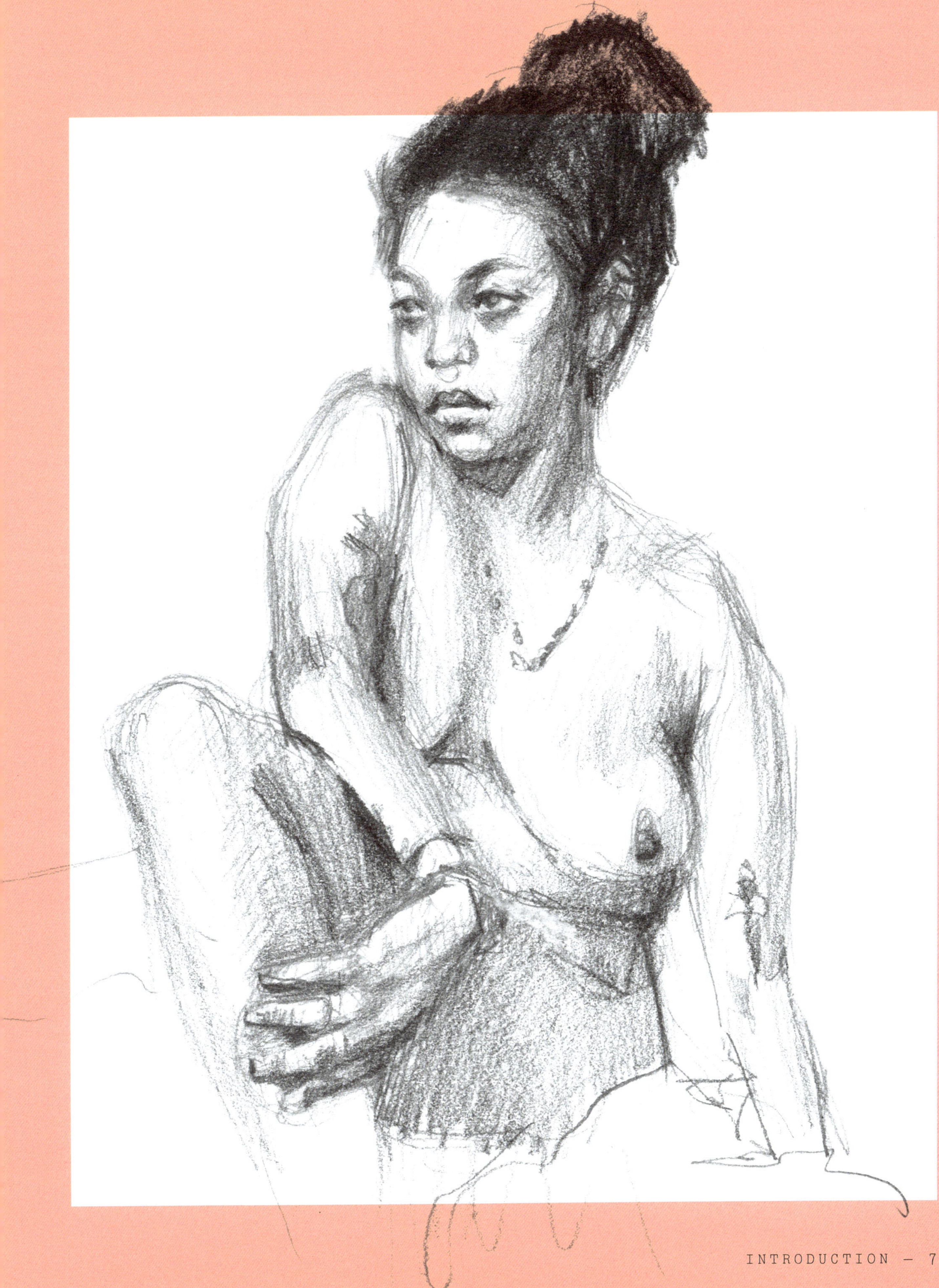

Materials

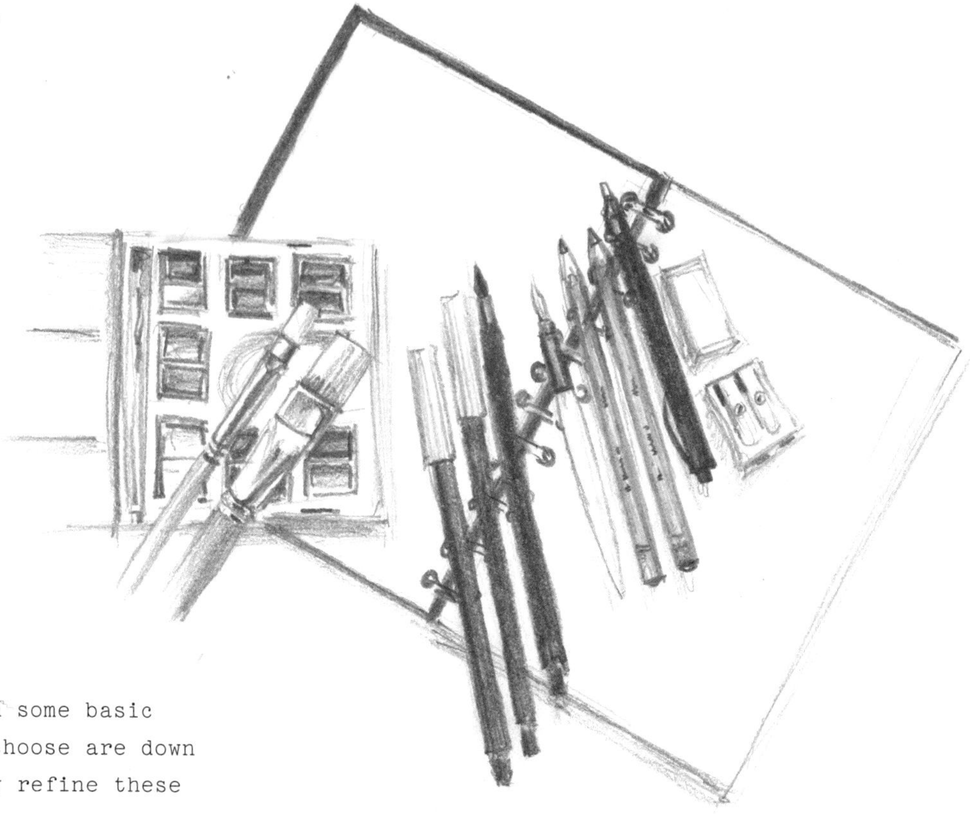

Although life drawing relies on some basic materials, the exact ones you choose are down to personal choice, and you may refine these over time.

It is sensible to invest in a sketchbook, or you could use a sheet of paper clipped to a drawing board. You could use masking tape instead of clips, but I always favour something reusable, such as pegs or bulldog clips. You will need to try out a few different sizes of paper before you work out what scale is most comfortable for you to work at. I use an A5 sketchbook, but some people naturally tend to make larger drawings. If this sounds like you, don't limit yourself to a canvas that is too small, forcing your drawings to be squashed. White cartridge paper is adequate for all of the exercises in this book.

Depending on what you aim to get out of life drawing, there are various options for materials. I find that pencil is great in order to learn and develop your fundamental drawing skills. It can be used for all the exercises in this book and is a good reliable staple for anyone hoping to push their work forwards technically.

You may wish to be braver and bolder in your work, in which case pen, with its unyielding permanence, might be the medium for you.

If you aim to be less rigid in your drawing, loosen up your marks and find some freedom and expression, you could use charcoal, graphite, paint or ink.

Introducing colour presents a whole new set of problems and each drawing can take longer, removing you from the realm of sketching and pushing you towards a more finished work. However, this doesn't always need to be the case. You may just want to express yourself in inventive colours, which can be achieved during a quick sketch. You might like to try watercolours, coloured pencils, pastels or oil pastels. You could also try felt-tip or marker pens. These are harder to blend – you normally need a good range of colours so that colour mixing isn't necessary; you can just use the raw colours available. They can give bold and vibrant results.

If you choose pencil, don't forget a sharpener and a rubber. A blunt pencil will limit you more than you think, and a rubber is essential for giving you the courage you need to make mistakes and then corrections. Don't believe any purists who tell you it's wrong to rub out!

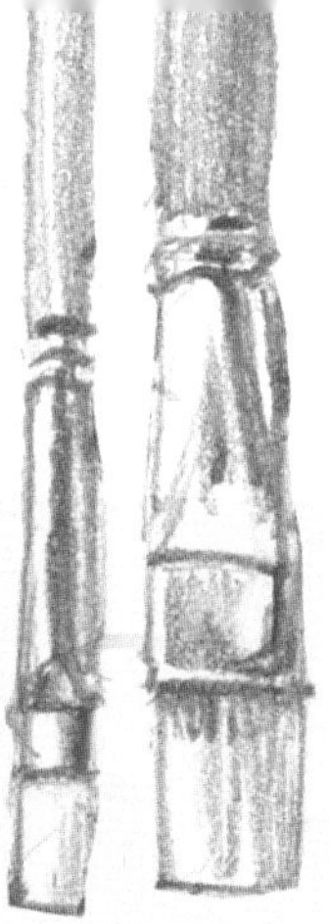

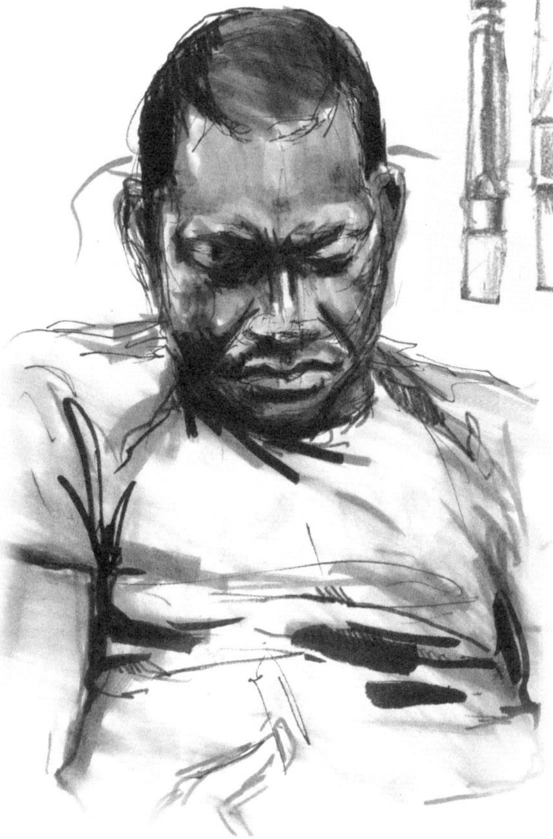

pen and ink

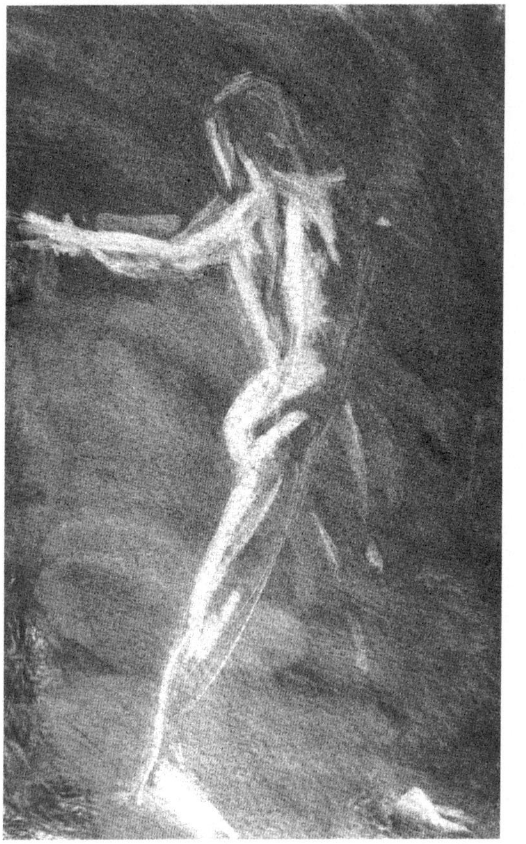

charcoal

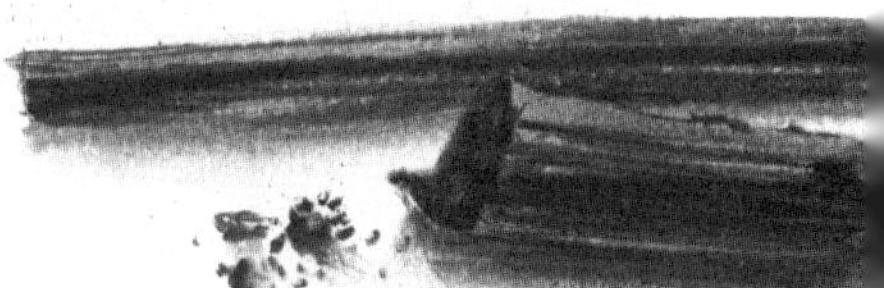

pencil

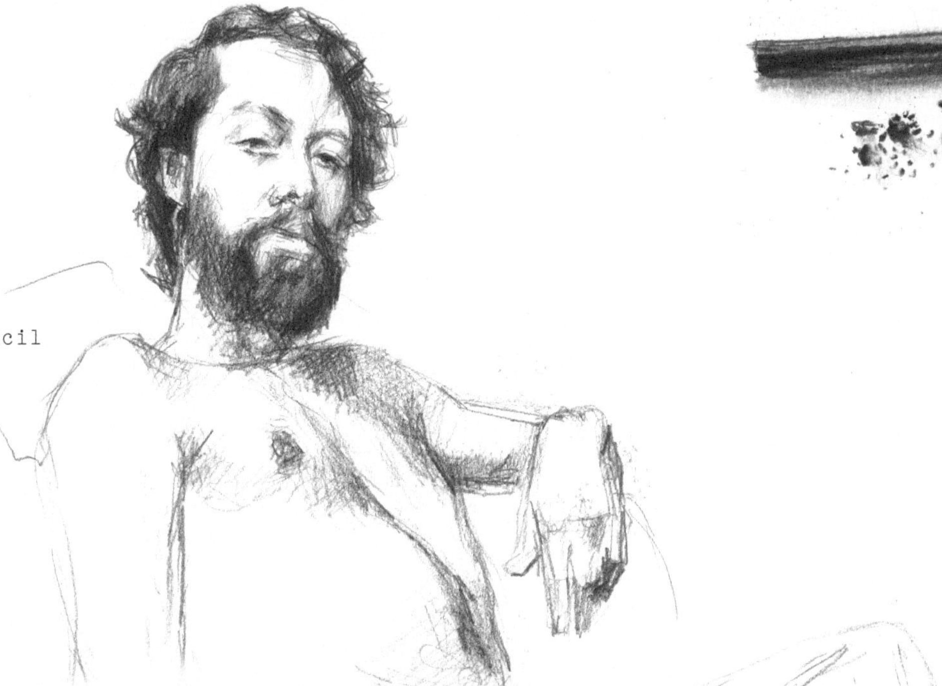

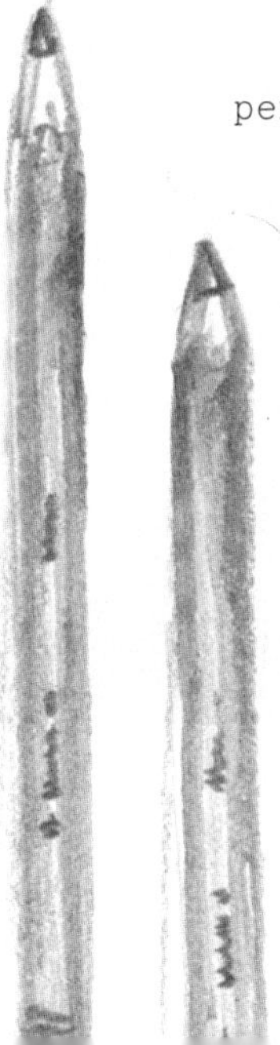

Pencil

You can develop your life drawing immensely using just a pencil. Pencils are an easy and accessible tool for quick poses, but can also be built up over time to create detailed drawings. Marks can be erased, thus encouraging risk-taking. Pencils can be used for measuring distances and angles. They are wonderful, eco-friendly, low-tech, reliable, traditional pieces of equipment that can be found anywhere.

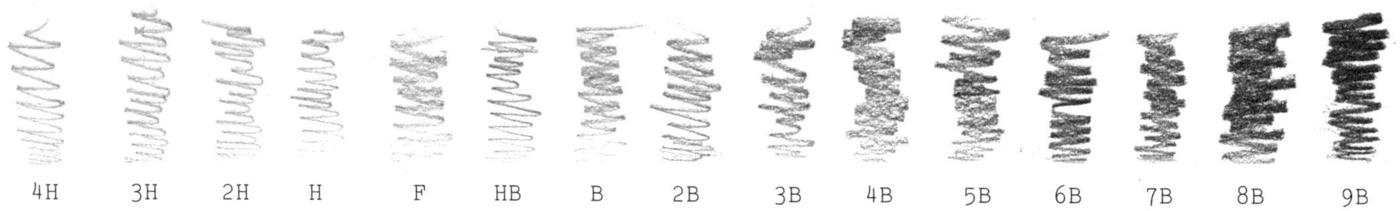

Tone can be achieved in different ways with a pencil. For all the following techniques, hold your pencil away from the tip to achieve a smooth arc and fill the area more evenly:

- Hatching in the same direction, going over your lighter tones to make them darker
- Cross-hatching – similar to above but making a mesh of pencil marks
- Random scribbling – building up tone intuitively, letting your hatching go in any direction that suits you
- Using the pencil flat to create a thicker line
- Smudging the line with your finger
- Cutting through shadows with a clean rubber to create highlights

Using two or three grades will deepen your tonal range and add so much more volume than one pencil will. Your trio of pencils can come from anywhere in the range; play around with different starting points to see what suits you best. If you have a very soft touch, you might like to try a 4H, 2H, HB combination. Or you might feel that more vigour can be elicited from a 4B, 6B and 9B. If you're unsure, try an HB, a 2B and a 5B.

Start off with a harder/lighter pencil (those graded H) to map out the figure and build up some light shading. As soon as you feel you are denting the paper, or the pencil marks are becoming shiny, it's time to move to a darker shade. Now you can develop tone and make certain lines more defined. If the marks are too grainy, you are pressing too softly to get your desired tone, so try a lighter pencil. You may find that you need a third pencil for a few very dark areas, but these may be very small.

You could try graphite for a darker and more expressive drawing. Graphite feels greasier and is harder to erase, but you can be more aggressive than you can with pencil, as it is more robust.

You might also like to introduce colour. You can use water-soluble pencils, but try them dry first. If you work lightly, you will find you can mix colours on the page, using layers of hatching and cross-hatching. You can achieve interesting effects as the colours aren't mixed on a palette like they are with paint but are mixed optically by the viewer.

There are some drawbacks to be aware of: pencil drawings can smudge and deteriorate over time in your sketchbook; pencils can be messy when you're transporting them and they can break easily.

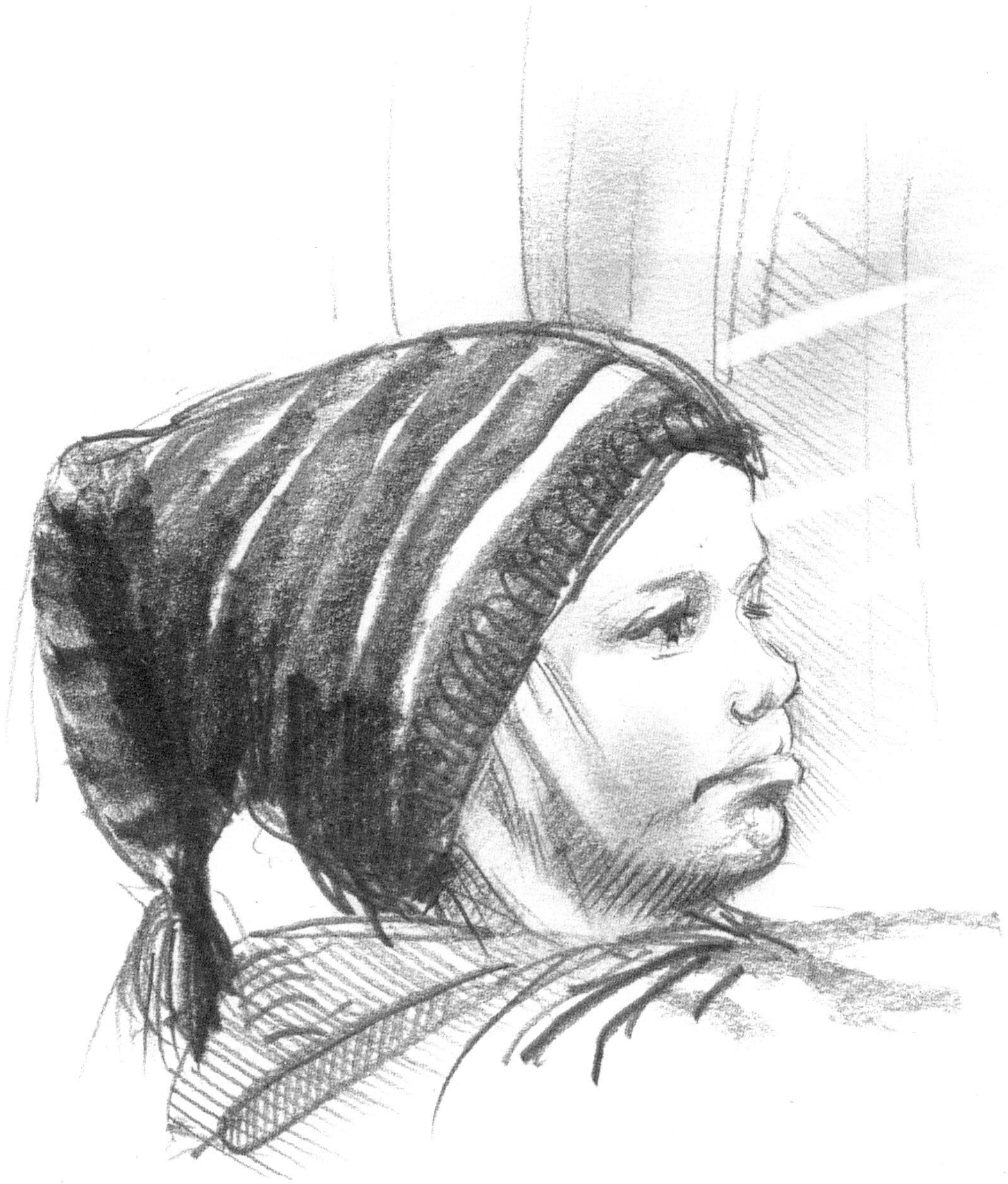

A rubber can be used as a drawing tool to create highlights and lighten areas of tone, not just to correct mistakes.

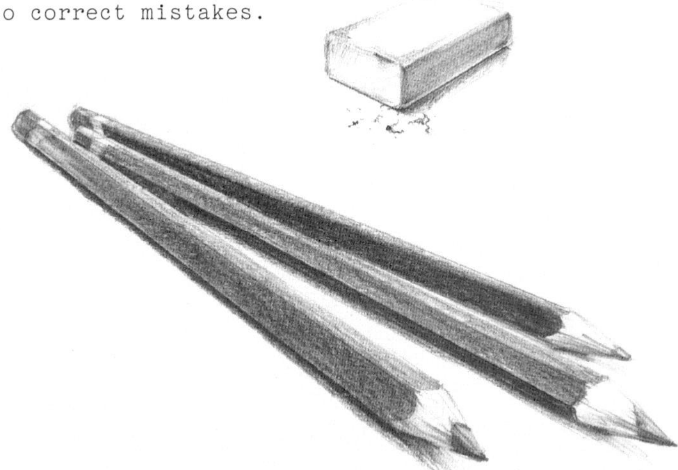

REMEMBER:

- Make sure you have a rubber so that you feel uninhibited and free to make mistakes.
- Keep your pencil reasonably sharp, and discard it when it becomes too short.
- Move up or down grades if your line becomes too indented and shiny, or too grainy.

Pen and Ink

I find pen and ink to be the most convenient of materials, enabling me to work whenever and wherever I am – pens can be carried loose in my bag or pocket without making a mess and they are perfect for both quick sketches and detailed drawings.

However, they are normally permanent, so you need to be sure of where you are putting your marks. This limitation can be helpful in encouraging careful observation, but is not for the faint-hearted! Pens may also present difficulties in building up tone smoothly, because they are usually darker than pencil and therefore contrast strongly with the white of the paper.

Ballpoint pen

The ballpoint pen may not be regarded as a lofty aide to fine art, but I love its versatility and accessibility. Although you can't rub it out, if your marks are light enough, mistakes can be accommodated. Build up tone using gentle hatching and cross-hatching. For darker areas you can apply more pressure until you have a wonderfully dense thicket of dark lines for the deepest shadows.

Fine liner

It's difficult to allow for lighter tones, but careful hatching can give you tonal variation within the darker range. Fine liners are wonderful for line drawings, enabling fluid and decisive marks for confident draughtsmen. For inspiration, look at Hockney's impeccably observed figures. No mark is made until he is sure of where to put it. You can find more expression within Emin's figure drawings – the stark and aggressive quality of the lines creates emotion out of very little.

Ink with water pen

This combination will allow you to cover areas quickly and in a painterly way. Using a water-soluble pen, map out the structure of your figure first. Use your water pen to draw the ink from these lines into the shape. Some types of pen are more soluble than others. You may find the lines can disappear altogether, so you are just left with a tonal drawing. Or you might have a pleasing variety of strong lines and watery shades. You can also flick and splash the wet ink around to create an exciting variety of marks.

Brush pen

These pens are similar to felt-tip pens. Many have two ends: one thin and one thick. With the thick end you can cover your page quickly and so retain some spontaneity – a rapidly executed sketch can capture something of the fleeting nature of a gesture, whereas a lengthier drawing may feel more static. The marks are permanent, so careful observation and considered mark-making are crucial. It will be clear to the viewer that no mark has been reworked or erased – all the artist's actions are assertively manifest in the final drawing. These pens are often available in different shades, and this is where I really see their benefit. I use a light grey, a mid-grey and a black. Using different greys, it is possible to build up your drawing tonally, as with a pencil. You can quickly build up subtle tone with the same pen, going over the same mark to deepen the shade before moving to a darker pen.

REMEMBER:

- Spend more time looking than mark-making.
- Less may be more – what can you leave out?

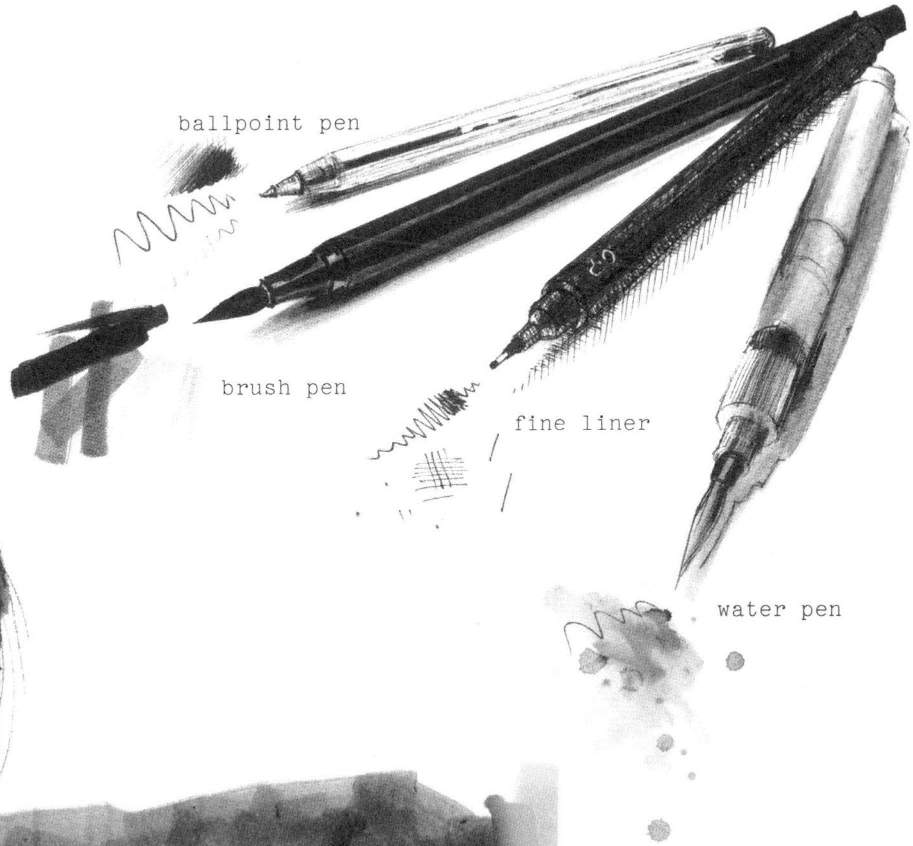

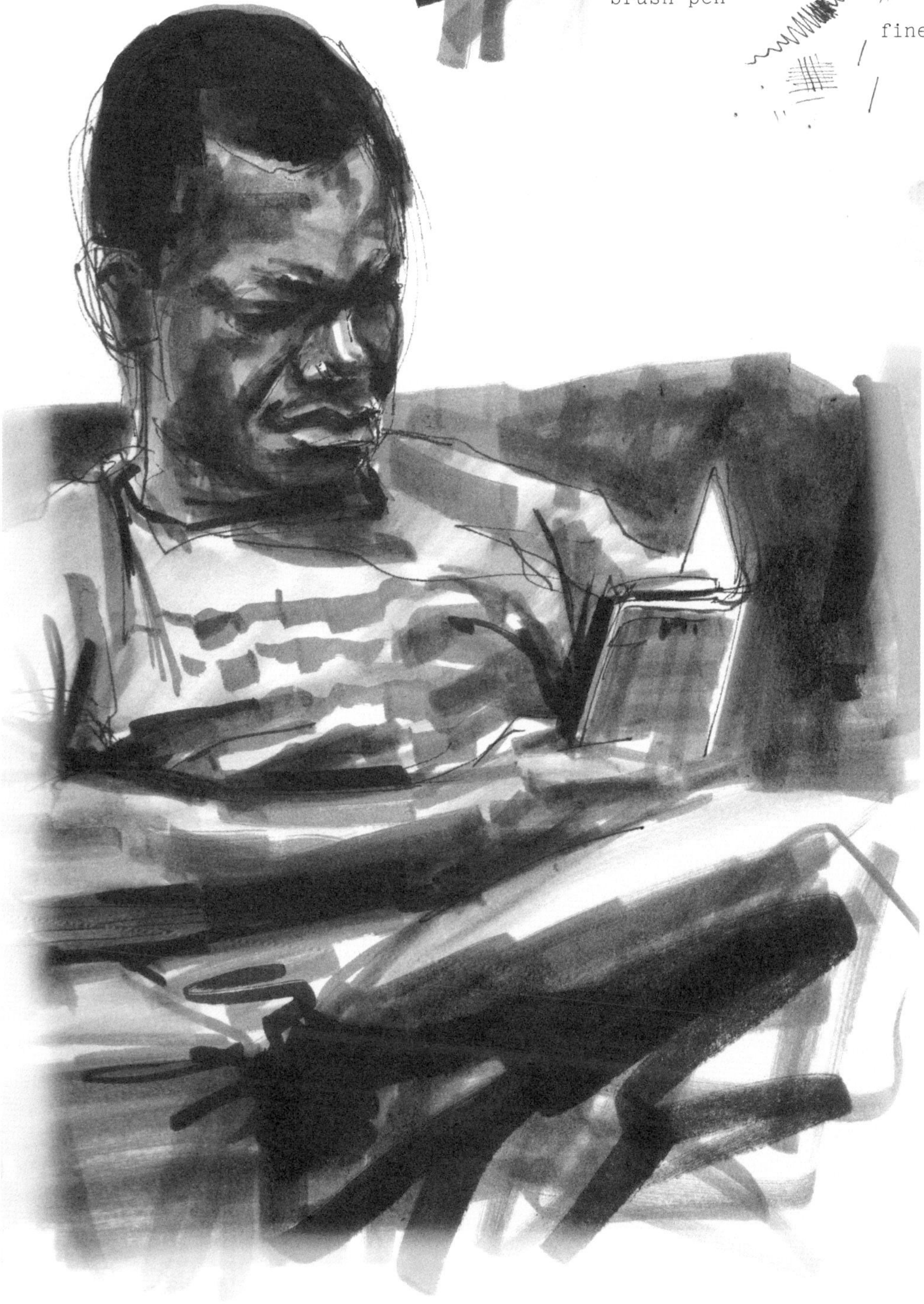

Charcoal

Although you can achieve less accuracy with charcoal than a pencil, you can fill up the page quickly with large and expressive marks. This is really useful when there is a time limit on a pose. Charcoal is very forgiving and can be moved around the paper easily with your fingers or with a rubber. It's also a wonderful medium for exploring tone. Because it is so dark, you can recreate a huge tonal range and get a real sense of depth and volume in your drawings.

You can use a thick stick on its side, ideally snapped into a length of a couple of inches – this will allow you to find form in very quick drawings, such as three- or even one-minute poses. The thin, fragile sticks will enable more detail. You can labour away for hours on a charcoal drawing, observing delicate nuances in light and building up deliciously dark shadows. Concentrate on large, simple shapes first and take time to develop the tone and the detail.

Your rubber will get dirty quickly with charcoal, so after two or three strokes, clean it on a separate scrap of paper. You might also like to chop it in half diagonally to get a point. This is more effective than moulding a putty rubber into the desired shape – putty rubbers are less likely to create sharp, clean highlights.

Once you've finished, use a fixative (outside the room) to prevent your work from smudging.

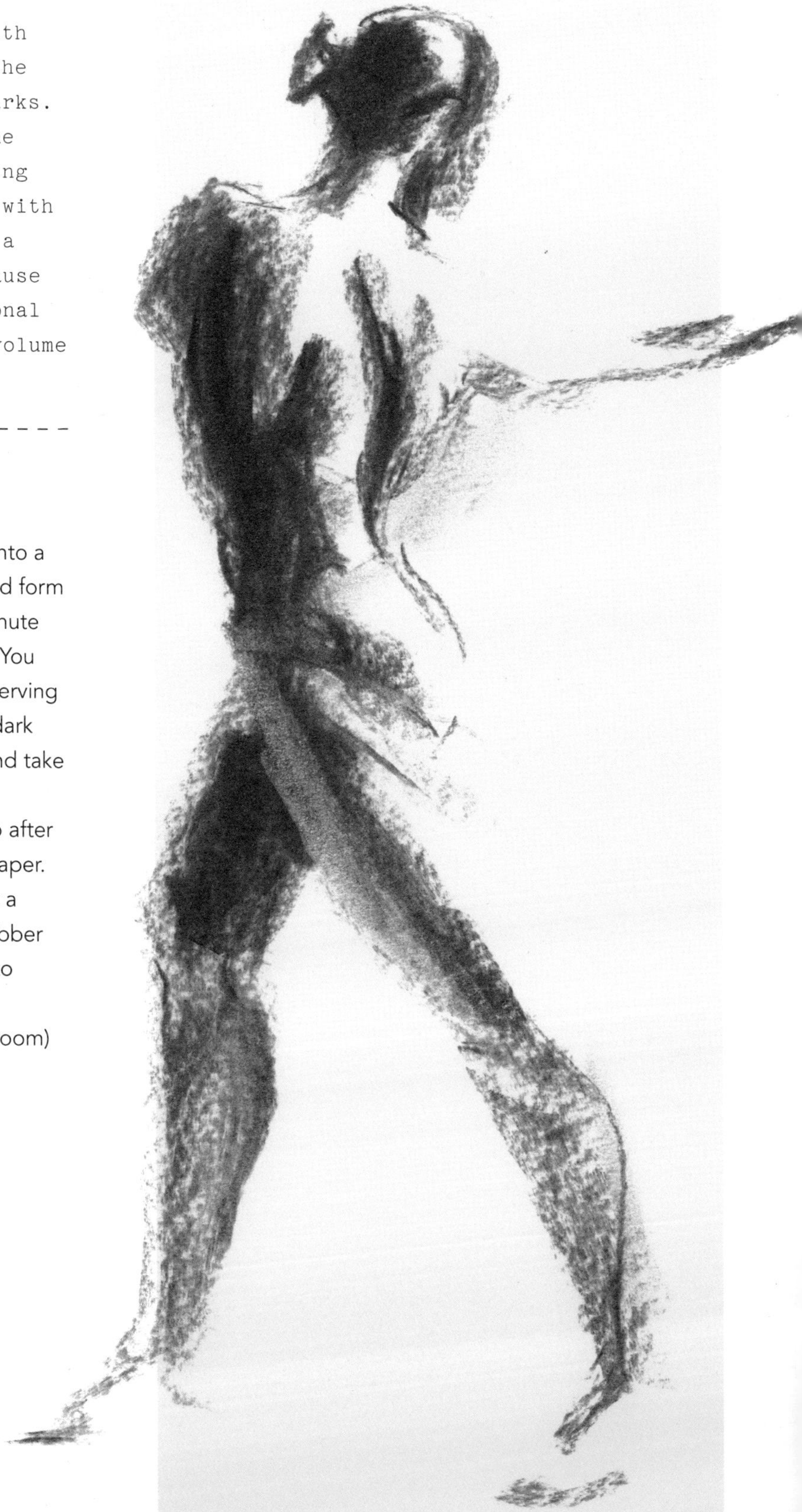

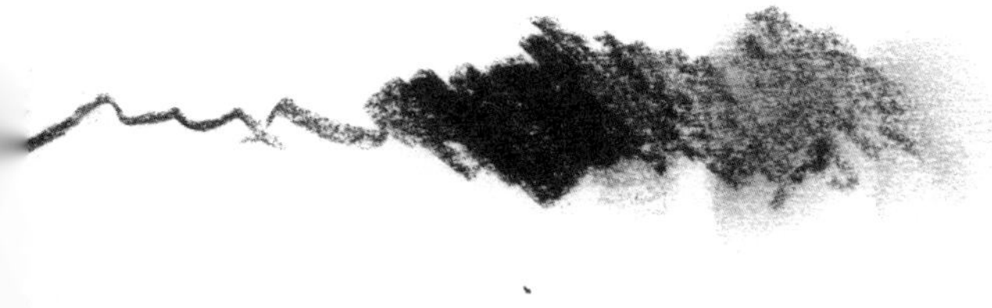

Paint

Time is limited in a life drawing class, so I wouldn't recommend setting up your oil paints. Acrylic can be a little swifter, due to faster drying times and less cleaning required. But for the sake of 'sketching', I would opt for something quicker and more manageable. Watercolours are very portable and offer a dynamic range of possibilities.

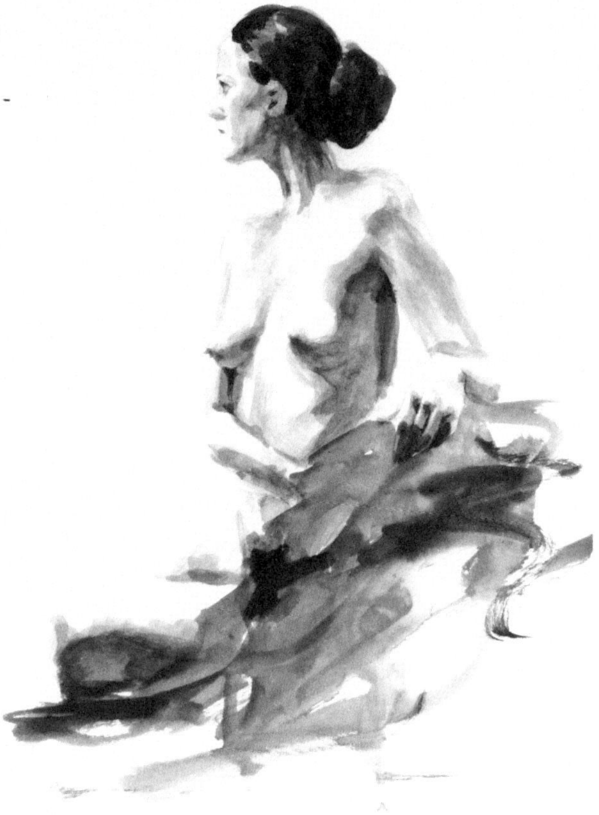

You could simplify colour to make a swift study, but you can also just stick to one colour and concentrate on tone. Ink can be used in the same way, diluted with water or left intense and dark. Use a wide brush, perhaps a chisel shape, to build up simple shapes for quick poses. A chisel brush has a flat tip that isn't angled or pointed – it produces block-like brush marks that allow for fast coverage and simple shapes, rather than detail. Or you could use a round brush, which can still be used for simple shapes, but which gives you more control.

For longer sketches, use a thinner brush and a very watery mixture (or a light pencil) to map out the structure of your drawing. Use a similarly light or dilute paint to build up shadows. When this layer is dry (or sooner if you want to take advantage of a smooth gradient or interesting bleeding), use a darker and less watery brush-full for darker shadows and details.

Explore different ways of getting paint onto the paper. Here are some ideas for making marks with your brush:

(A) Thick and thin brush marks
(B) Dry brush marks
(C) Flicking and splashing
(D) Use a clean, wet brush to lift dry paint and make soft highlights.
(E) Bleeding
(F) Score the paper gently (see how the pigment fills the indentation).
(G) Scratch the top layer of the paper away to get a crisp white highlight.
(H) Dab at wet paint with a tissue to slightly lighten an area.

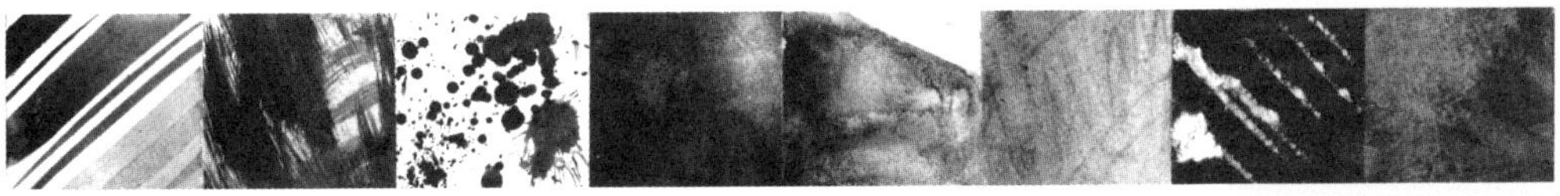

A B C D E F G H

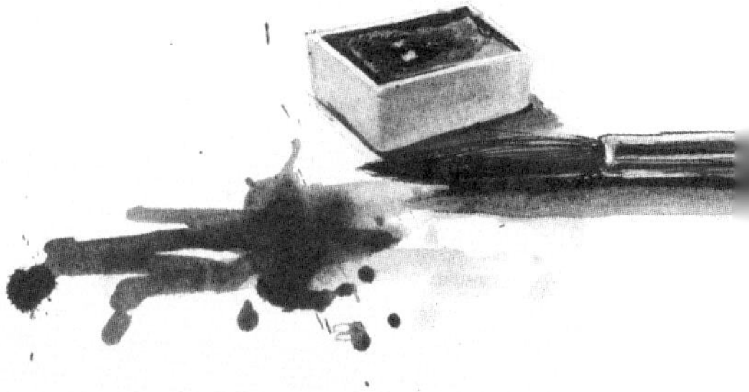

Sketchbook

A sketchbook is a very important space where much of your growth as an artist will happen. Having said that, it needn't be a hallowed and revered space, kept neat and well planned. It should be a place where you are entirely free to do whatever you like: experiment, play, be rigorous and disciplined, be free, be frivolous. Above all, use it often.

I use a small sketchbook that's easy to carry so I can always have it to hand. The work inside is not impressive or accomplished. I feel that when I use it I needn't answer to anyone, so I needn't be self-conscious about what I put down. You should treat your sketchbook as if it is only you that will ever see it. You may even want to make keeping it private a rule of yours, if this encourages you to be unselfconscious and brave. Your drawings needn't be finished, polished works of art. They may be just a few lines intended to jog your memory. Or they may be merely the physical residue of your having observed and processed a particular view.

Even the great masters have rough and erratic sketches in their books. Turner and Constable have some very scruffy drawings in theirs, perhaps made in hostile weather or in a hurry. If even Turner and Constable make scruffy drawings, we as learners can too.

It isn't always necessary to strive to make realistic representations of the world; we can aim for emotive and expressive responses instead. John Virtue's sketchbooks, which he fills at a terrifying rate on his daily walks, can be read not so much as *aide-memoires* for final paintings, but as stand-alone works of art in an abstract visual language that need make sense to only him, though we may find them striking and beautiful. John Ruskin, on the other hand, made very clinical and strictly observed studies of trees, water and architecture – not very romantic or expressive, but nevertheless important in their objectivity. Kurt Jackson makes beautiful sketches of landscapes to inform his paintings, but he also makes quick sketches of the inconsequential and the quotidian, for example: musicians in pubs, his family watching TV, loaves of bread and insects.

Here are some things that could appear in sketchbooks:

- Disciplined and meticulous drawings
- Quick studies of day-to-day objects around you
- Thumbnail sketches to test out composition/tone/colour
- Experiments with materials
- Scribbles intended as an *aide-memoire* for later work
- Abstract doodles
- Train/parking/exhibition tickets to remind you of a trip
- Notes from meetings
- Shopping or to do lists
- Notes made on colour/smell/sound/experience

Try to keep your sketchbook with you at all times and try to make some sort of drawing every day. Even a one-minute drawing is better than nothing – it can still have value. Sketching every day improves your fluency with mark-making and you will quickly notice improvements in your drawing in general. Regular sketching is also very good for mindfulness and all-round well-being.

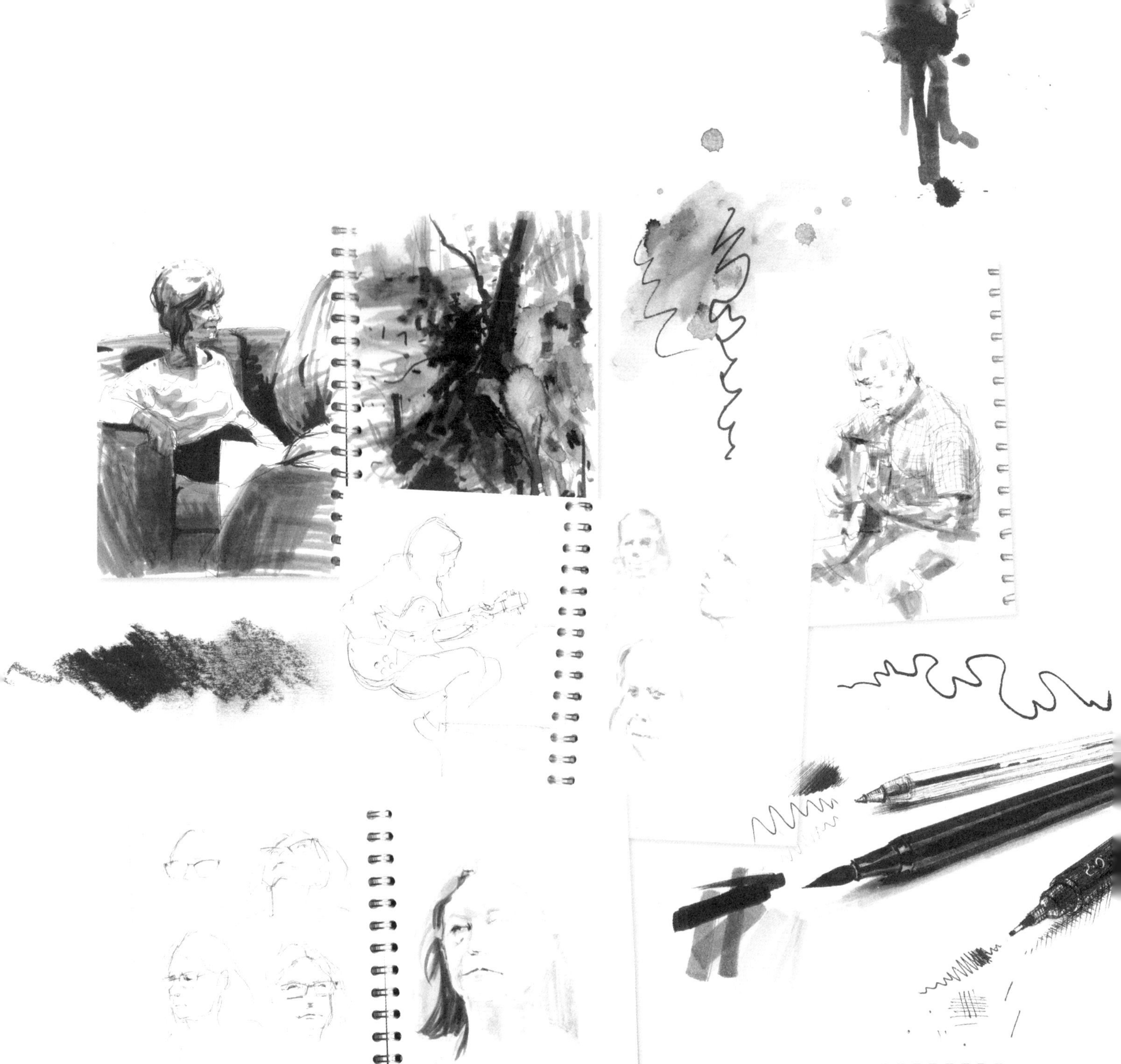

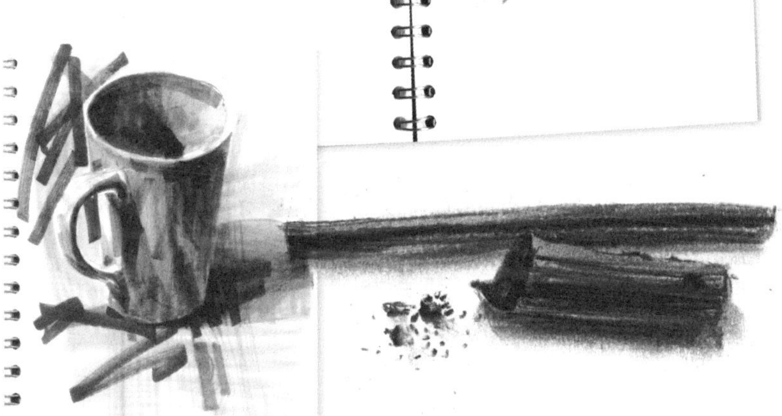

REMEMBER:

- Be uninhibited in your sketchbook – keep it private if necessary.
- Use your sketchbook as a visual diary.
- There are no mistakes in your sketchbook – just experiments.

The Life Drawing Class

Firstly, in consideration of the model, cover any windows allowing a view into the room with curtains or blinds and place a sign on the door to avoid unwanted interruptions. Turn on a heater or fan according to the model's needs in the prevailing conditions.

It is best to stand or sit at an easel. If you prefer not to, you can rest a board or sketchbook on your knees or on the back of another chair. Whatever you do, make sure your board is not flat, as it would be on a table, and certainly don't angle it away from you. Both flat boards and those angled away from you will cause you to unintentionally overcompensate at the top of the drawing, so that when you hold it upright, your drawing will be ill-proportioned. A slight slope is enough, although if the board is on an easel it may be almost upright. It shouldn't, however, be completely upright – it is more tiring to work at this angle, and is slightly less stable since the board is likely to fall towards you.

Have your paper at a suitable height for you – if it's too high your arm will get tired, but if it's too low it will feel awkward. Position the easel so that you can see both your work and the figure simultaneously. You shouldn't have to peer around your work in order to see your subject, neither should you have to turn your head from subject to paper, just your eyes. Having the shortest possible distance from the view of the model to the view of your paper will reduce the amount of information lost in transit. But do make sure there is room to move back from your paper. If you're standing, make sure you have space behind you; if you're sitting down, make sure you can lean back, or hold your board at a distance every so often. This will allow you to measure easily and to look for errors. It is important to get some distance from your work at regular intervals as this will help you assess it as a whole.

Make life easy for yourself. It is a matter of personal preference as to whether the easel is to your front left or front right. Check there is enough light on your work and have your materials on a stool or table next to you. I find that when I'm really engaged in my work, if a particular pen or some other implement is slightly out of reach, I am loathe to break my concentration to get it, even if the drawing suffers as a result.

It's nice to have a break for tea and coffee, to give people a chance to have a chat about their work. Life drawing is a sociable activity that allows creative people to connect. If your class is only an hour, it isn't necessary to have a break, but classes generally last at least two hours, sometimes three. If the class lasts all day, I would suggest a small break at least every hour.

You may wish to listen to music, and this is often a good idea as it can help you focus. If it's a group session, the tutor may put some quiet and appropriate music on. I have found it best not to stick to a single musician or a genre, but to use a mix, so there's something for everyone – no one wants easy jazz for two hours. Alternatively, you can bring headphones and listen to a personal playlist.

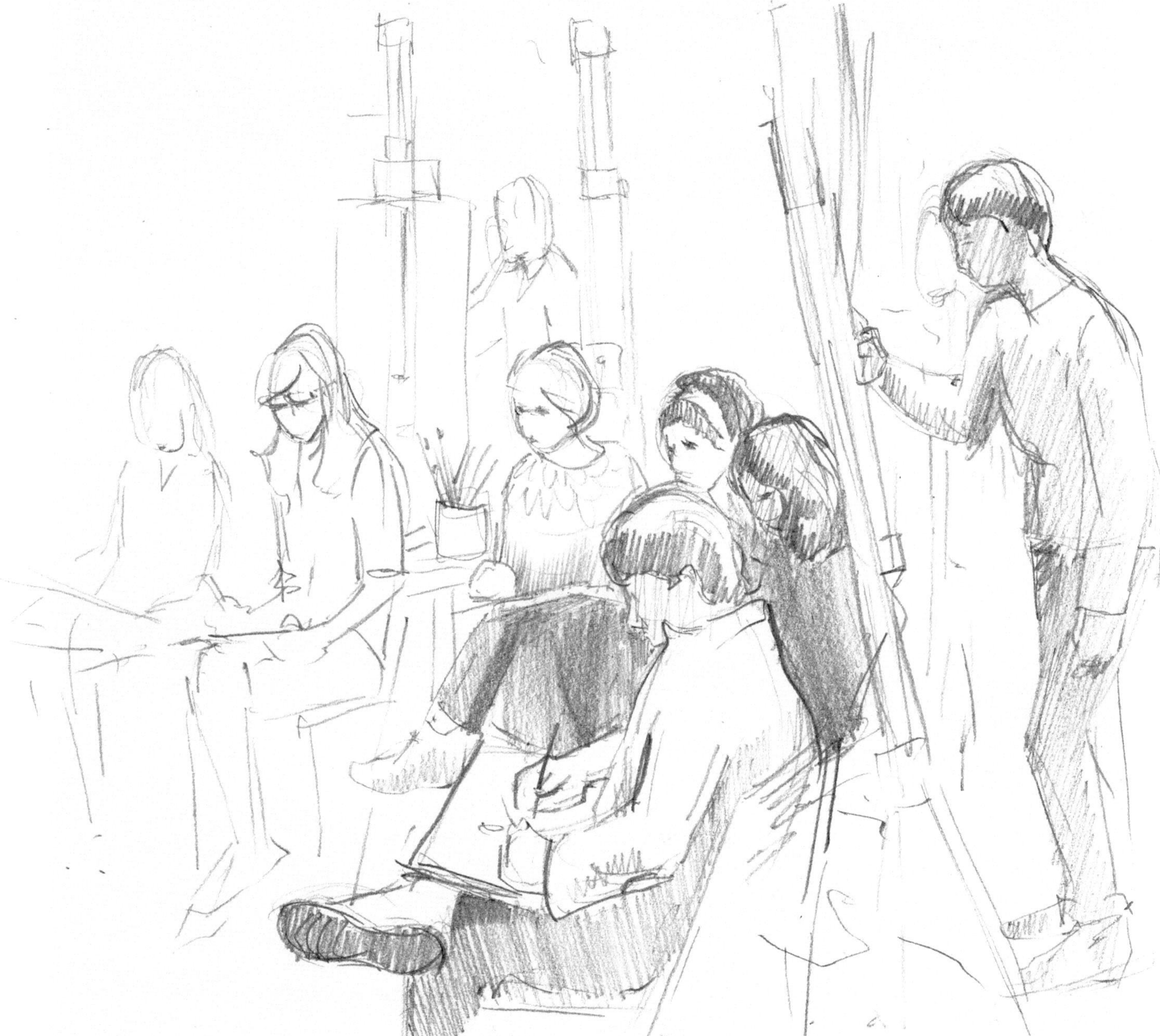

Class Etiquette

It is essential that you as a student get what you need from the class, but this should never come at the cost of the needs of the other drawers or the model. There are certain rules of etiquette that should be followed. I mention them here because they are not always as obvious as they sound but should always be kept in mind.

It is best to have one person in charge of the poses, whether they direct the model, or merely have the final say in order to avoid a conflict of interest among all the drawers. This will most likely be the tutor. Whoever is in charge should have an awareness of what will work for everyone who is drawing (i.e. making sure each student has a view of the model's face at some point, and that the figure isn't foreshortened for the same drawer during too many poses).

Avoid giving directions to the model yourself. Unless you have a model to yourself, it is better not to make suggestions, unless you're asked or you really feel you're getting the raw end of the deal. An experienced model will know what they are doing and what is sustainable for the allotted time. An inexperienced model may be more likely to take pointers from even less experienced drawers, so be careful to avoid this.

Giving criticism to other students will depend on what the drawer aims to get out of a lesson. If you know that they attend classes as a creative release, rather than with an aim to learn, criticism isn't necessary. If the drawer truly wants to develop, criticism is essential. Even in brilliant drawings, there is normally something that could be developed upon. However, tact is obviously key, and encouragement should also be given. When receiving criticism, try to have an open mind and accept the benefit of a different point of view.

If you ever get a chance to model, I would recommend it – either for a life drawing or for a portrait. Until you have tried it yourself, it is not always apparent how challenging it is, or what might cause discomfort. As you can imagine, being nude in front of a room of people can be daunting – one can feel vulnerable, so it is a good idea to stick to certain rules, even if they don't seem *that* crucial:

- The model should be told when they're halfway through and also when they are a couple of minutes from the end. Time can begin to lose its meaning when you're sitting completely still for a long period.
- Never ask, even politely, that a model consider continuing for longer. The temptation is strong when it's a lovely pose, but they may feel they can't refuse when they're in a room full of people. An experienced model will have chosen a pose that they can hold for the right amount of time, not expecting it to be extended.
- Assume that photography is not allowed, unless otherwise stated, even in a portrait or clothed class. Private sessions may be different, though there is a good argument for relying purely on direct observation, and structuring your drawing to fit into the given time frame.
- The temperature should be right for the model, and their comfort should be checked frequently.
- It is fine to direct the model back to the exact pose after they've had a stretch – this can be helpful as you have a better view than they do.

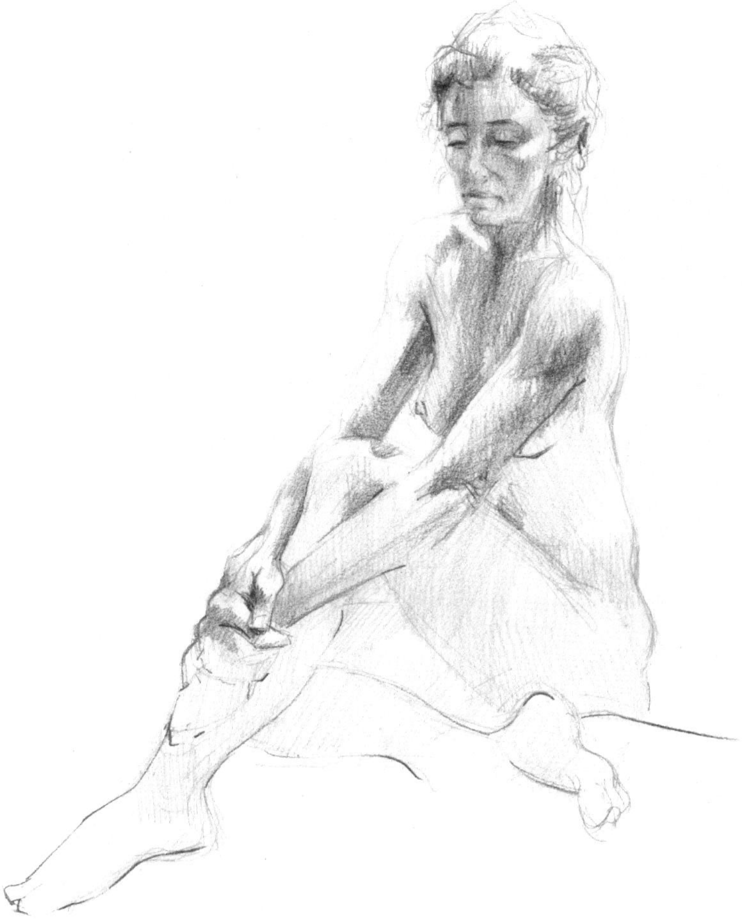

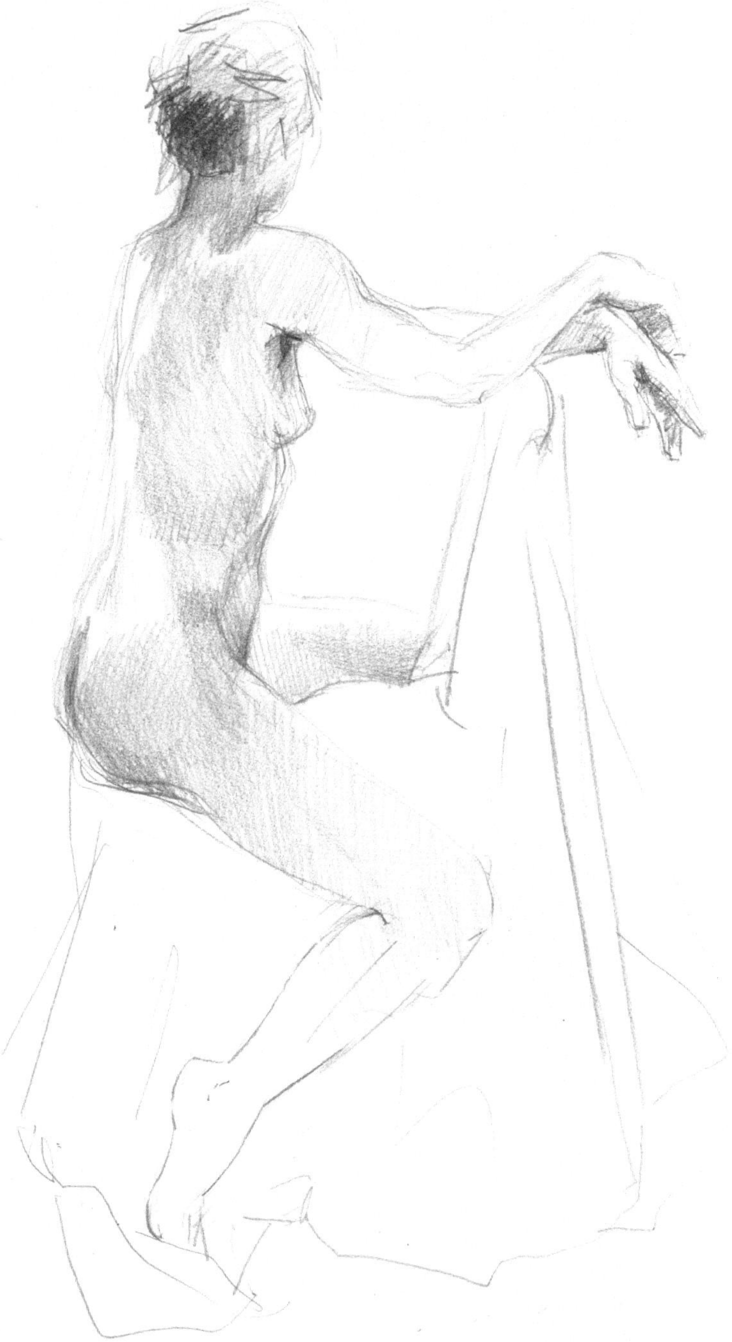

REMEMBER

Although I emphasize that life drawers should look objectively at the model and see shapes and forms rather than recognisable features, it is obviously necessary to keep in mind that a model is still a person with feelings. Be careful when commenting on the model's features, even if you are doing it from a detached perspective. I have seen people forget themselves in this. It is perfectly possible to suggest that things have been drawn too large or too small without sounding offensive.

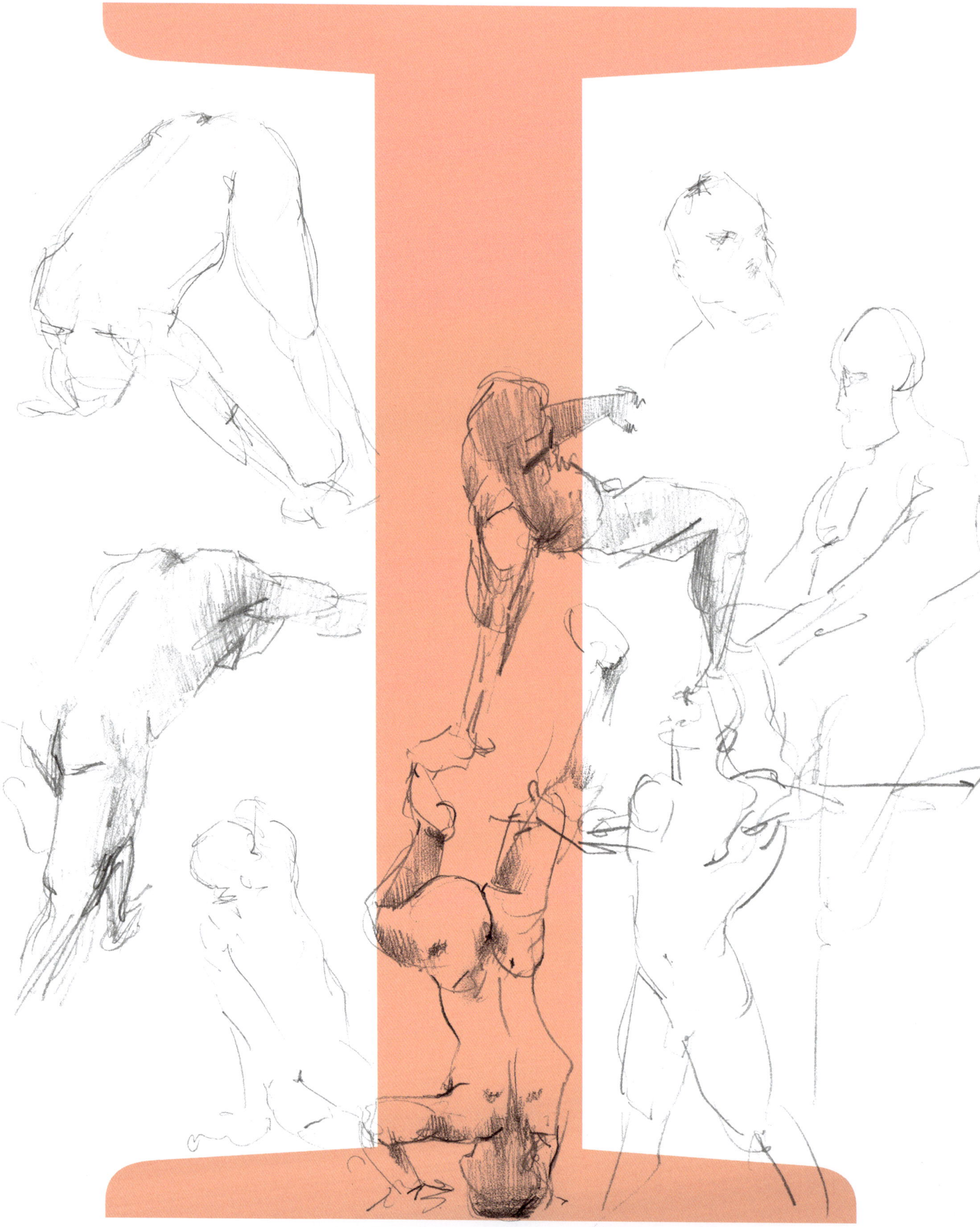

Freeing Up

Being able to draw quickly is a useful skill, allowing artists to make drawings of fleeting or non-static subjects. The speed and unpolished feel of the marks can give a sketch a spontaneity that reflects the movement or impermanence of a moment.

There is little point labouring over a drawing until it is as detailed as a photo. Such drawings can look turgid, stiff and overworked and also beg the question, ‘Why make a drawing rather than just take a photo?’ A drawing should offer something a photo can’t, rather than aiming to mimic one. This could be a sense of movement or drama through accented marks, or it could be the conscious omission of unnecessary details.

Though these drawings may be unfinished and unrefined, they will benefit from a fluency in mark-making and an adherence to observation. A relatively accurate portrayal of the figure, no matter how simple, gives reality and credibility to a quick, expressive drawing.

The exercises here teach you to observe with an open mind, so you are free to react honestly and make the most accurate marks possible. They also seek to nurture an ability to ‘free up’ – encouraging quick but well-planned hand movements to economise and make fewer, better marks.

Basic Figure
Capturing Gesture and Essence

It is useful to be able to draw a figure quickly and fluently. It will enable you to make a complete work during a one-minute pose and will also allow you to apply your skills to moving subjects, making it possible for you to capture something of real life outside of the studio.

As your experience and technical ability increase, you will be able to get a structural 'underdrawing' down before you concentrate on developing other elements of your drawing such as building tone or adding colour. It may also mean that even if you continue the drawing for an hour and a half, the original freshness of your quick drawing remains.

A quick drawing tends to elicit a feeling of spontaneity – concise and swift marks will add a sense of immediacy to your work. They can also convey a sense of movement, which you can then apply to situations outside of the class. I have found that capturing a basic figure quickly has enabled me to make more accomplished drawings of tricky subjects such as children, animals, musicians and passers-by.

It is worth looking at the sketches of Constantin Guys, a 19th-century Dutch artist who lived in Paris at the time the city's boulevards were being widened by Haussmann. Guys captured the rise of the bustling middle classes in a flurry of carriages, twirling dresses, dancing and jostling. This influenced artists like the Impressionists who were able to convey the sense of that which is ephemeral and fleeting.

When time is limited, it might feel that you need to get your pencil to your paper quickly, but actually you can complete your drawing effectively if you spend more time looking. Extended observation will give you a clearer insight into where to put your marks, so you can be more assertive and efficient. In quick drawings, you obviously won't have the time to go into lots of detail. Think about being economical in your mark-making – never use two strokes where one will do. What can you omit?

When observing the model, if you squint or let your eyes go out of focus, only the essential features will jump out at you. Try to determine what the essence of the pose is and how you can rapidly represent it. It may be a gesture, it may be some tension in the muscles, tendons or the skin. You could show this with long straight lines, sweeping curves or heavier marks.

If you're using a thick brush, or a thick piece of charcoal, you can quickly include important shadows, which can indicate twists and bends. Successful blocks of tone may render outlines superfluous, providing further opportunity to economise. For slightly longer poses in any medium, you can use your swiftly created framework to act as a base for expressive or more nuanced tone. This tone can describe stress, folds, muscles, tendons, bones and sinew, which might be integral to the essence of the pose.

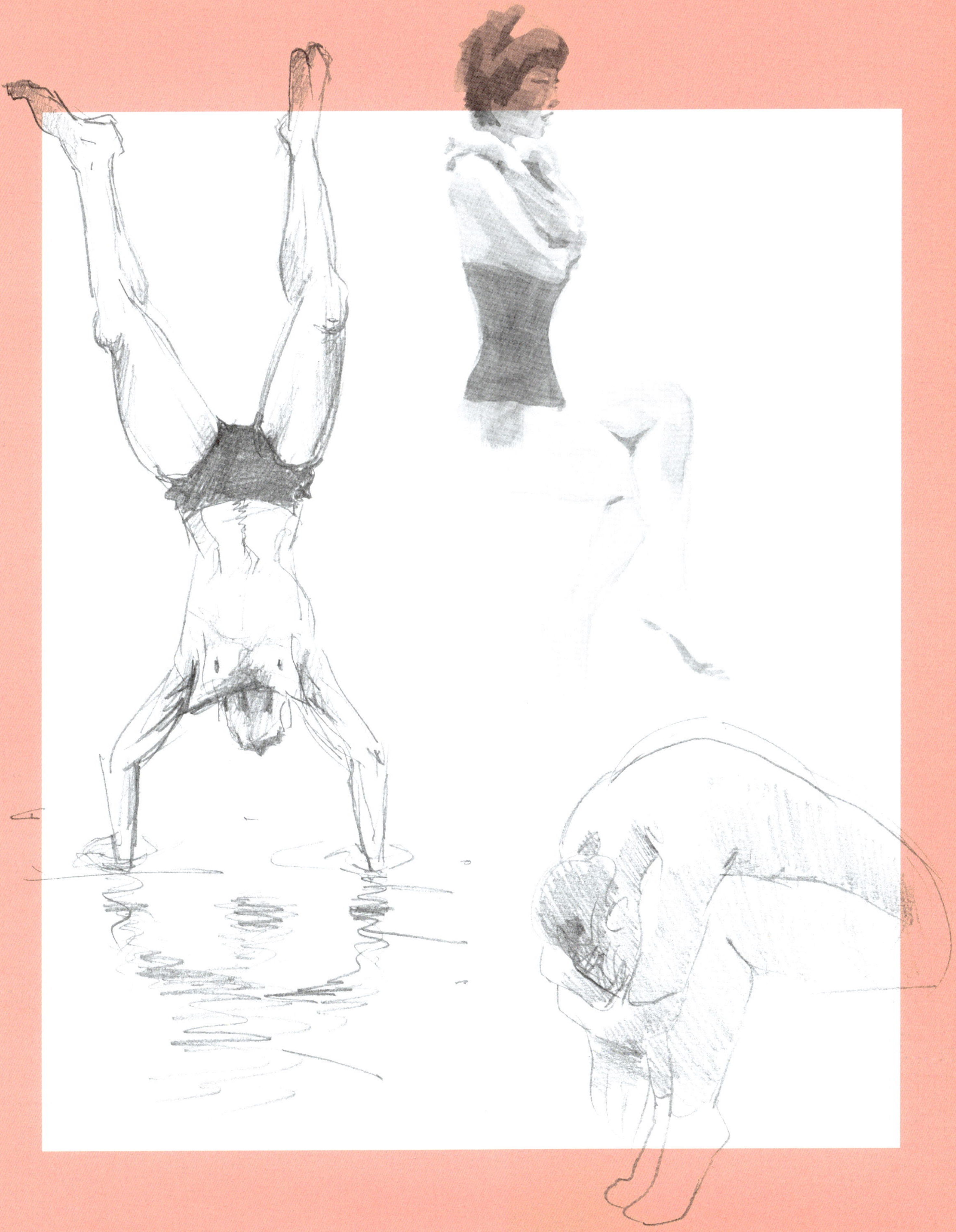

Quick Pose Exercises

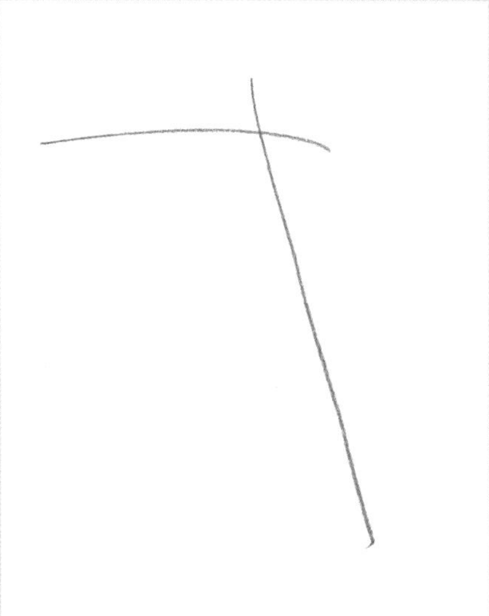

1

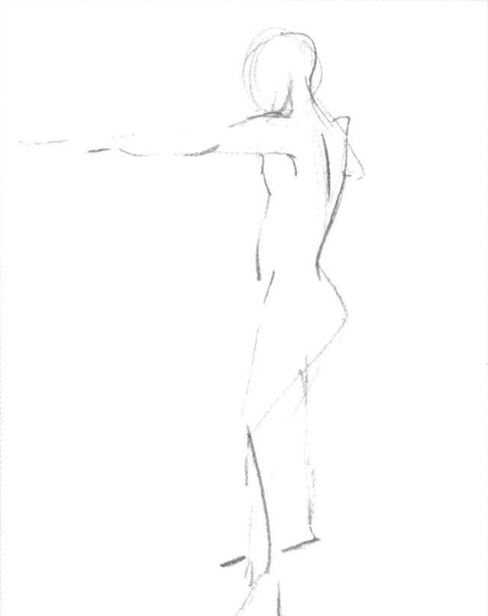

2

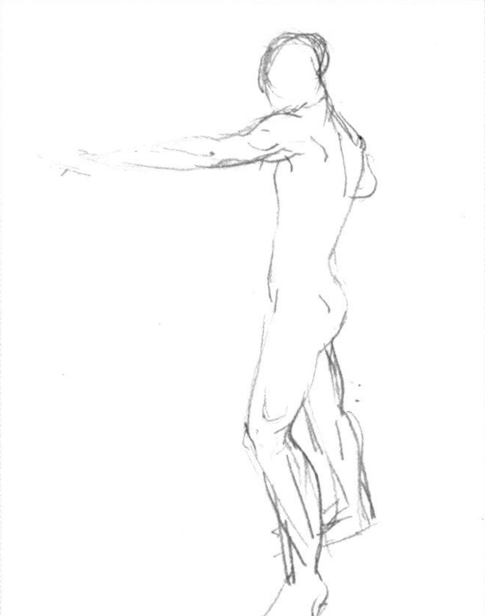

3

1. Two-line drawing
Look closely at your model for twenty seconds. Fully absorb the image and decide what is absolutely essential, and what can be omitted. Now use only two lines to transpose your impression of the figure onto the page. This should look and feel quite abstract.

2. One-minute drawing
Here you will really be thinking about the essence of the pose. You may not have time for accuracy, and certainly not detail, but the fundamental shape or structure will appear on your paper in a very energetic way. Spend the majority of the minute looking for important gestural characteristics, perhaps notable bends in the body, or stresses in skin and muscle, perhaps sweeping curves or long straight lines formed by the torso and limbs. Let your hand hover over the paper and make marks as economically as possible.

3. Three-minute drawing (to be continued in next step)
Force yourself to spend more time looking than making marks. Try to get the entire figure down in a few informed and decisive lines. Although this is a short pose, you have time to make decisions about what must be included and what can be left out. You also have time to think about the accuracy of your lines. You may make decisions about the strength of your marks in order to emphasise an essential feature.

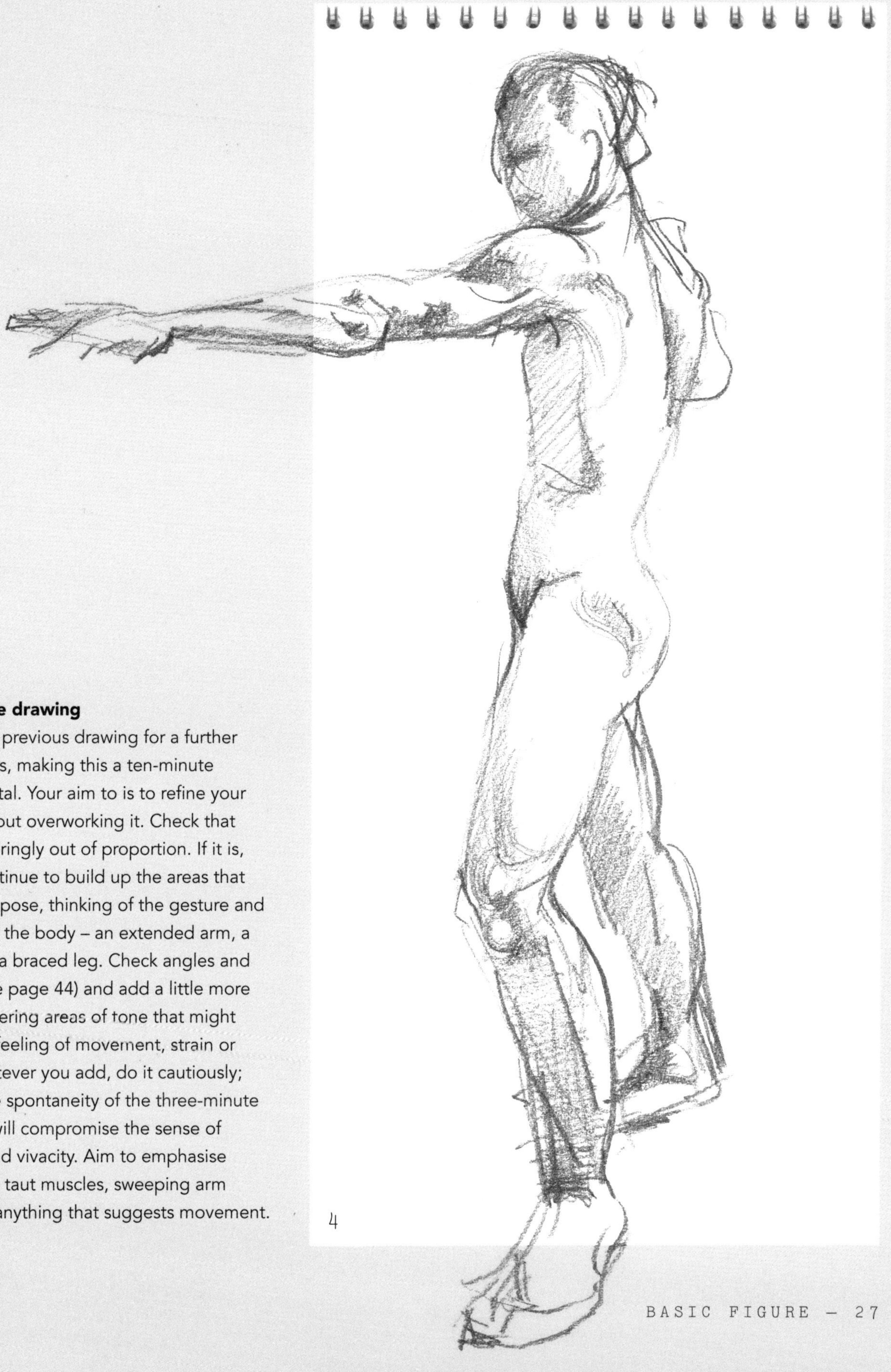

4. Ten-minute drawing

Continue the previous drawing for a further seven minutes, making this a ten-minute drawing in total. Your aim to is to refine your drawing without overworking it. Check that nothing is glaringly out of proportion. If it is, adjust it. Continue to build up the areas that underpin the pose, thinking of the gesture and the shapes of the body – an extended arm, a curved back, a braced leg. Check angles and distances (see page 44) and add a little more detail, considering areas of tone that might enhance the feeling of movement, strain or tension. Whatever you add, do it cautiously; don't lose the spontaneity of the three-minute pose as this will compromise the sense of movement and vivacity. Aim to emphasise twists, bends, taut muscles, sweeping arm movements, anything that suggests movement.

Looking Objectively

Most mistakes that are made in a life drawing class arise from preconceptions about what a person looks like. You might have an idea of what a mouth is, and then proceed to draw that idea of a mouth rather than the actual mouth of the model.

I often hear people mention such 'anatomical rules' as: the eyes are situated approximately halfway down the head; the distance across the eye is similar to the distance between the eyes; and the top of the ears are level with the eyes. Similar annotations appear with Leonardo da Vinci's drawing of the 'Vitruvian Man' – these rules may be anatomically accurate, but they are unhelpful in a life drawing class. Every model is amazingly different but, more significantly, their position in relation to your viewpoint will almost always cause you to have to reject any formulaic approach.

Robert Hooke mentions in his book *Micrographia* (1665) the importance of 'a sincere Hand, and a faithful Eye, to examine, and to record, the things themselves as they appear…' He places this above 'imagination, or exactness of Method, or depth of Contemplation (though the addition of these, where they can be had, must needs produce a much more perfect composure)'.

The artist's job is to process a three-dimensional image into a two-dimensional one that can be represented on a flat piece of paper. This is a challenging task, and I suggest that the best way to do it is to see your subject as they would appear on your picture plane – two dimensionally. Depth of field shouldn't be assumed – we can't know for sure how far back something stretches without walking around the model. If you accurately represent the shapes as they appear from your fixed position, depth can be implied. This is called foreshortening. Foreshortening can refer either to the figure, where features are distorted due to the effects of perspective, or your drawing and how the effects of perspective are represented. For a full explanation of foreshortening, see page 48.

I like to keep in mind Cézanne's assessment of his fellow artist: 'Monet is only an eye, but my God, what an eye!' I interpret this as referring to Monet's reliance on pure visuals, with no exaggeration or use of artistic licence to illustrate a point or opinion, just innocent, objective representation. The adherence to pure visual perception is so honest that any meaning or complexity within the subject is transmitted without the artist's intention. The Impressionists strove for this simplicity and honesty in representation.

A way to channel this simple honesty is to pretend you are seeing a human for the first time. All you have to go on is their two-dimensional appearance, you can't make any assumptions about what is behind them or what lies under their skin, much less their history or character. The only information you have is what you can see from your position next to your easel.

Empty your mind and begin to see your subject as a collection of shapes and tones, no more or less important than the background behind them or the furniture they are posing on. To aid you in this, let your eyes go out of focus in order to simplify the shapes and distance yourself from a familiar concept.

Spend a lot of time looking, rather than drawing. I was taught to look for 85 per cent of the time and make marks for 15 per cent. This may be counterintuitive, but if you force yourself to do it, you will notice an increase in accuracy, as well as an appreciation of subtleties that you may have previously overlooked. Try looking for eight seconds and drawing for no more than two. After making a couple of drawings in this way, just try to keep this ratio in mind before you commit marks to the page.

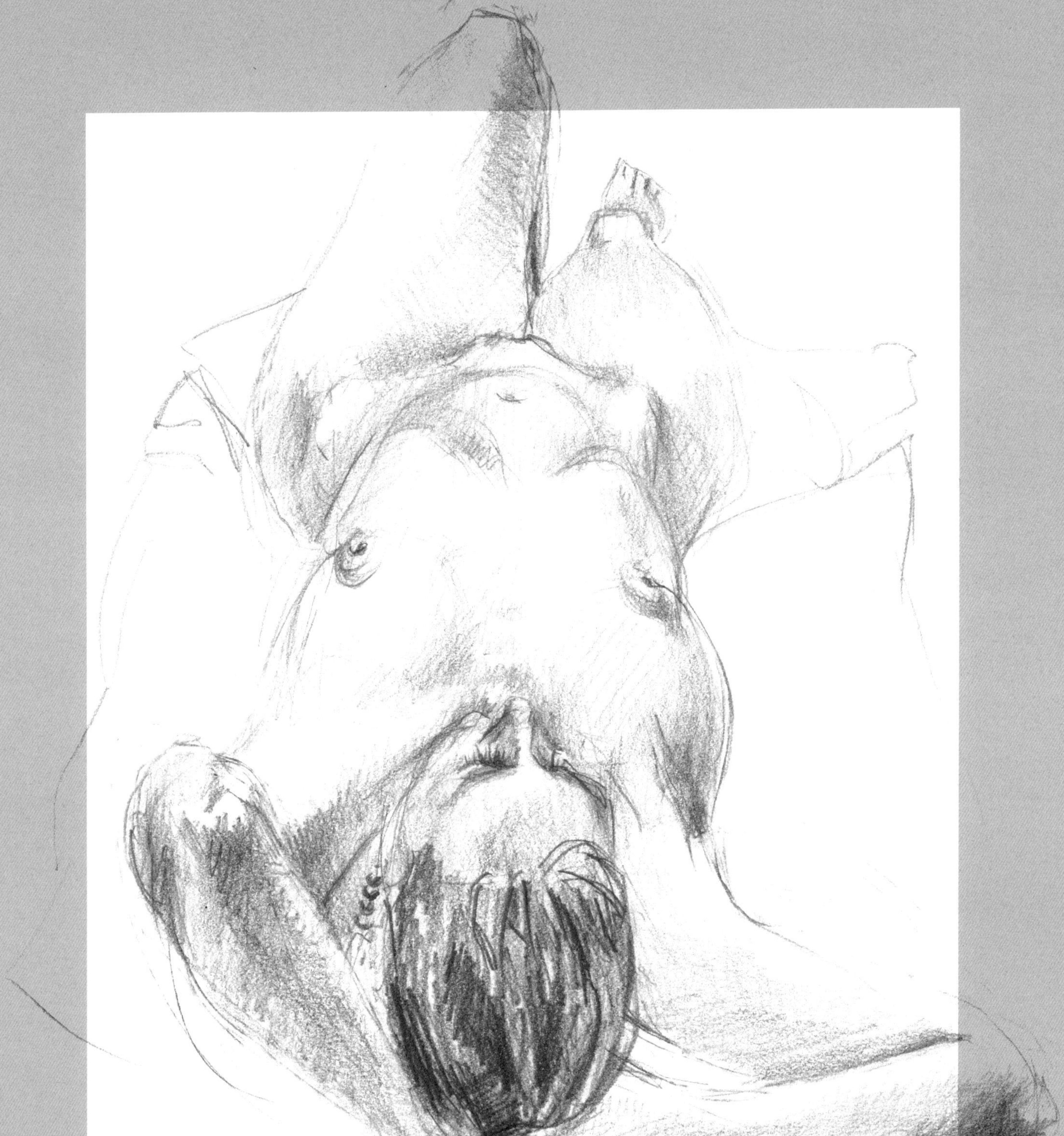

REMEMBER:

- Draw what you see, not what you think you see.

Observation-Based Drawing Exercises

In 'blind drawings', you draw from the model without looking at your paper. You have no choice but to concentrate on observation. The model will only hold the pose for a very short time as these blind drawings don't last long, perhaps just a minute or two each. You must be strict and stop yourself from glancing down – you might want to put your work on your lap under a table, or under a cloth. If you're working at an easel, turn farther away from it.

1. Blind drawing

Spend some time looking at the figure first. Then start drawing as you continue to look at the figure. I suggest you start at the head, as you might with any figure drawing. As your eye travels down, allow your pencil to echo the outline as you perceive it. Think mainly about the outline, but include any other features such as the hairline, eyes, jawline and breasts. It is fine to take your hand away from the paper; although you may find it impossible to recontinue the same line once you leave it, this is irrelevant for the purposes of this exercise and the end result needn't be coherent. The exercise ends when you feel you can do no more, when you accidentally look back at your work or when the time is up on the pose.

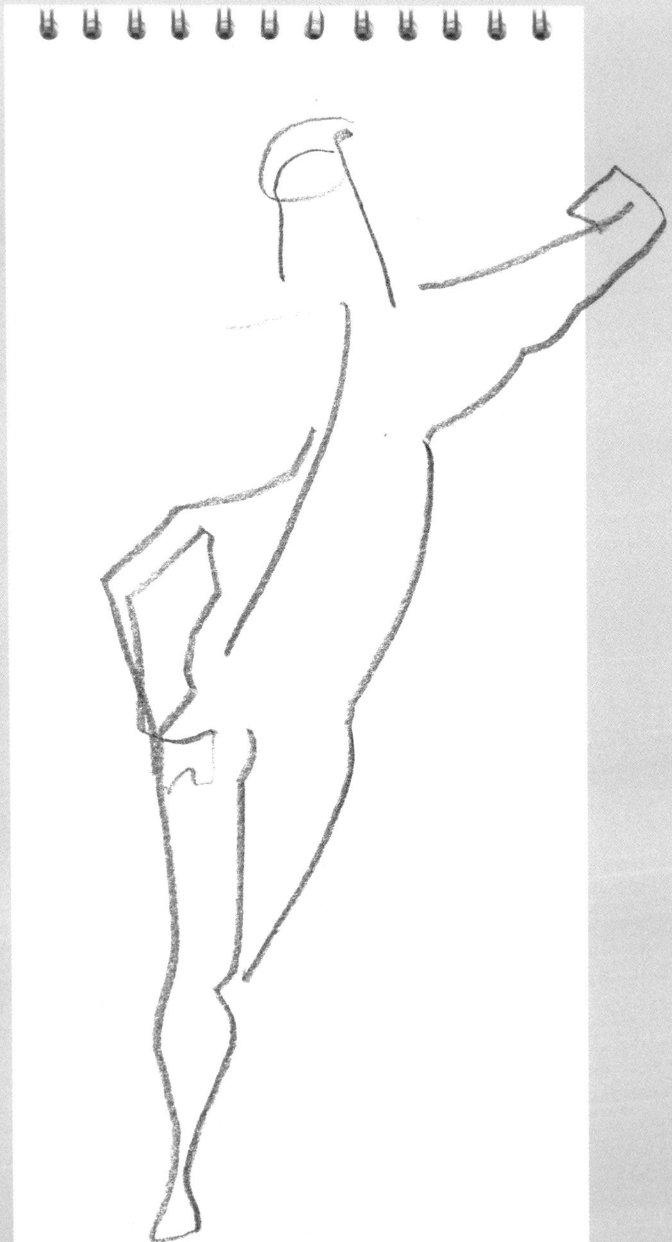

1

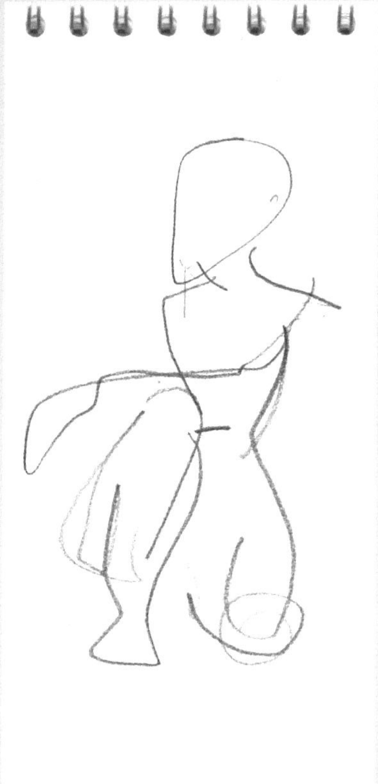

2

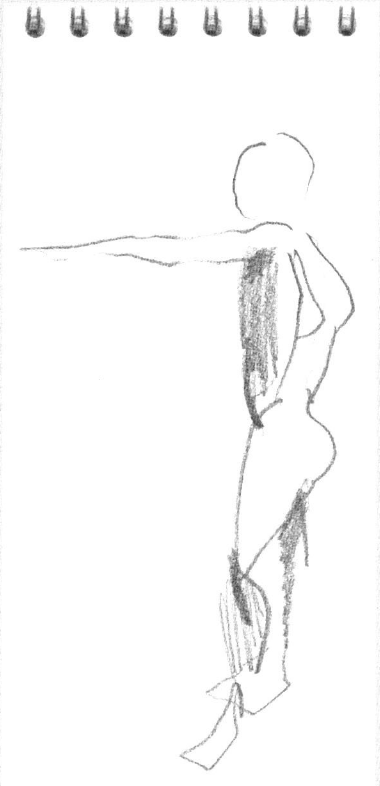

3

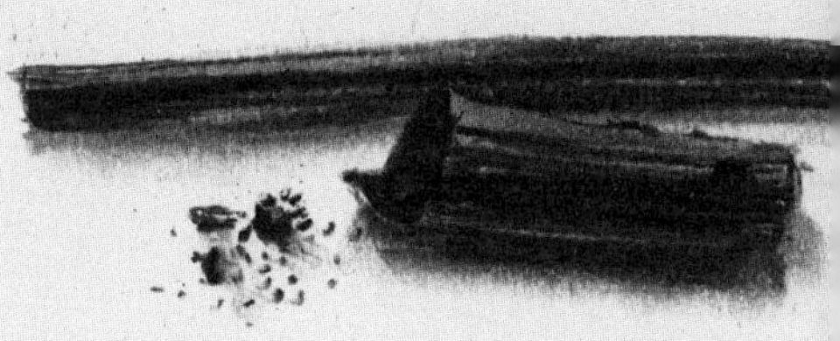

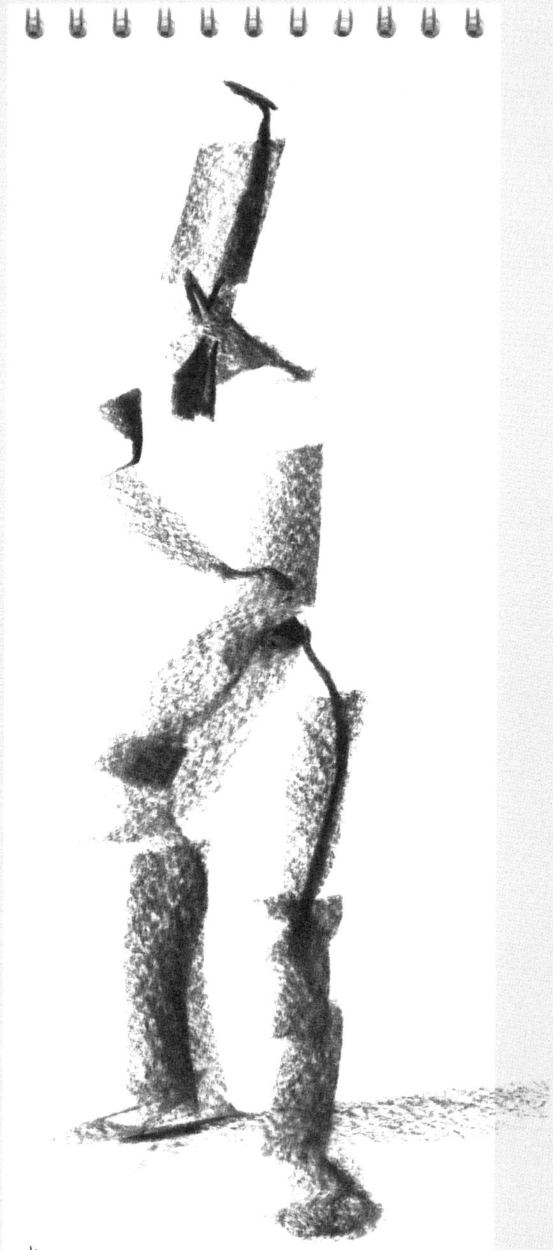

4

2. Gestural blind drawing

Although the resulting drawing is unimportant, the act of mark-making is linked to the 'looking' function, so try to let your actions reflect what you are seeing. What you may end up with is lots of convincing components but arranged together discordantly. In this pose, concentrate specifically on gesture and shape, as is described on page 24. Think about which features and shapes convey action or movement. What strikes you as essential? Is it perhaps an outstretched limb or a twist in the torso or neck?

3. Blind drawing with tone

In this blind drawing, think not just about line, but about tone as well. Let your eyes go out of focus to ascertain where the most important or deepest shadows appear.

4. Blind drawing using charcoal

For this exercise, try using a thick piece of charcoal. See blocks of tone, rather than lines. Again, going out of focus will aid you in noticing these patterns and ignoring detail.

Drawing with the Weaker Hand Exercise

It is often said that our weaker hand has an emotional rather than a logical function. With it, we certainly have less control when writing and drawing. Relinquishing this control leaves us freer to make mistakes. It allows us to be less concerned with the final drawing and more focused on the act of observation. I find that drawings made with the weaker hand are often surprisingly convincing, but look as if they're drawn in steel wool. The image is transferred from your eyes to your paper via a different route, tapping into the more creative and perceptual functions of your mind, rather than the verbal and analytical.

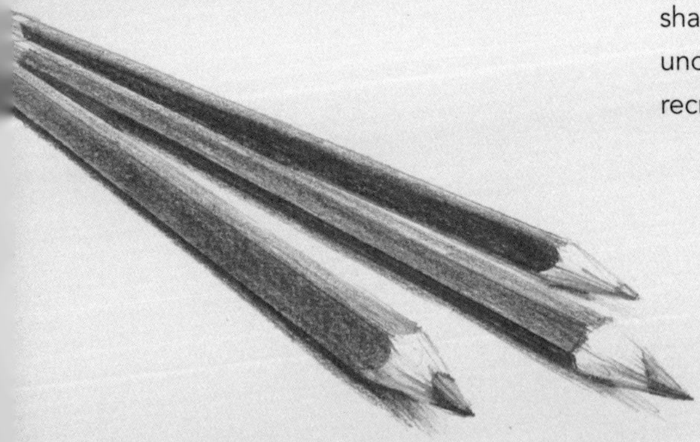

1. Clear your mind and look at the model carefully. Spend more time looking than drawing – remember the rule about looking for 85 per cent of the time. With your weaker hand, first sketch out a vague outline, starting with the head, then torso and arms, then legs, looking for opportunities to break the figure into manageable shapes (refer to the section on 'Shape', pages 36–39).

2. Let your eyes go out of focus and choose which lines and areas of shadow stand out. Depending on the pose and the lighting, this could be anything – perhaps the eye sockets, the shadow around the neck and chin, the spine or shoulder blades, the shadow around the pubic area and under the knees. Let your hand recreate these features on your paper.

3. Now you have a structure mapped out, go into slightly more detail. Look hard at the position of the nose, lips, ears and hairline. Think of the shape and size of the hands and feet in relation to other parts of the body – don't worry about individual digits, just look at the shape of the hand or foot as a whole.

4. Rub out any drastically wrong lines and try to strengthen the correct ones. Try to refine and add a little tone to consolidate your shapes. What do you notice about your drawing? Does it feel successful as a whole? Although the lines are shaky, is it accurate? Is it more expressive than a drawing made with your dominant hand?

1

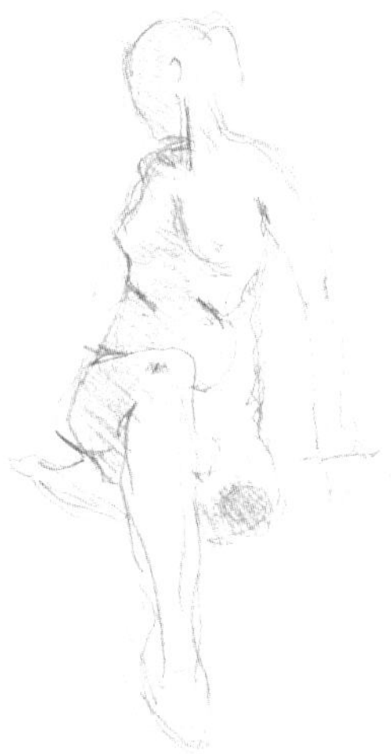

2

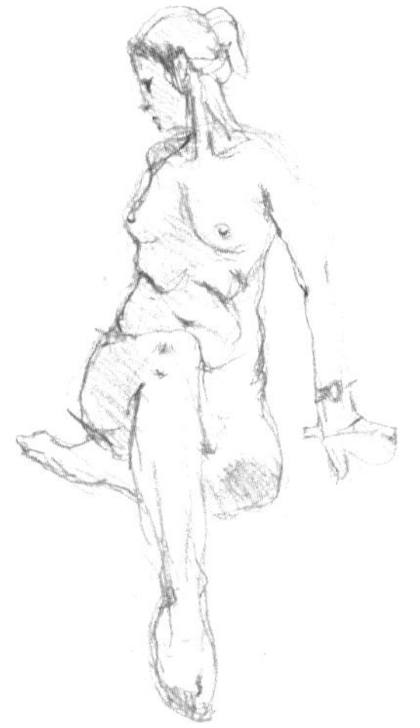

3

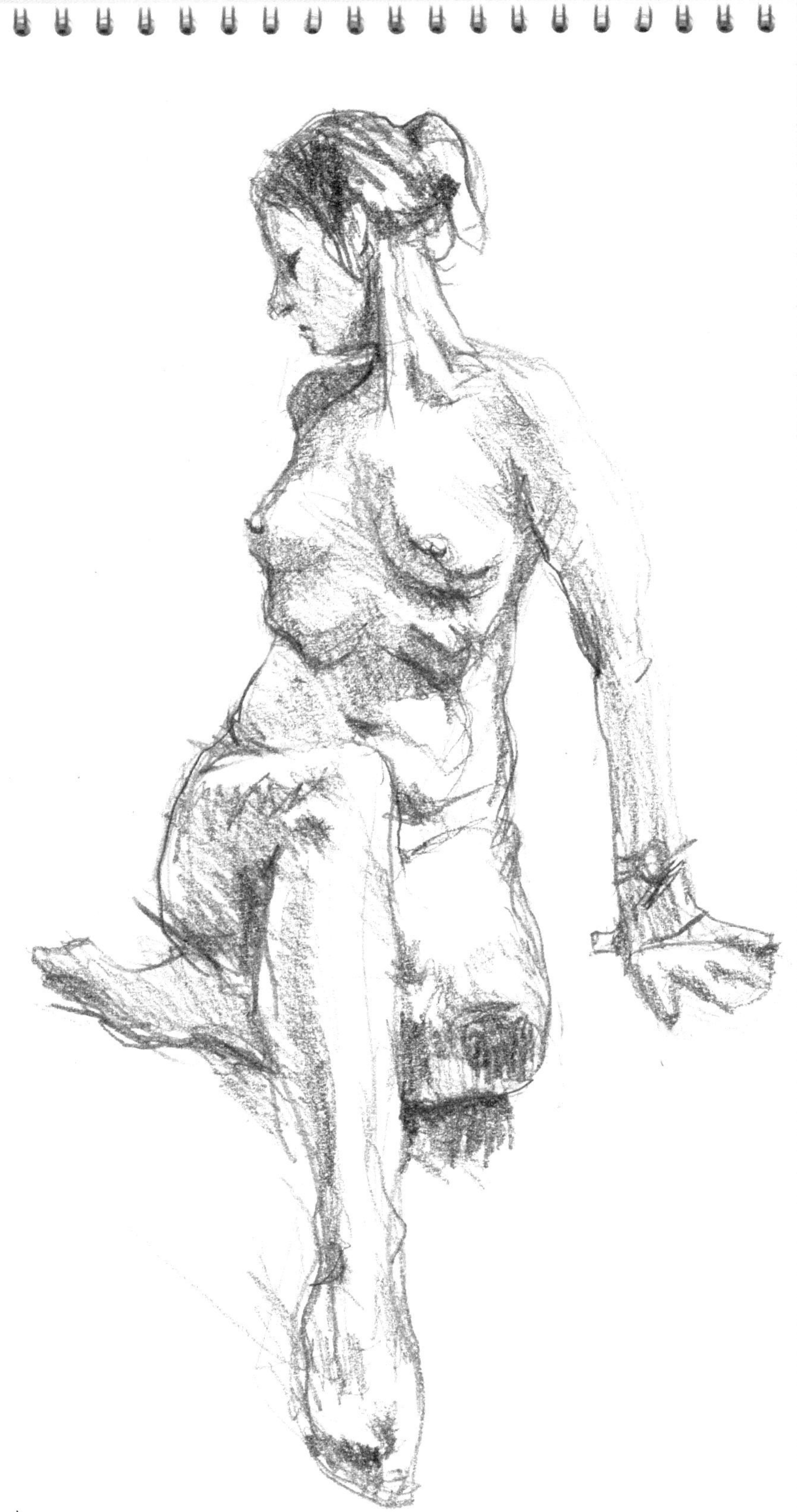

4

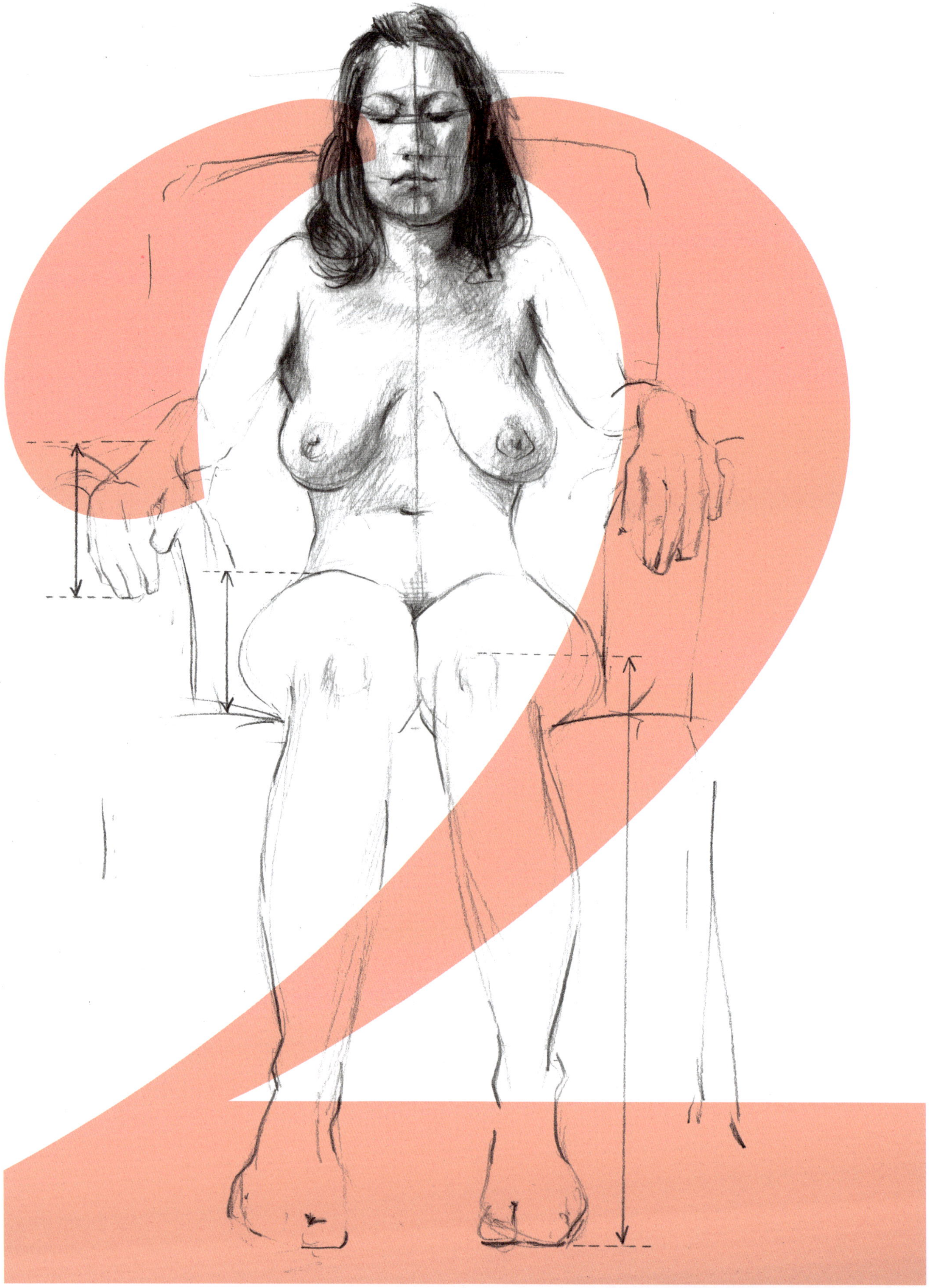

Construction

When we look at the figure, we see a familiar collection of three-dimensional shapes. To draw these shapes we need to process our view into a two-dimensional image, so that we can represent this on a flat piece of paper. To do this, it is helpful to detach ourselves somewhat from what we already know of the human body. This chapter encourages you to regard the figure objectively without preconceived ideas or assumptions about anatomy. All of these notions will come across in your drawing without you thinking of them. For example, when you faithfully copy the outline of the arm, even if you do so without considering or understanding the muscles underneath the skin, the line you have drawn will describe the shape of the muscles underneath the skin because they are what cause the bumps and curves of the outline.

The exercises here, ideal for both quick and longer drawings, will help you break the body into manageable shapes. Measuring by eye gives a level of accuracy, but there are also methods offering a more certain sense of proportion. These measuring techniques are essential to ascertain the correct angles and distances needed to convey a sense of perspective in foreshortened poses, where features may be distorted due to your viewpoint.

Shape

The quickest and most direct way to achieve proportion in your figure sketching is to concentrate on shapes. Don't think of drawing a human figure with a shape you recognise as a head, an arm, a torso, and so on, but concentrate instead on the shapes as they appear to you, without thinking about their meaning. This will ensure structural accuracy, which will then implicitly *describe* the shape of a head, an arm or a torso, even if there happens to be awkward foreshortening (the effect of perspective appearing to distort shapes – see page 48).

It is a daunting task to try to reconcile all parts of the body, getting them in proportion to each other. To make this easier, look for sensible points at which to segment the body. The idea is to construct the whole figure from simple shapes. You can decide on these points of division by letting your eyes go out of focus to simplify your view. Take note of dividing 'landmarks', which are visible marks or shadows that appear on the surface of the skin (as a result of the underlying skeleton or muscles, cast shadows, folds in the skin or blemishes) and provide a point at which to divide the figure. Such landmarks may include the shoulders, the waist, the spine, the hips, the groin, the knees, the ankles, the elbows and the wrists.

Once you have divided the body into manageable chunks, it is easier to assess visually how large one part is and where it sits in relation to the next. Try not to let your familiarity with body parts come into your assessment.

Although I advocate being completely objective and forgetting about the meaning of the shapes, I find it easiest, for whatever reason, to start with the head. This might be just because it is normally at the top, and that is a sensible starting point. I equate this with handwriting, where you habitually start to form a letter of the alphabet at a certain natural point.

You can set these shapes down as close to your estimations as possible, but still spending the larger proportion of your time regarding the model. If you keep your marks light from the beginning and completely eschew detail for the time being, you can portray a recognisable person very quickly. This is great practice for improving proportion in your very quick sketches, without having to do any measuring (which will be explained later in the 'Measuring' section, pages 44–47).

When you have the whole figure sketched out in simple blocks, it is helpful to get some distance from your work and judge it as a whole. Does anything feel wrong? If so, compare it directly to the model. Continue to look at your drawing in terms of shapes, rather than anatomy. At this point you can make adjustments if you need to – you won't have the trauma of having to erase a lovely area of detail that is just undeniably in the wrong place. You can then begin to add detail, knowing that your structure and proportions have been consolidated first.

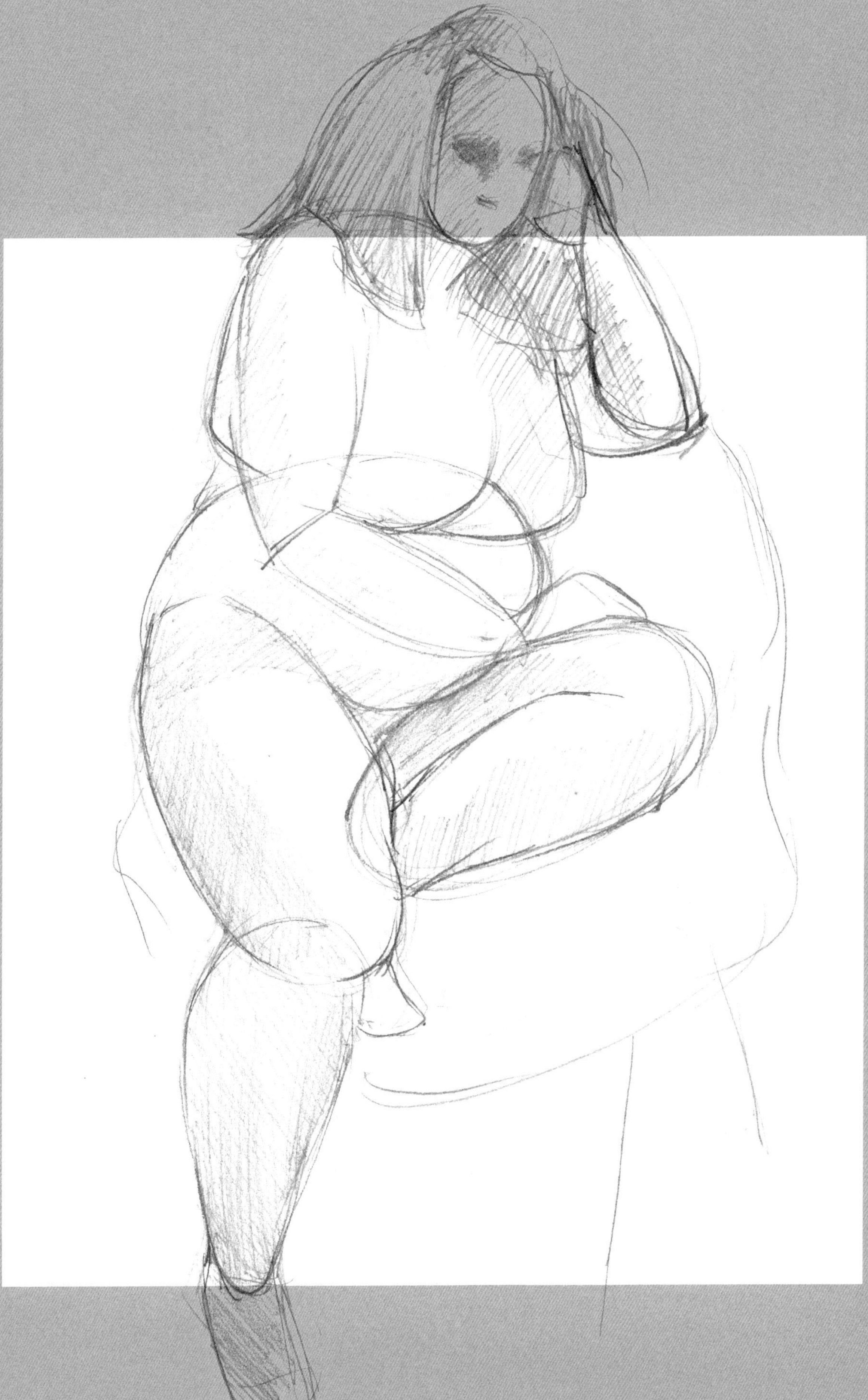

Shape Exercise

1. Look carefully at your model through very unfocused eyes. Gauge the shape as a whole – think in terms of a forensics outline at a crime scene. Mark this down in very light pencil. This helps you fit your entire figure onto your page, so you don't later discover you haven't left enough room for the feet.

2. Look at the model again for a while. Choose a few points at which you can split up the figure. Although these will change from pose to pose, some sensible shapes might be the head; the shoulders to the navel; the navel to the groin; the waist to the buttocks; the thighs and knees; the lower leg; the foot; the upper arm and the lower arm. Scrutinise each shape one at a time, letting it become totally detached from its nomenclature and associations. See it as a disembodied form and think about its angles and symmetry. Mark them down one by one, with a similarly light touch.

3. Check the relationships between each of these shapes. The relative position and size of each shape is crucial in order to establish the proportions of the figure as a whole. Make any adjustments you need to. Be led by intuition. If you feel something is not quite right, this is the stage to rub it out and alter it. As you check the sizes you can be more sure of the outlines and you can begin to reflect the shapes you wish to represent, rather than sticking purely to geometric shapes.

4. Look at the joining lines that connect the shapes. Mark them in slightly darker. Think about the angles of these lines. Using a rubber, you can begin to lighten the outlines of the shapes drawn in steps 1–3, thus allowing the contours of the figure to become stronger.

5. Look at the refined shapes and areas within your figure drawing and find landmarks to break them down even more.

Let's take the head as an example: how far up do the eye sockets, nose and lips appear? What are the angles between each? Mark their positions without going into detail. Do the same for the rest of the body. You now have a well-proportioned structure on which to build more detail if you wish.

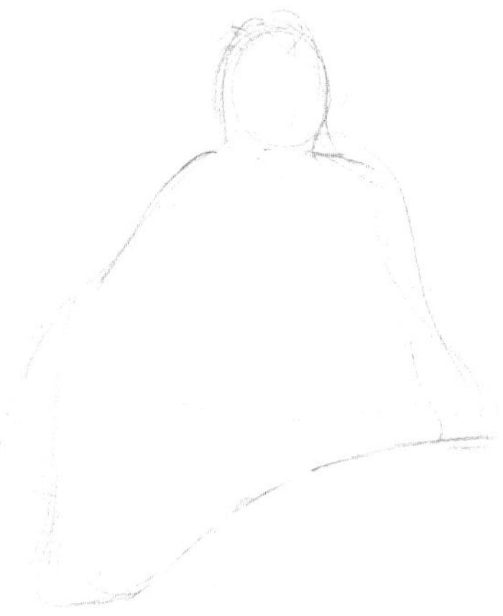

1

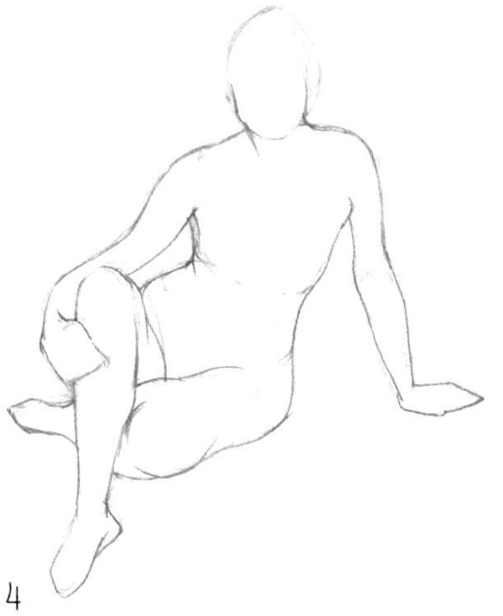

4

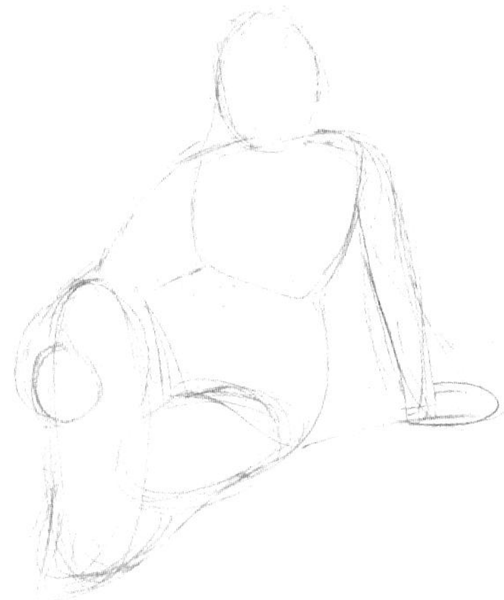

2

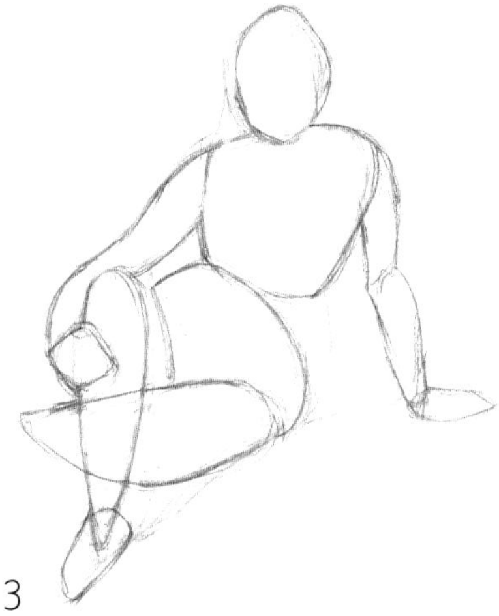

3

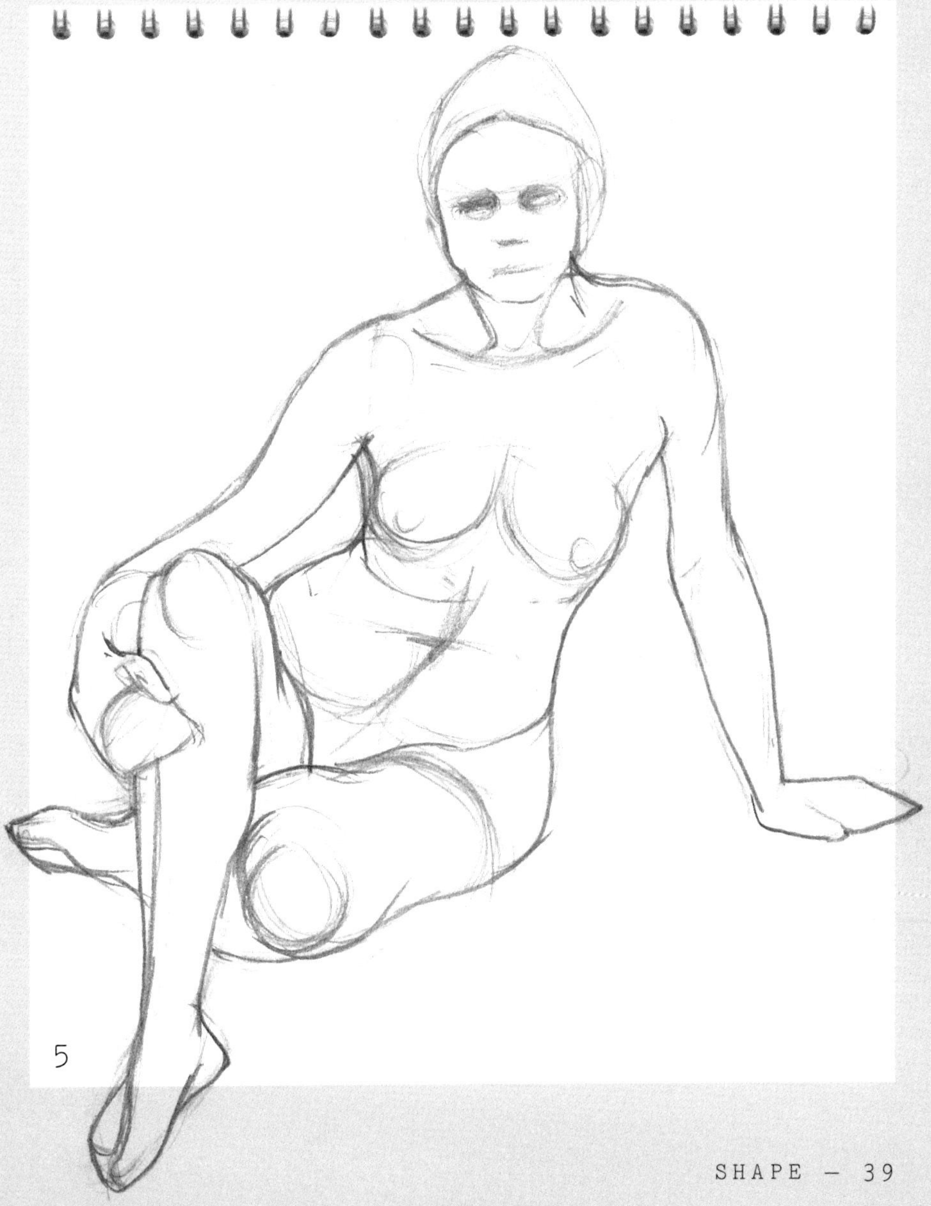

5

Construction Lines

Construction lines are another way to segment the figure into manageable chunks. These are not necessarily formed by the shapes you see, but by virtual lines that you impose. If you imagine that the Shape Exercise on the previous pages, 38–39, explained how one might draw the earth as a round shape, this exercise makes use of lines of latitude, longitude and the equator – imaginary lines – to describe the volume and tilt.

Construction lines provide further sensible 'landmarks' to work with, and an armature to underpin the structure of the figure. They are the 'workings out' – if you draw them lightly, you can rub them out later so that they don't appear in your finished drawing. You might, however, feel they add something to your work. Euan Uglow leaves evidence of his construction lines and marks all over his finished paintings. He uses them as a means to achieve absolute perfection in the accurate proportions of his strictly observed figure drawings and paintings.

Construction lines can be used very effectively in portrait drawings, as well as for the figure as a whole. It may be tricky to choose their placement because they don't actually exist, but you can situate them between real points on the body, such as from the centre of the collar bone to the navel, to the pubis (see fig 1). On the head, try from the centre of the forehead down the nose to the centre of the chin or, perhaps, from the top of one ear through the eyes to the other ear (see fig 2). These lines, like the equator, will appear flat and straight as you look at them head on, but will curve and move to one side, or become higher or lower as the figure rotates or looks upwards or downwards. In these slightly more dynamic poses, construction lines can be very helpful in mapping out the spatial relationship between various features.

Don't think of imposing a line down the middle of your drawing, but rather imagine a line drawn down the middle of the figure, bending as they move, then draw this visualisation.

You can also use construction lines as scaffolding between two points, to consolidate the angles. These needn't curve with the position of the figure but can be a straight line joining two points, for example, the outer edge of the shoulder to the top of the head. Drawing construction lines between key points and identifying the angles helps you to judge the distances between features within the figure as a whole (see the dotted lines in fig 1).

Construction lines can make clearer things that aren't quite so obvious, such as how much lower one point is than another. For example, the knee of the leg closest to you may seem lower because of the effects of perspective. When someone tilts their head upwards, their ears are no longer level with their eyes, they seem to move lower on the head, while the eyes move higher. A construction line connecting the eyes and ears in this pose will form an arc and account for this change in height.

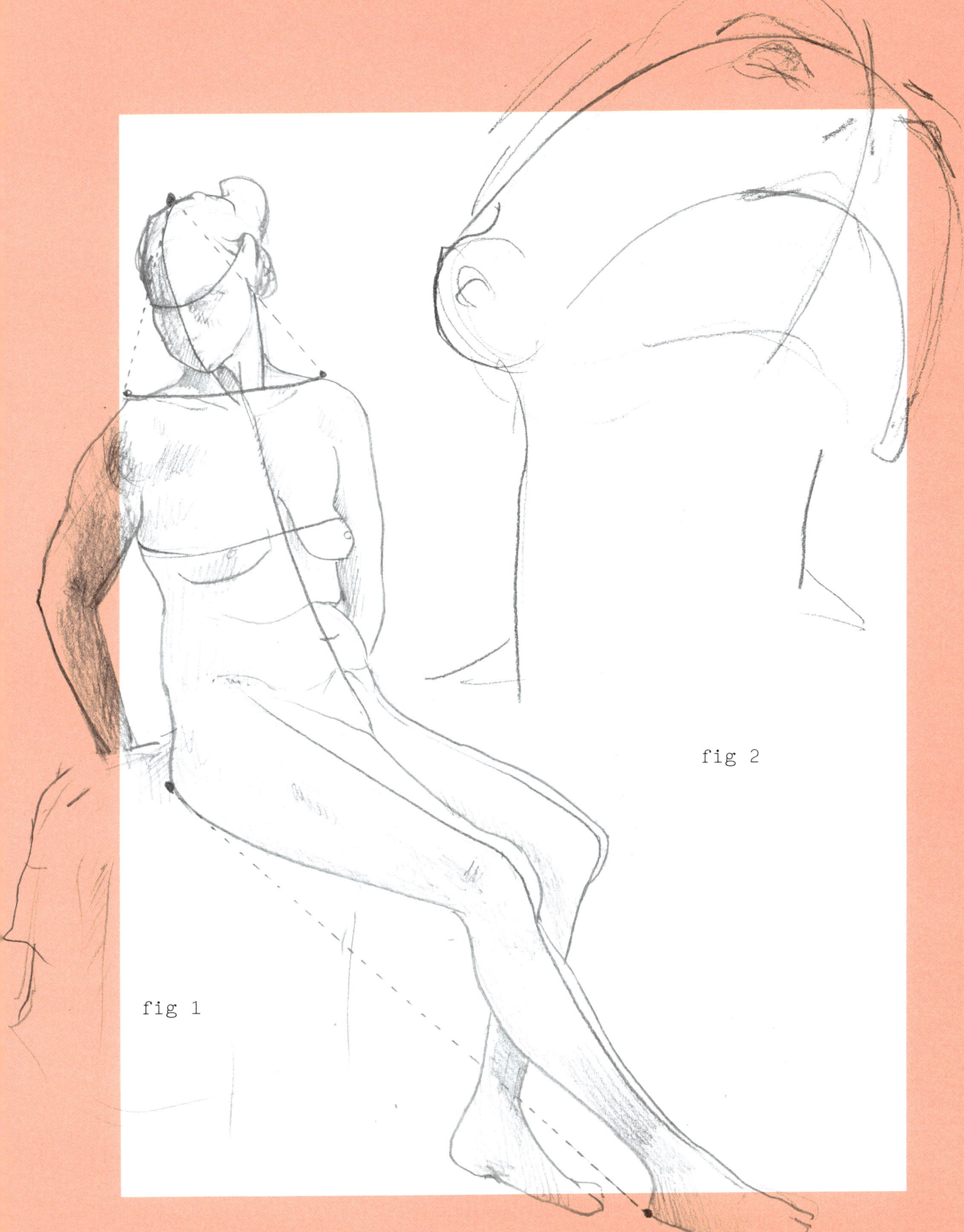

fig 1

fig 2

Construction Lines **Exercise**

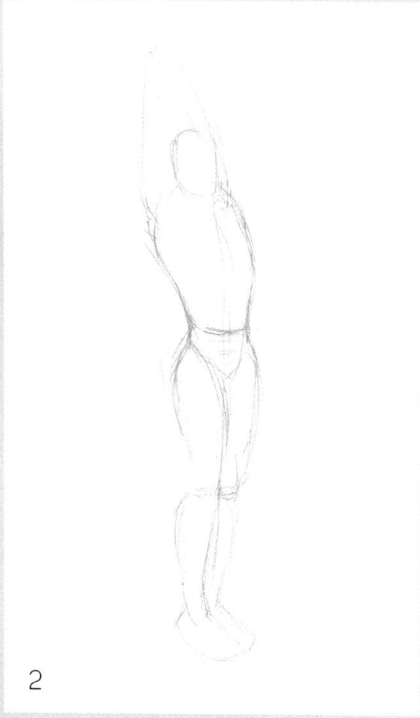

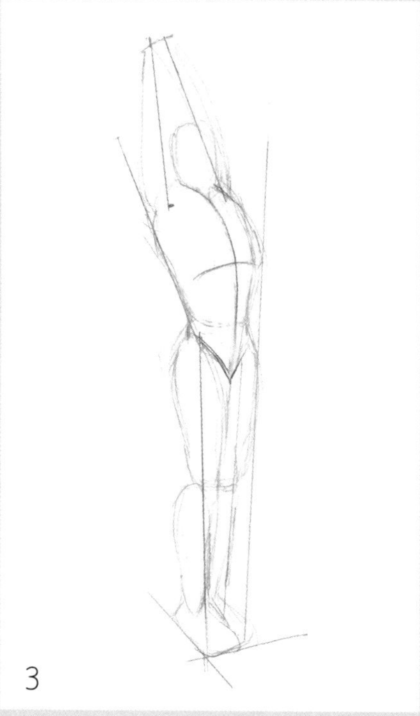

1. Look hard at the figure and try to imagine a line running down through the centre of the body. This line might be bent or curved if the model is bending. Mark the line in lightly on your page.

2. Referring to the previous Shape Exercise (see page 38), let your eyes go out of focus and break the figure down into simple shapes. Using your line from the previous step as a guide, take time to draw the shapes in the right position in relation to each other. Again, use your pencil lightly.

3. From a distance, check if your shapes appear to be in the right positions and are proportioned correctly so far. Attend to any obvious errors at this stage. Is your central construction line in the correct place or does it need tweaking? You might find it helpful to use straight construction lines from shoulder to fingertips, and from hip to toes, to make sure the overall angles of the limbs are correct. These lines will be single straight lines joining two points and won't necessarily run centrally through the limbs, which will curve and bend.

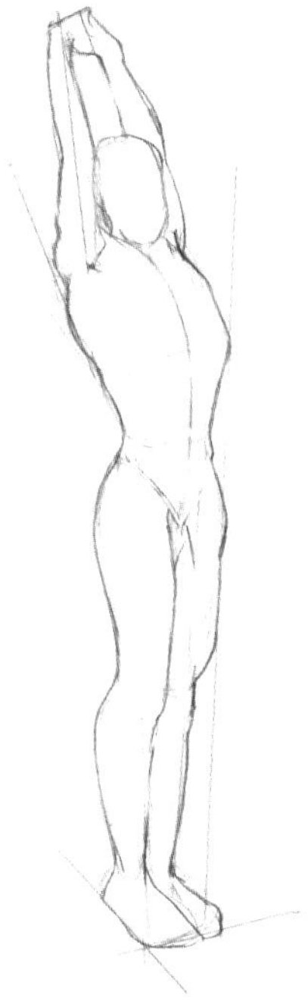

4

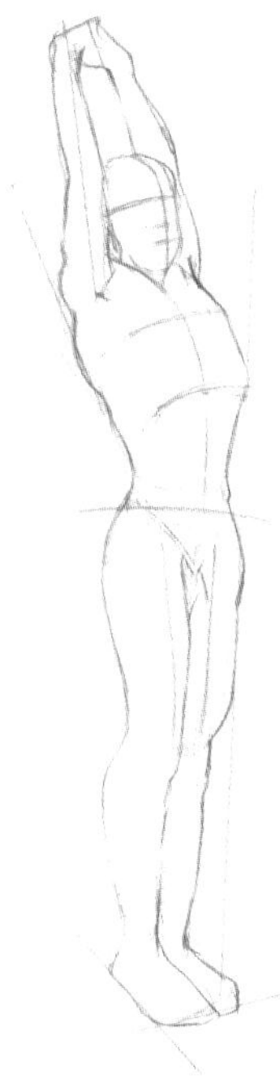

5

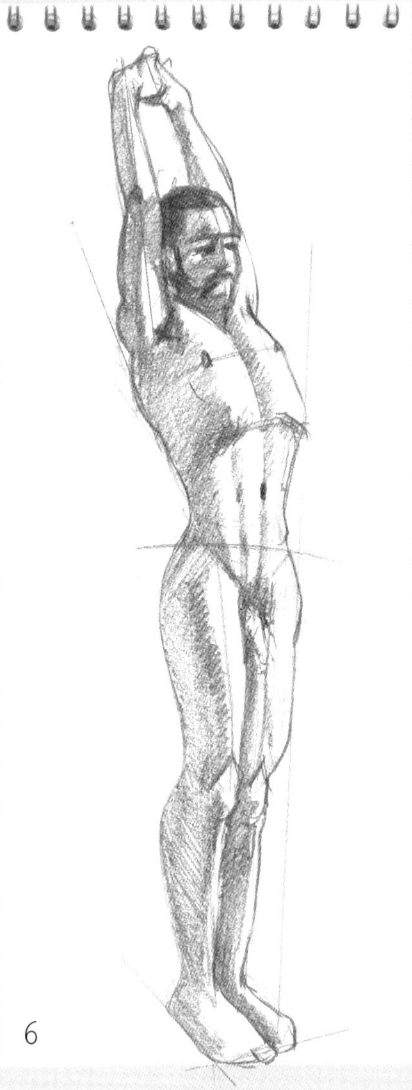

6

4. If you need to adjust the limbs after putting in these construction lines, do so. When you are satisfied, strengthen some of the outlines of the shapes, and join them together. You can erase some of the lines that made up your original shapes, leaving only those that refer to the actual contours and outlines of the figure.

5. Now draw in more specific construction lines. Imagine a vertical construction line that bisects the face and continues up and over the top of the head – how close to the centre or the side is this line? Next, perhaps a horizontal construction line to inform the positions of the eyes and ears – how far up the head is this line? Does it curve slightly or dramatically? The line from hip to hip or shoulder to shoulder is often quite useful for indicating the stance of the figure.

6. Use these new construction lines to add further features, such as the eyes, nose, mouth, nipples and navel. Keep your shapes vague and light so that they can still be moved if necessary. You can now add tone to make your drawing look more developed.

Measuring

Adopting a detached objectivity in order to see the figure in terms of pure shape is an effective way to improve the sense of proportion in your quick sketches. However, to achieve an even higher level of accuracy, you can use any of three simple methods for taking measurements using your pencil.

These methods rely on measuring the figure as a two-dimensional image, which appears in your picture plane. In other words, imagine looking at the model through a window: for each of the following methods, hold your pencil as if it were pressed flat against that window, able only to rotate clockwise and anticlockwise (not tipping forwards or backwards). Imagine the window is at your full arm's length – this will keep your pencil at a constant distance so that your readings don't fluctuate with a slight bend in your elbow.

Even if these methods yield dubious results, check them, then trust them – never ignore them. The rest of your drawing will benefit.

Horizontals and verticals

Hold your pencil horizontally in front of you as if it were a spirit level. This will give you an indication as to whether the features line up as expected. For example, the eyes may not actually appear at the same height. You will also see what else on the body appears along that horizontal line.

You can use your pencil as a plumb line in much the same way to see which features line up against a vertical axis. This may tell you where the foot needs to be in relation to hips or shoulders, giving your drawing a more realistic sense of balance and gravity. If the feet are not in the correct place, they may appear not to be able to support the weight of the figure, and your figure may seem like it is about to topple over.

Angles

Holding your pencil flat against the imaginary window at arm's length, you can align it with a leg or an arm of the model, and then move the pencil to your paper, trying to retain the angle. Unless you're working at an easel, hold your board or sketchbook up so that you've got as little distance to travel as possible, so you don't lose the position. You can also measure the imaginary line between two points, which can be useful when trying to place construction lines. Using just angles, you should be able to triangulate all the key points on the figure and avoid using the slightly more time-consuming distance method below.

Distance

This method requires that you already have something down on your page, because it relies on comparative distances. Let's use the head as a 'control measurement' in this example. Hold your pencil at arm's length, with the point meeting the top of the figure's head. Slide your thumb down until you reach the chin. Now you can use this measurement to check how many 'head distances' you have from chin to toe, by keeping your thumb in place and moving your pencil down in line with the body. Or you can move your pencil to another part of the body and find a similar control distance. Looking back to your drawing, you must make it reflect your findings. Don't transfer the 'thumb to pencil-nib' measurement to your paper directly, but use the knowledge of the comparisons you have made.

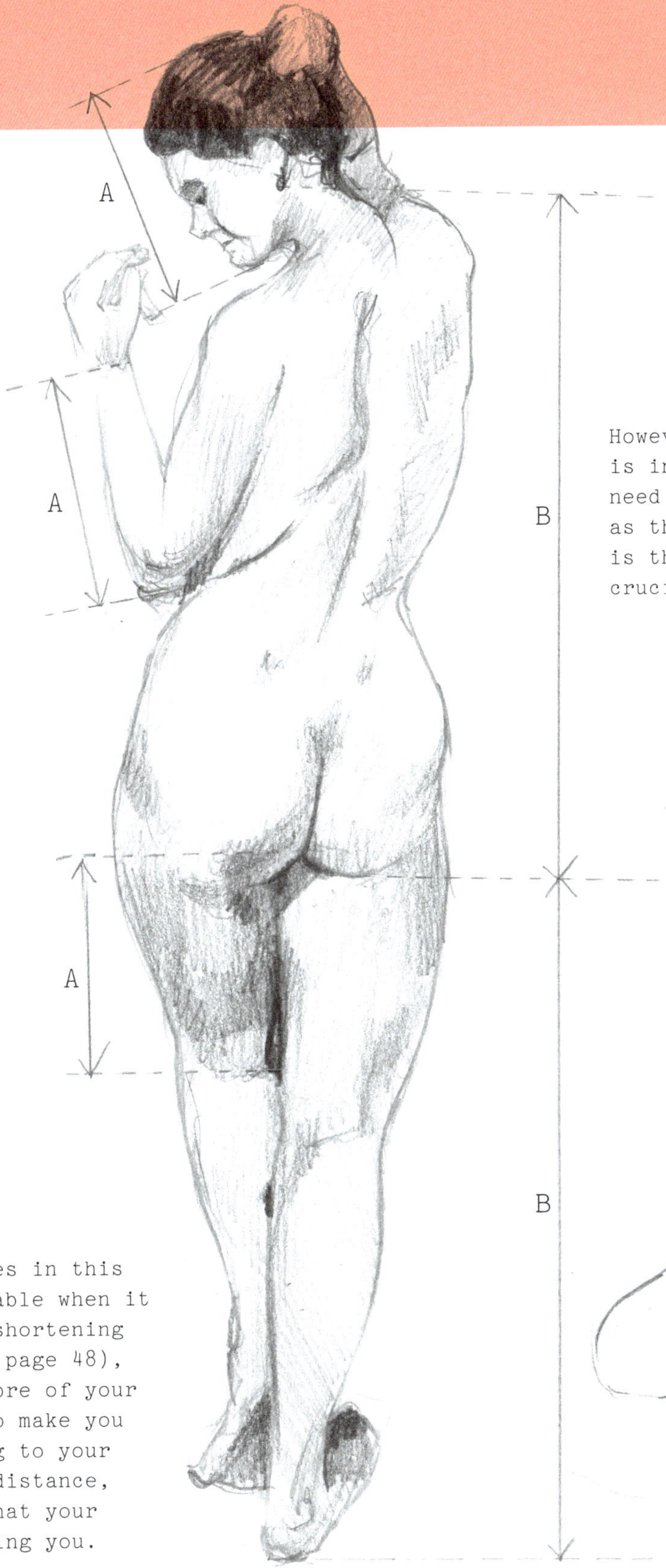

However large the head is in your drawing, you need to use *that* distance as the measure. This method is the most accurate and is crucial to foreshortening.

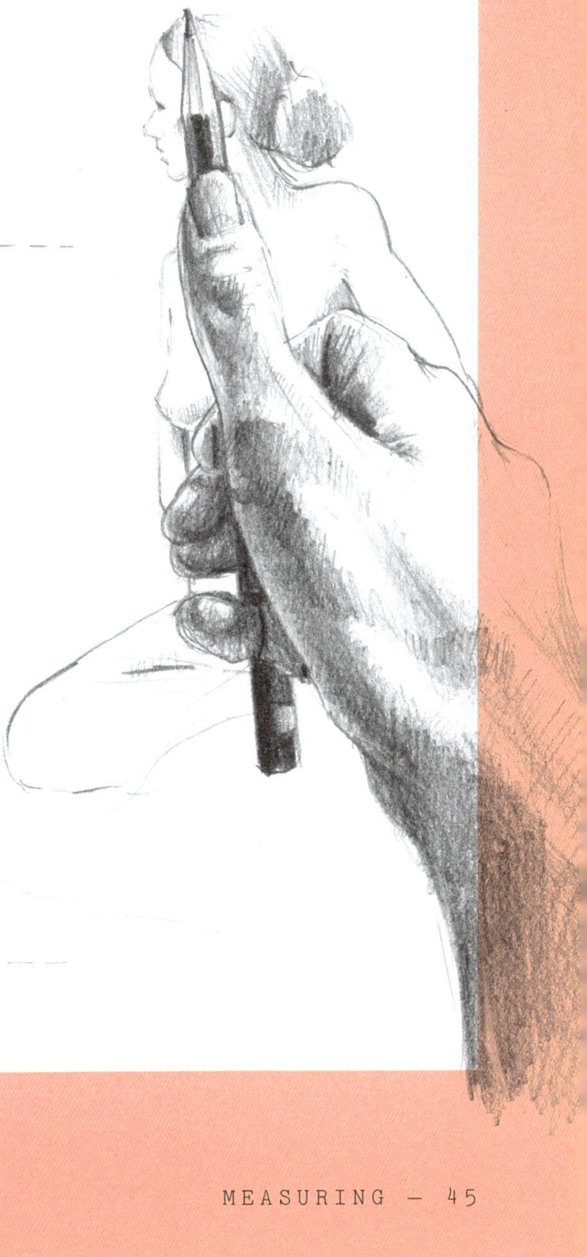

Checking angles in this way is invaluable when it comes to foreshortening (explained on page 48), when every fibre of your being tries to make you draw according to your knowledge of distance, rather than what your eyes are telling you.

Measuring Exercise

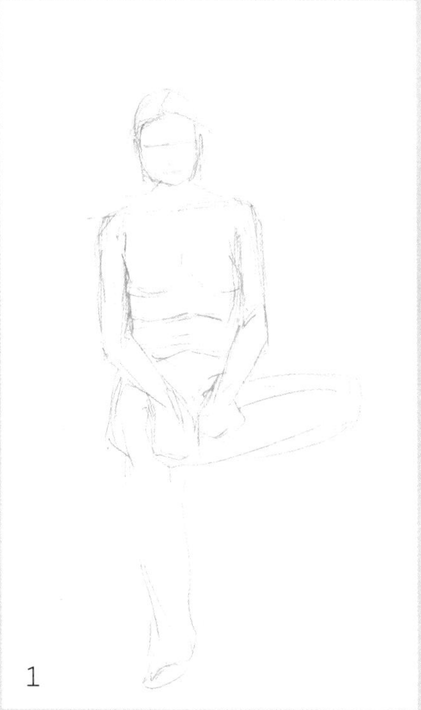

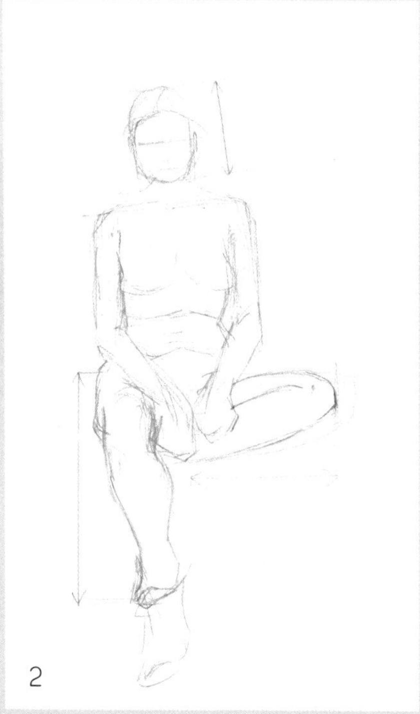

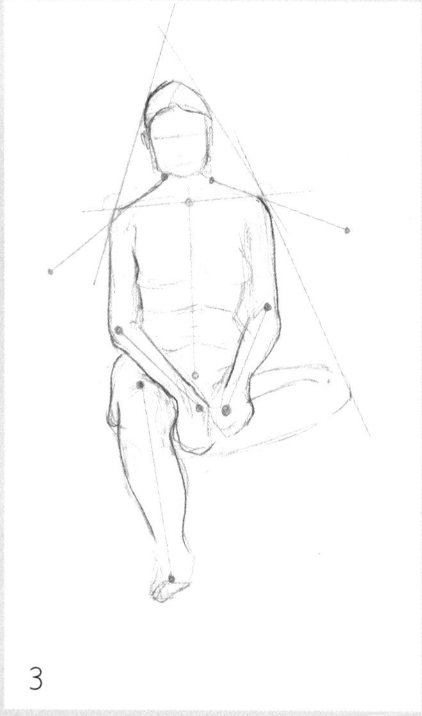

1. Having broken the figure down into its main large shapes, quickly draw it out as you see it. Make very light marks that can easily be erased. Do not include detail. Refer back to steps 1–3 in the Shape Exercise on page 38.

2. Use your pencil at arm's length to see if all the shapes are correct in height and distance from each other. Align the nib of your pencil with a point on the model (e.g. the top of the head) and slide your thumb down to the other side of the shape you are measuring (e.g. to the chin). Move your pencil around to find similarly sized features. Measure the head in your drawing and check it against features that should match it in size. Make any alterations needed. Always trust your measurements, or you will have problems with perspective later.

3. Next, use your pencil to check the angles on the figure. Select points on the figure and align your pencil with them. Then transfer your pencil to your paper, keeping the angle the same. You can use this method to begin to consolidate your outlines. Think about the slope of the shoulders and the overall angle of the legs and arms, from hip to toe and shoulder to fingertips. Are the limbs straight or do they bend at the joints? If they bend, you will need two separate measurements (e.g. from hip to knee and from knee to toe).

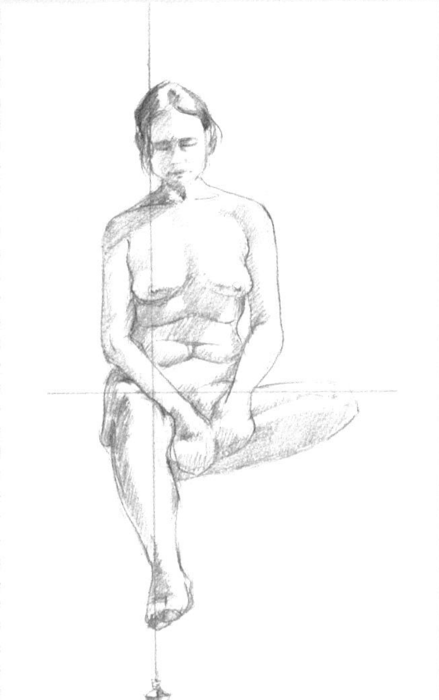
4

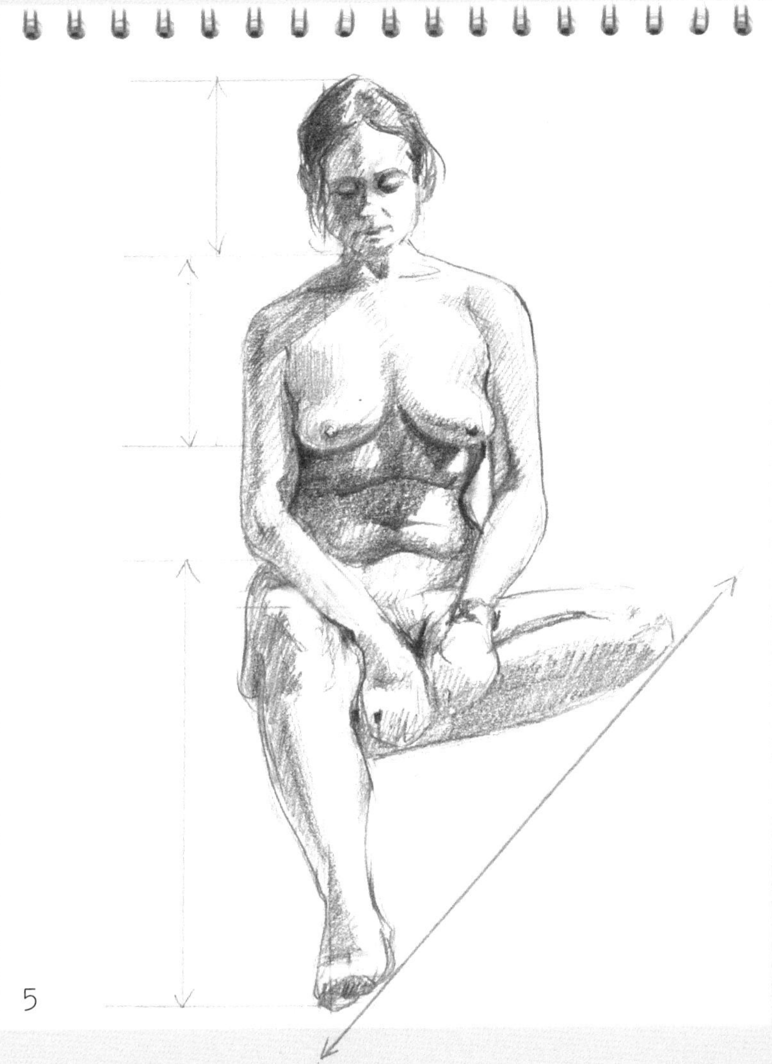
5

4. Get some distance from your work and check that everything is beginning to look in proportion. Check that everything lines up correctly against your vertical 'plumb line' and your horizontal 'spirit level' line. You can use the imaginary plumb line to check where the navel should be. Also make sure that the feet are in line with whatever should appear above them. You can start to add a little more detail and tone now. Use the plumb line method to ensure that any tone or detail lines up correctly with what is directly above it on the figure.

5. Again, check your drawing as a whole. Use any of the three measuring methods to check that your sense of perspective is correct and everything is in proportion. Trust your eyes and don't try to ignore small mistakes – they can have a large knock-on effect. If a limb is extended towards you, it will appear shorter due to perspective, so you must trust any surprisingly short measurements. Similarly, if the angle of the hips is imperceptibly wide, the knees will be visibly too far apart. The feet, in turn, will be in a more drastically incorrect position.

Foreshortening

Foreshortening is the distorted appearance of three-dimensional objects as they recede into the distance. In your drawing, it may be necessary to manipulate the familiar proportions of the figure so that they replicate this depth of field in two dimensions. This is not an easy process: it is difficult to detach yourself from the familiar length of an arm and draw it directly as it appears when extended towards you – short and squashed.

The painter Andrea Mantegna provides an early example of foreshortening in art. In his painting *The Lamentation over the Dead Christ* (c. 1480) he is not altogether successful – we can see that the legs and feet appear much too small, but the arms are too long.

We know that the farther away an object is, the smaller it will appear. Think about train tracks travelling away from you towards the horizon, seeming to get narrower and closer together until they disappear. These follow lines of perspective. The point at which they seem to disappear is the vanishing point. In your drawing you must create the illusion that parallel lines travelling away from the viewer (orthogonals) will converge at a vanishing point in the distance. Fig 1 shows how the light (the image in front of us) reaches us from the figure, via the picture plane. The light travels in straight lines from all points on the figure – I have just illustrated a few. The picture plane is the imagined 'window' corresponding to the surface of the drawing, perpendicular to the viewer's line of sight.

Fig 2 shows how the light would hit this picture plane and thus how the image appears to the viewer. This is consequently how it should appear in the drawing. We see here how much the shapes seem to be compressed – distances are much shorter than we expect; closer body parts appear much larger than we imagine; certain parts are lost from sight, hidden by the length of the body. This diagram offers proof to refer to when you second-guess your measurements and attempt the counterintuitive process of manipulating the figure in foreshortening.

Obviously in a life drawing class it is impractical to work out the proportions of the figure using this lengthy and empirical method. To create a convincing sense of perspective, you must draw the image as it would appear on the picture plane. The only sensible way to do this is to look completely objectively, as always, detaching yourself from familiar notions of proportion. It is necessary to see the figure purely as a collection of shapes. Refer to the section on 'Shape' (pages 36–39) and simplify the figure accordingly. Jenny Saville and Lucian Freud often use exaggerated foreshortening to create drama, placing the viewer uncomfortably close to the figure, or in a strange position above or below.

For severe foreshortening (such as a limb pointing straight towards you, or a figure lying down with their feet close to you and their head farther away), you will also need to measure with your pencil. Holding your pencil in front of you, check the relative sizes of the shapes. These measurements are always surprising, and it is always worth trusting them.

Achieving accurate angles is also very important in foreshortening – you want your orthogonal lines to converge at the correct vanishing point. Look back at the 'Measuring' section (pages 44–47) to see how to check angles and distances. You are not measuring the proportions of the model but your *view* of the model. So take care with how you hold your pencil – it should be flat against your 'picture plane', don't be tempted to let it lean forwards to follow the receding lines of the foreshortened figure.

fig 1

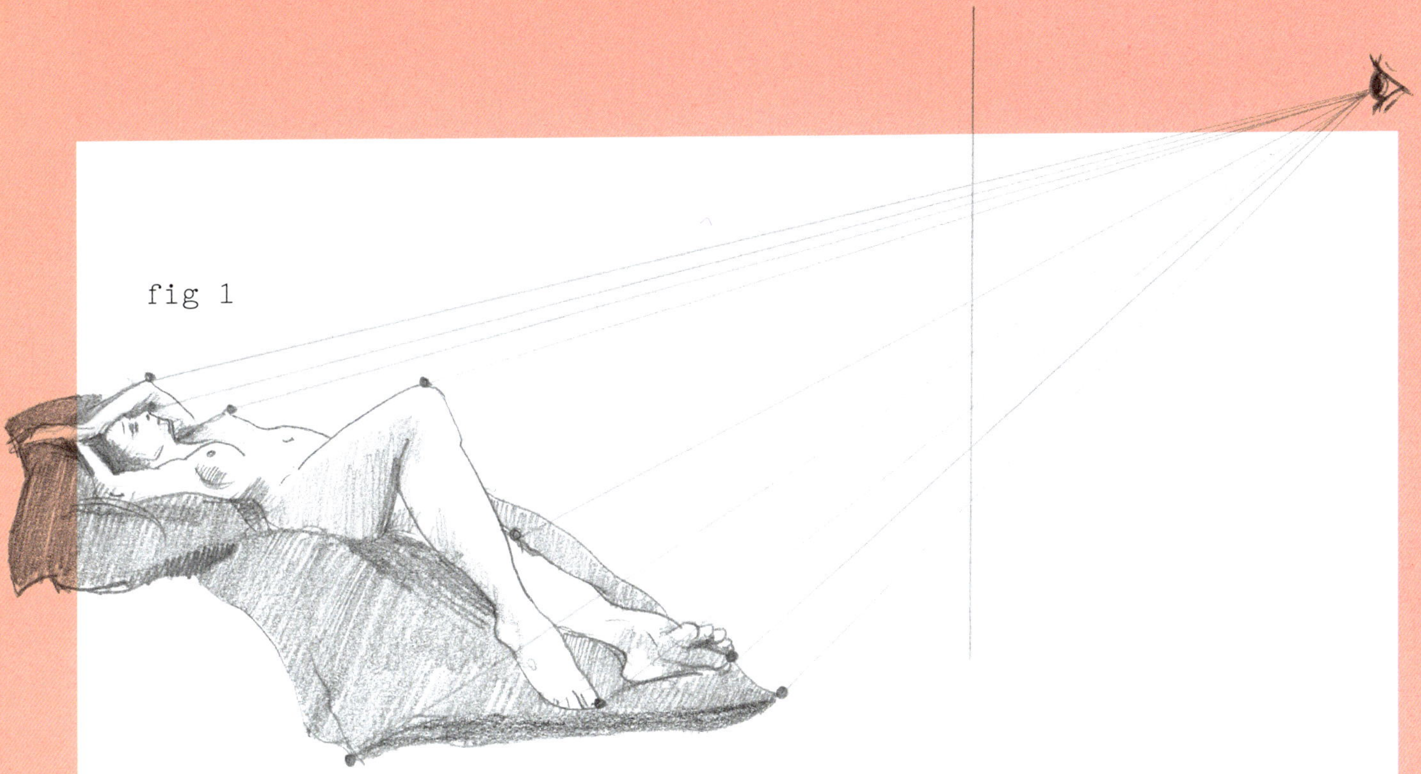

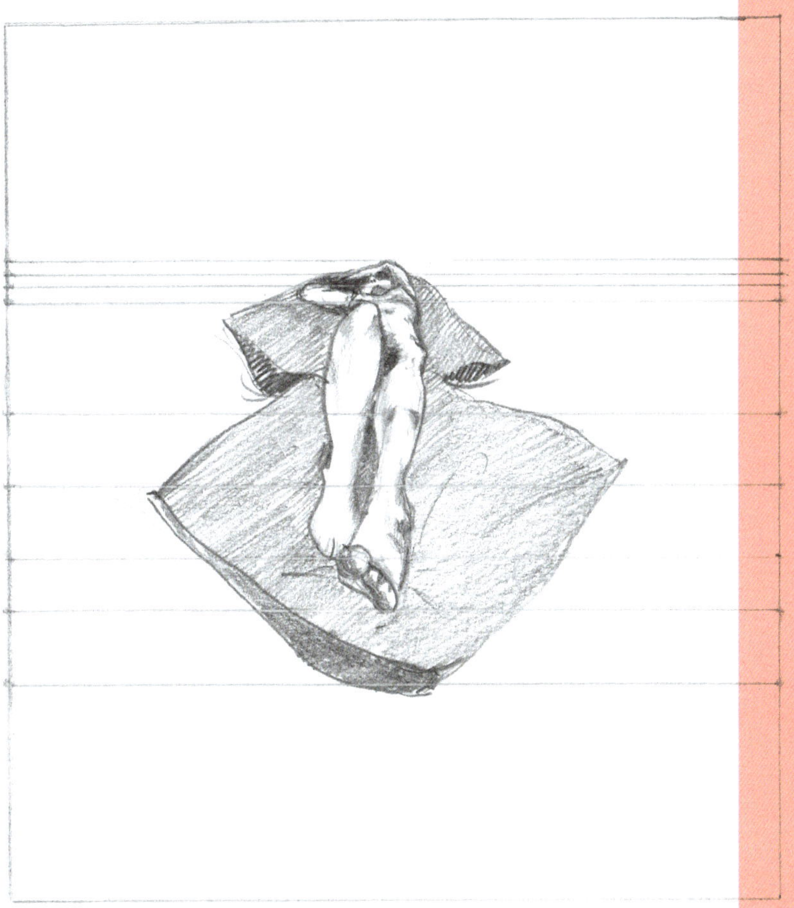

fig 2

REMEMBER:

- Draw what you *see*, not what you *think* you see.
- Trust your measuring, rather than prior knowledge.
- If parts are hidden, don't draw them.
- Regularly check angles and distances.

Foreshortening Exercise

1. First establish the orientation of the model on your paper – it is crucial to identify the position of the figure in relation to your viewpoint. Do this by measuring the width and height of the figure as it appears in your picture plane. Let your mind empty, let your eyes go out of focus; see the figure not as a person but as a collection of shapes (refer to the Shape Exercise on page 38). Draw these shapes faintly so that they can be adjusted later.

2. Check the angles of the outer limits of the figure, such as from the top of the head to the shoulders or the length of an arm or leg, for example. I have chosen to measure a straight line from the curve of the buttocks to the point of the heel. Add these faintly as construction lines. You may need to alter your shapes to fit these construction lines.

3. Measure the shapes carefully using your pencil (refer to the Measuring Exercise on page 46.) Start with the nearest and largest shapes – compare their dimensions with shapes farther away from you. If the measurements seem wrong, check them again, then trust them. Alter your drawing accordingly and refine your outlines.

4. Move on to the smallest and furthest away shapes. It might transpire that these are too small to measure with a pencil. Perhaps you could group some of them together to measure them, or rely on angle-checking instead. Don't move closer to the model as this will distort your view. Remember, some detail may be obscured, or too small to include, and it is fine to omit such detail: you will be reflecting the image honestly.

5. Your figure may not make sense until you add some tone to describe the different aspects of some distorted parts of the body (see the chapter on 'Tone' for more help, pages 52–61). You may need to measure areas of shadow in the same way that you measured the form – it is important that they are in the right position. This addition of tone will indicate volume and so emphasise depth of field.

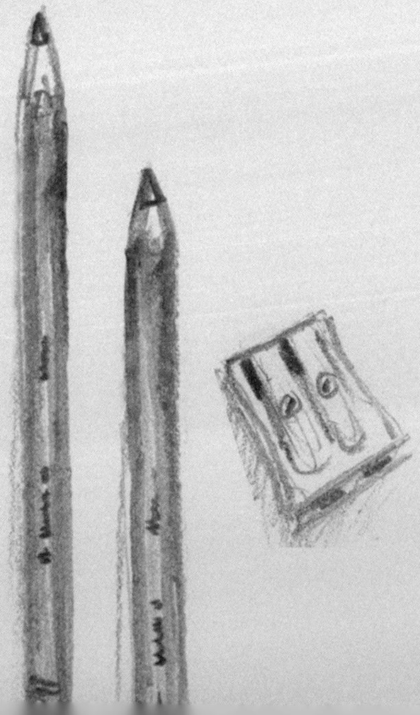

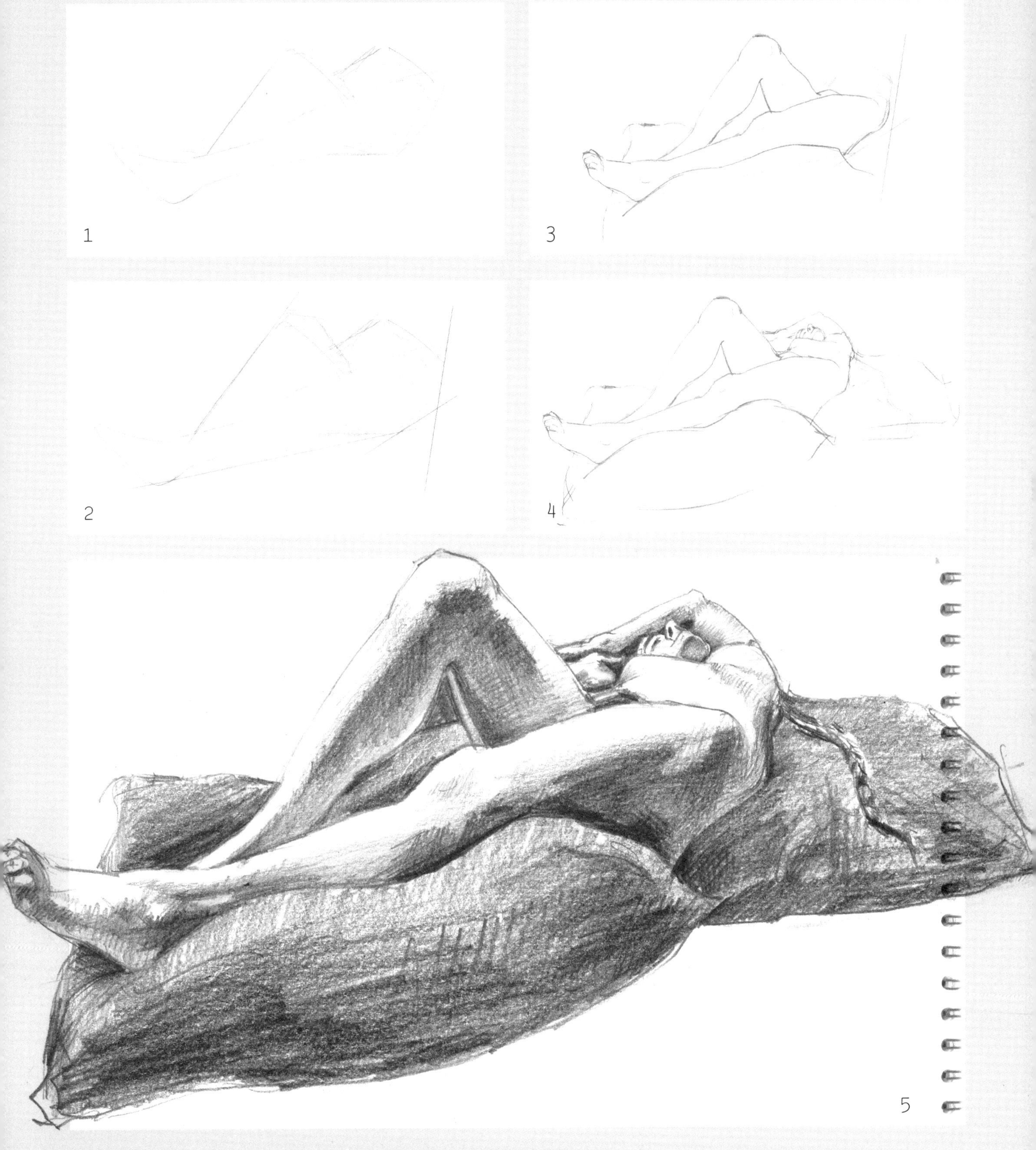
1
3
2
4
5

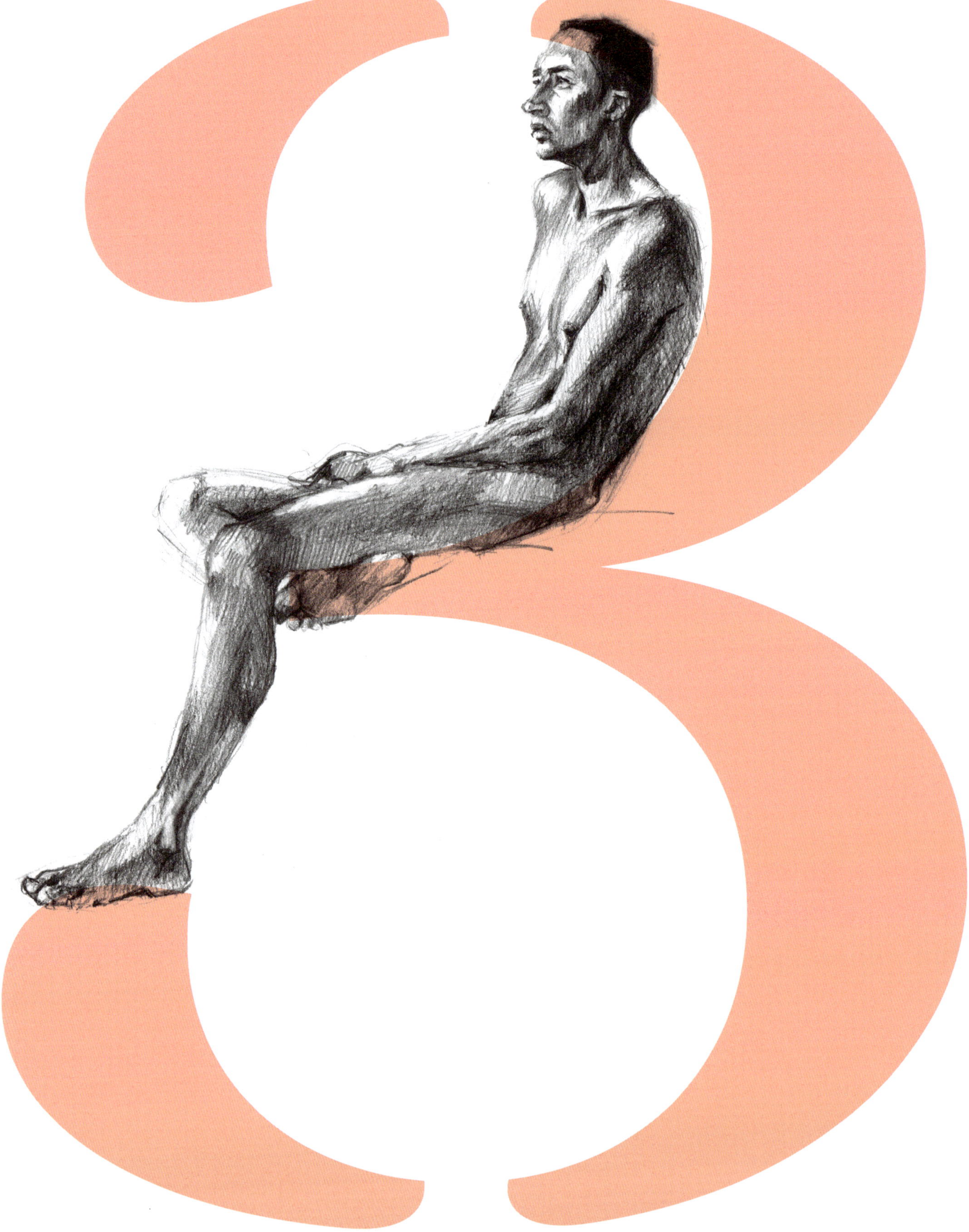
3

Tone

The use of light and dark adds body and volume to a quick line drawing. This enhances the realism and credibility of a sketch. It can also give an idea of the context, surface, colour and position of a subject.

We can use tone to work out whether the form of a drawing is accurate. Tone provides useful landmarks where lines and details are not present. It can also indicate colour in the skin.

In this chapter I will highlight the importance of tone and explain ways of applying it to a drawing, using a range of techniques and media. The exercises in simple tone will encourage you to add basic tonal values to quick sketches, demonstrating how to see light and dark simply and to represent it quickly.

I will also look into complex tone, with reference to the nuances within light and shadows. The exercise in complex tone will encourage you to look at subtle changes in light while utilising an appropriate tonal range, one that can represent the spectrum of natural light effectively.

Simple Tone

'Tone' in the life drawing classroom means 'light and dark' and refers to the way in which we can use shading to render light fall, highlights and shadow on the figure. A competent representation of even very simple tone, also referred to as 'value', will give your figure drawing an immediate sense of definition and volume. We see the world around us in tonal values, rather than lines, so acknowledging this in our drawings helps them to make sense.

Tone can instantly develop a simple drawing into something much more realistic. Pure line drawings can sometimes make life more difficult than it really needs to be, while using tone means you can hide some of the trickier parts of detail in the shadows. This isn't to say that you should be lazy, only honest: sometimes drawing parts of the figure feels difficult because these areas are less clear, having less light on them. Instead of worrying about their accuracy, let them be similarly obscured in your drawing. It will reflect your honest observation of the figure. Similarly, some outlines may be unnecessary if they are separating two areas of similar tone. If the boundary isn't obvious, don't agonise over making it accurate.

Occasionally large areas of your drawing may seem incorrect and you may be unable to work out why, having measured and checked them several times. More often than not, the reason these parts look strange is because the tone is missing. Tone may provide a much-needed landmark, and when you add it, your composition can suddenly make sense. This often happens when drawing feet, for example, or the jawline and neck.

We can use tone to indicate various qualities:

Context
- Position of the subject
- Position of the light source
- Type of light (daylight, firelight, stark fluorescent or spot lighting, candlelight)
- Atmosphere/drama (chiaroscuro/up-lighting)

Shape
- Aspect/orientation
- Volume
- Depth
- Underlying shapes such as bones and muscles

Surface and texture
- Glossy/shiny
- Matt
- Wet
- Bumpy/rough

Colour
- Pink cheeks
- Tanned skin
- Veins
- Hair colour

Some of the different shades you can get from a range of pencils are shown here.

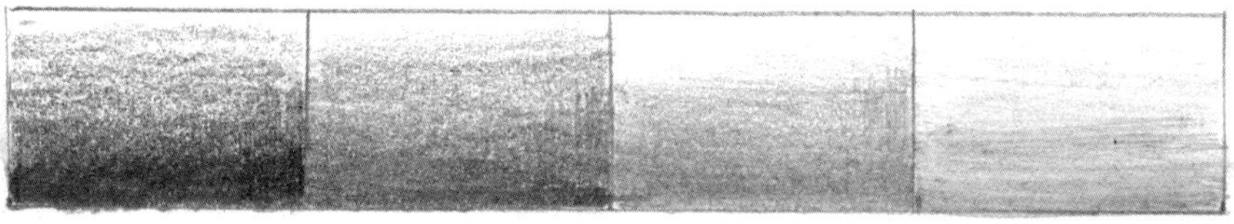

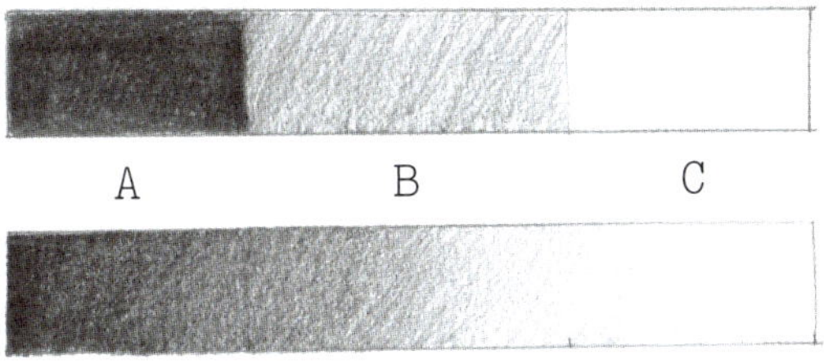

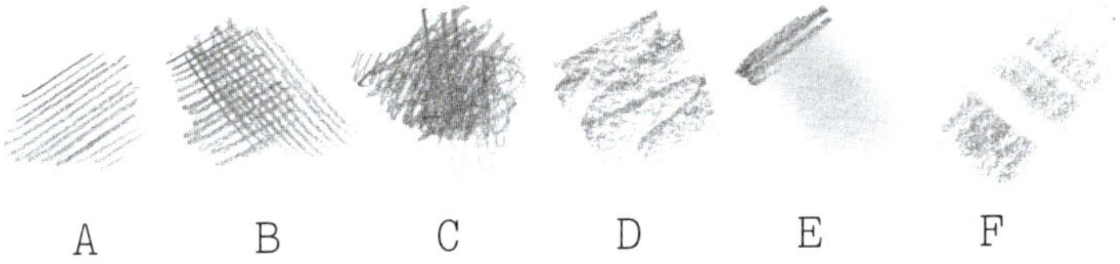

In quick drawings, and when using simple tone, it is sufficient to use just two tonal values (including the white of the paper). Think of stencils – these can look very effective, even though the tone is so basic. The images below are split into just three relative values. The diagrams above illustrate the use of these shades – the darkest shadows (A), the mid-tones (B) and the lightest highlights (C). The diagrams show how you can divide tone into just three shades or allow gradual increments.

Even in longer drawings, it is very sensible to begin with the most basic shadows. To make it easier to see this simplified version of tone, squint or let your eyes go out of focus.

It may also be enough to use the roughest and most cursory of techniques for shading. Some very loose hatching will adequately indicate the position of the limbs and torso, whether they are facing the light source or away from it. One thick brushstroke will satisfyingly throw half of the figure into the appropriate level of shadow.

Here are some ways you can use your pencil to create shadow:

(A) Hatching in the same direction
(B) Cross-hatching
(C) Random scribbling
(D) Using the pencil flat to create a thicker line
(E) Smudging the line with your finger
(F) Cutting through shadows with a clean rubber

Simple tone in charcoal can be achieved in a similar way to pencil, especially by using a piece of charcoal flat against the paper (D), smudging with your finger (E) and removal with a rubber (F). Pen can be used only for hatching (A), cross-hatching (B) and random scribbling (C). Felt pens and brush pens can be applied in simple blocks, similar to how you might use the flat pencil to create a thicker line (D). Paint and ink probably won't be applied in hatching, but in simple blocks with a brush, and can be smudged and blurred with a wet brush or tissue, rather than your finger.

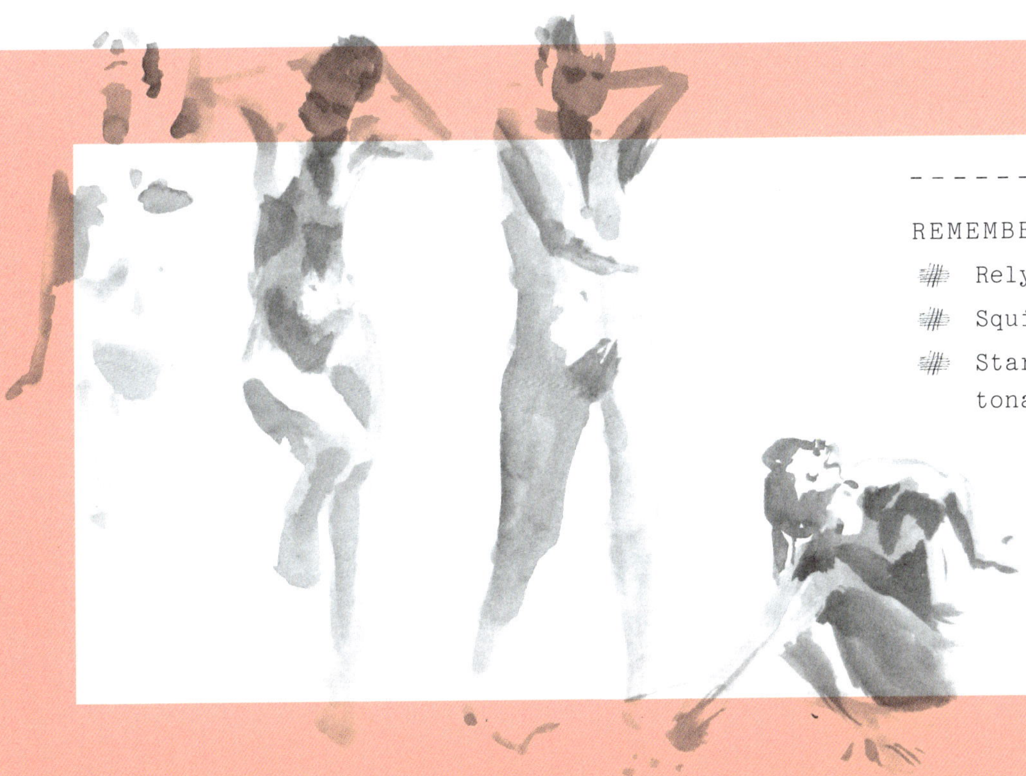

REMEMBER:

- Rely only on observation.
- Squint to simplify tone.
- Start simply, add more tonal variation later.

Simple Tone Exercises

1. Spend no more than two minutes lightly sketching out your figure in pencil. Look closely, paying attention to proportion, but don't spend too long on any one part – time is limited and there is no need to include detail. Accuracy is helpful but not paramount. Your pencil marks should remain faint; treat them as a guide.

2. Let your eyes go out of focus to see tone in a simplified way. Spend no more than three minutes blocking in the main areas of shadow, hatching to cover the areas quickly and evenly. Which areas really stand out? Which features disappear into the shadows? Use only two tones: the white of the paper and one value of grey.

3. Repeat step 1 on a clean sheet, skipping step 2. This time use a thick brush and a grey watercolour, or some slightly diluted black ink, to block in the main areas of shadow. Spend five minutes in total on this exercise. You will need to take greater care because the marks fill the page quicker, and you will not be able to rub them out.

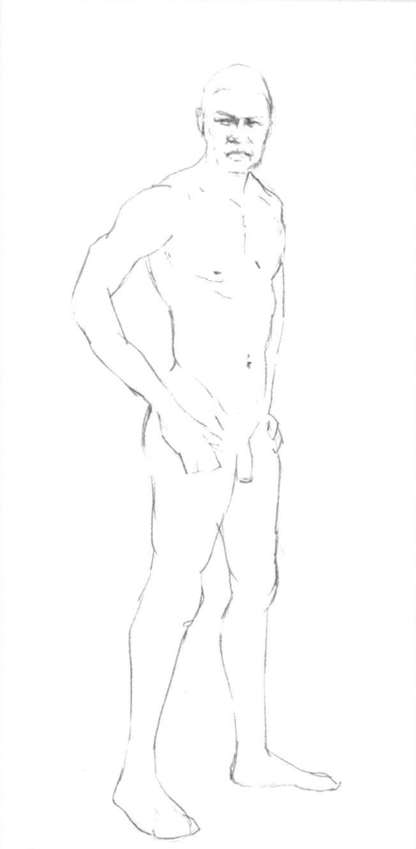

1

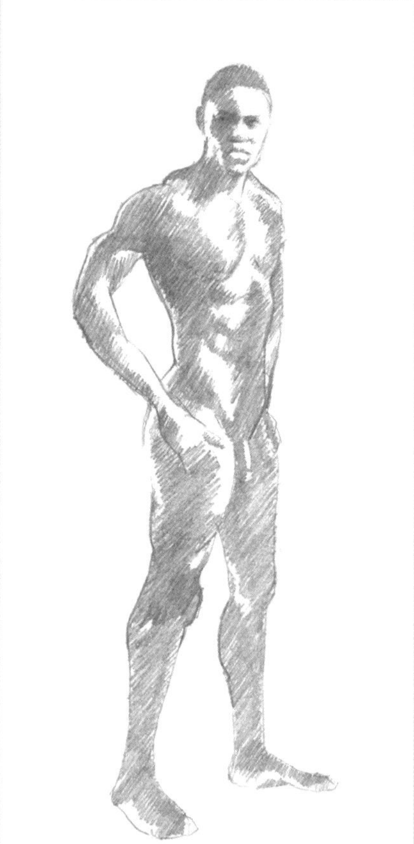

2

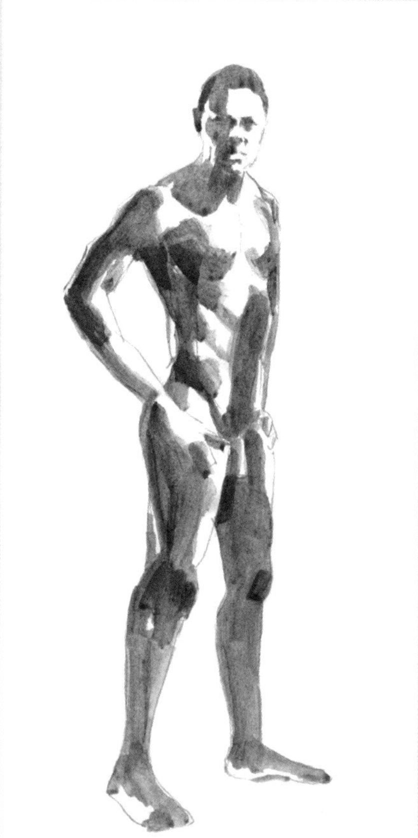

3

4. On another clean sheet, use charcoal to sketch the outlines of the figure, then use the edge of a thick piece to block in the shadows. If you feel confident, do this without first setting down an outline. You can use the extra time saved to make some simple developments to the shadows, introducing three tones.

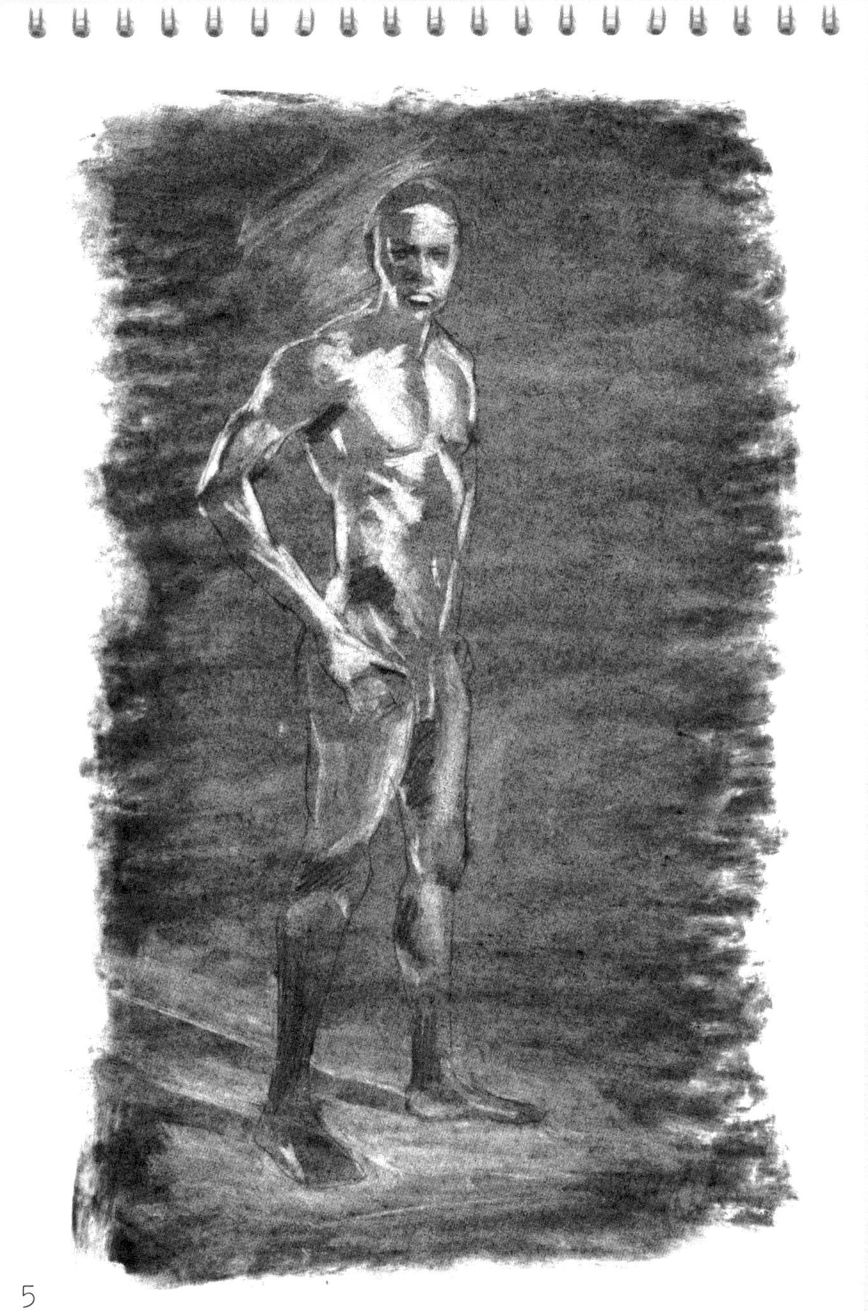

5

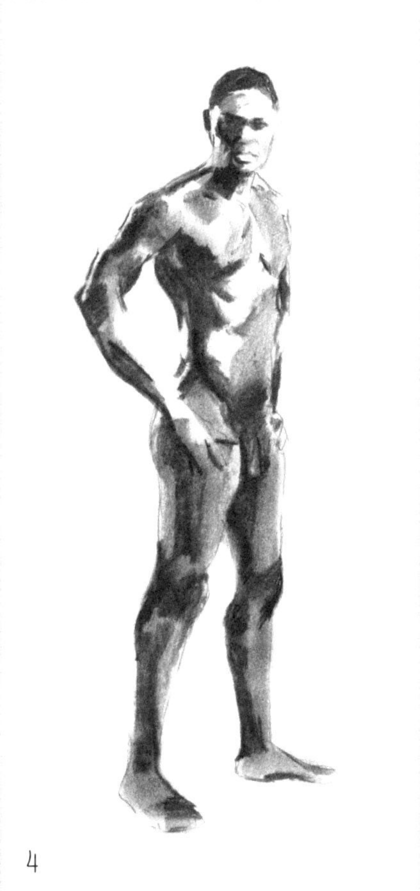

4

5. Pre-charcoal a piece of paper: smoothly coat the whole sheet in a layer of charcoal or graphite. Repeat step 1, then use a clean or newly sliced rubber to carve out areas of light rather than shadow as these fall on the figure. This time you are subtracting rather than adding tone to the drawing.

Complex Tone

For longer figure drawings, there are lots of nuances of tone to appreciate – some of which are not obvious and can be gleaned only through very careful scrutiny. However, once you have noticed these subtler effects, they are easy to represent, and can make a huge difference to the quality of your drawing. Simple tone adds depth, life and volume, whereas more nuanced, complex tone can add realism and draw attention to small changes in skin colour and texture, as well as the contextual light.

The spectrum of visible light is much larger than can be represented on paper, so it is necessary to use whatever materials you have at your disposal to make the widest possible tonal range. You cannot create a value lighter than the white of the paper, so this is your starting point. If you are working in pencil, you should use various grades to widen your options. You might even want to use a black pen in certain very dark areas, if it will appropriately deepen the shadows. When working in either charcoal, pen, paint or ink, it is possible to achieve very deep blacks, much darker than in pencil, so their tonal ranges are large and you probably don't need to mix media to enhance the range further.

It is still necessary to compress the real spectrum into something that can be represented by your materials. Keep the relationships proportional, though smaller, or allow some detail to be bleached out, or lost to shadow. Imagine taking a black-and-white photo. A camera will curtail the natural spectrum and lose the lightest or darkest details.

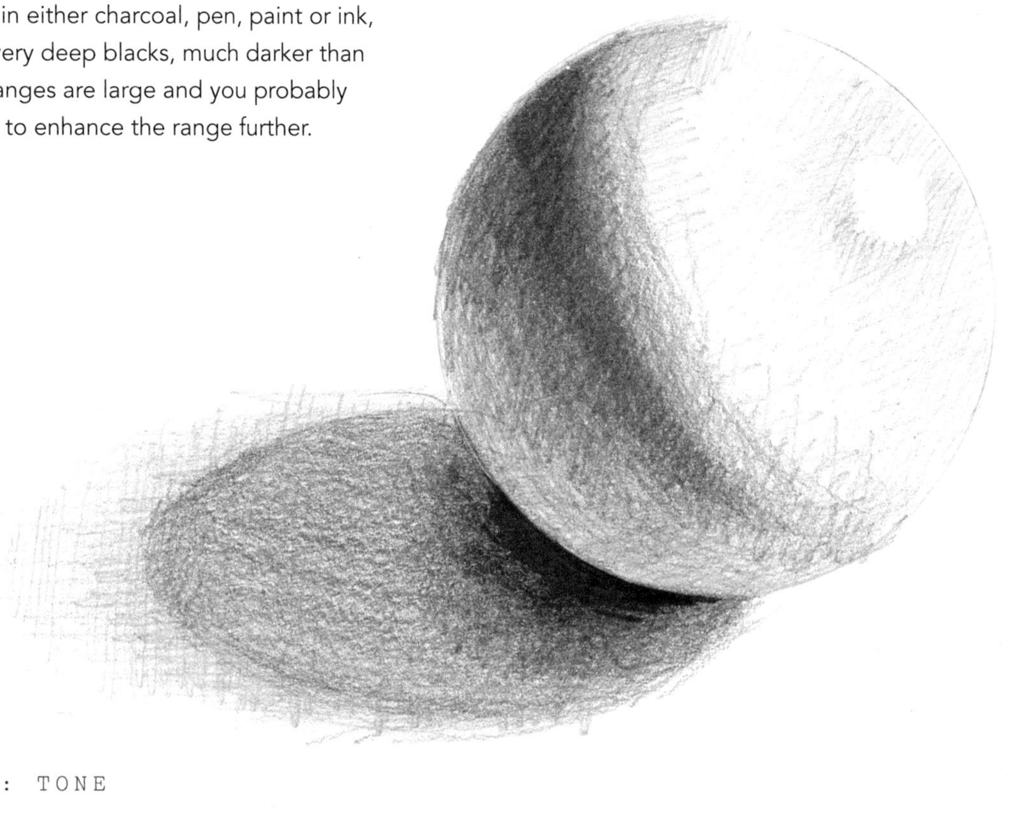

Although in practice you will rely on innocent observation of the tonal relationships, it is useful to know these terms as they are often used in the life drawing classroom:

Form Shadow

(A) Highlights
The lightest part of your drawing where the skin reflects the brightest light. This will probably appear white.

(B) Local colour
Not shadow, but the very light shading you may put in to show the colour of the skin.

(C) Core shadow
The main area of shade – this is all you would realistically represent during a short pose.

Within the core shadow you may have:

(D) Reflected light
You often see this on the underside of a breast or thigh, where light bounces off a nearby surface.

(E) Terminator
The border between light and shadow.

(F) Occlusion shadows
There won't be too many of these; they are the very darkest areas, where no light can bounce around. You normally find examples of this tucked tightly between the arm and the torso, or in folds of skin.

Cast Shadow

(G) Cast shadow
This is the shadow made by the object.

Within the cast shadow you find:

(H) The penumbra
The area of half-shadow at the edge of the cast shadow – some stray rays of light are scattered in this marginal area.

(I) Occlusion shadow
This is the darkest area, where the form and the cast shadow meet, where no light gets in.

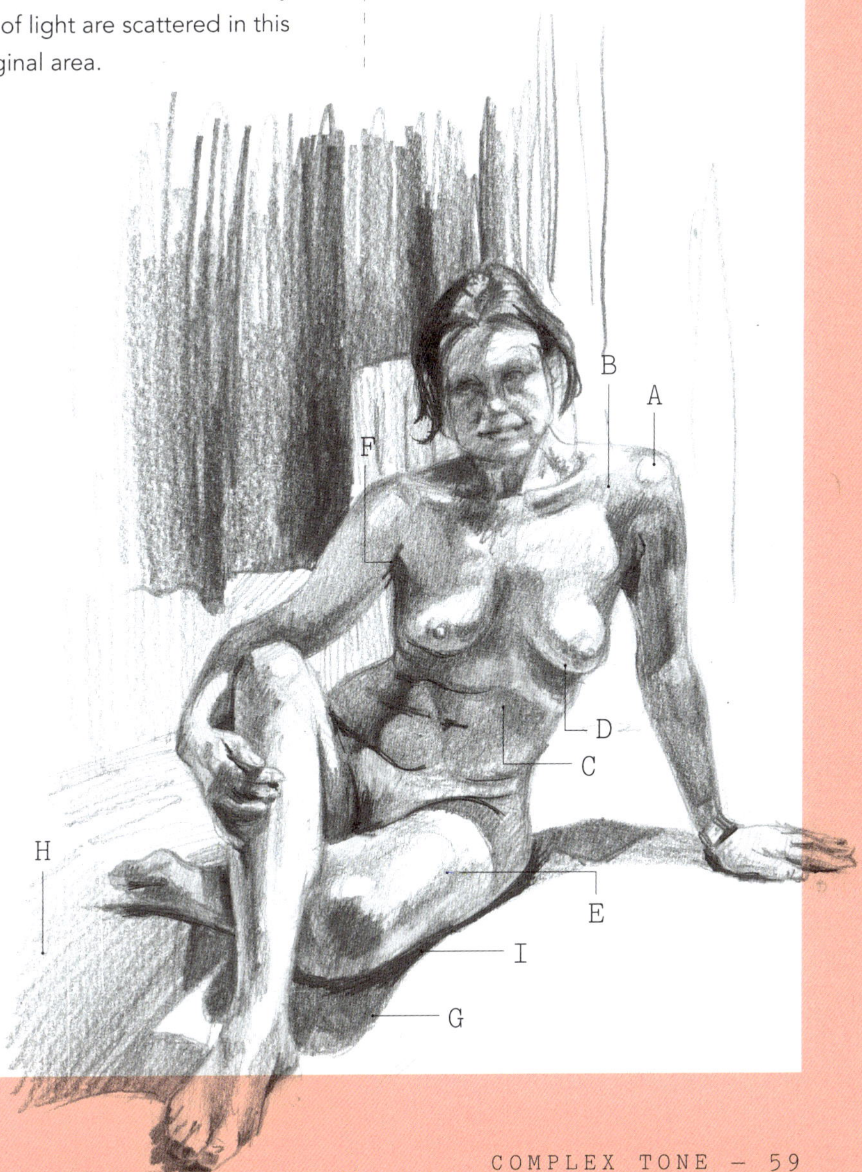

Complex Tone Exercise

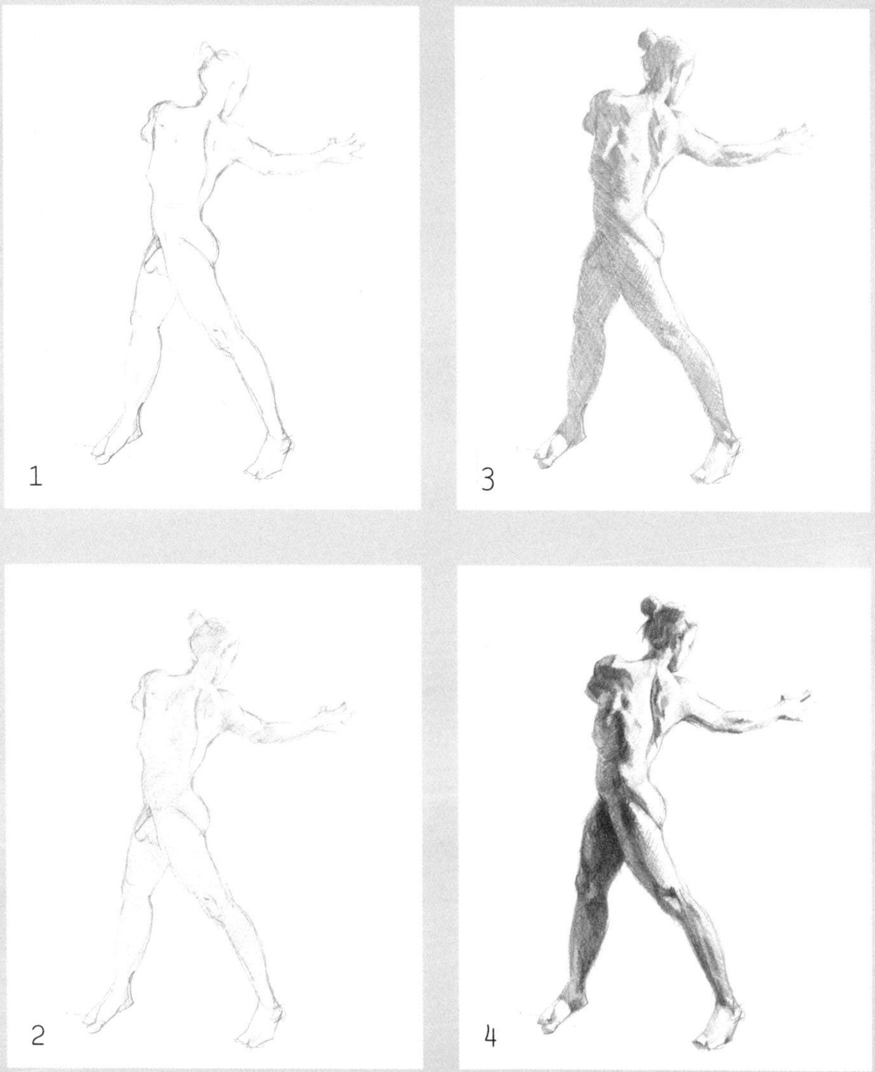

1. Spend five to ten minutes mapping out the figure carefully with charcoal or pencil. Add only minimal detail such as the position of facial features if they are visible.

2. Work from light to dark, increasing in a smooth gradient rather than a predetermined set of increments or using a tonal key. Add the tone in layers from top to toe, not by area. Decide where the highlights should be, including on the hair. Which parts of the paper should remain white? Everywhere outside of this, very lightly add local colour. You may need to be slightly heavier where you have colour on the skin or hair. The hair balances out the tone of the whole figure.

3. Observe carefully where the core shadows fall. Mark them in using a smooth and even covering of hatching, cross-hatching or brush marks.

4. Look for deeper areas of shadow within the core, and shade accordingly from top to toe. If you're using pencil, or a grey pen, you may switch to a darker one. With charcoal, use slightly more pressure. If you're using pen, build up the layers of cross-hatching.

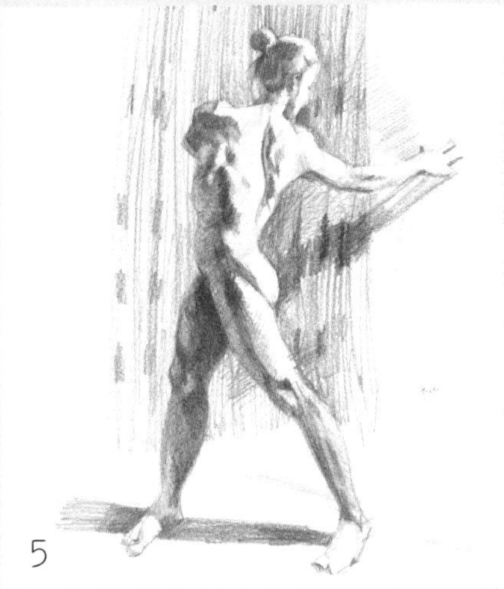

5

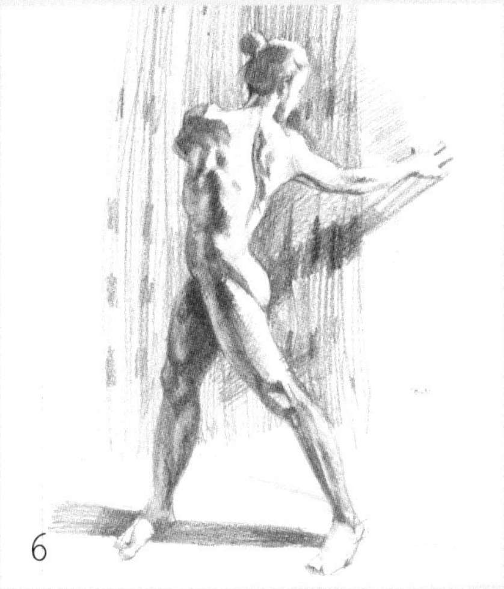

6

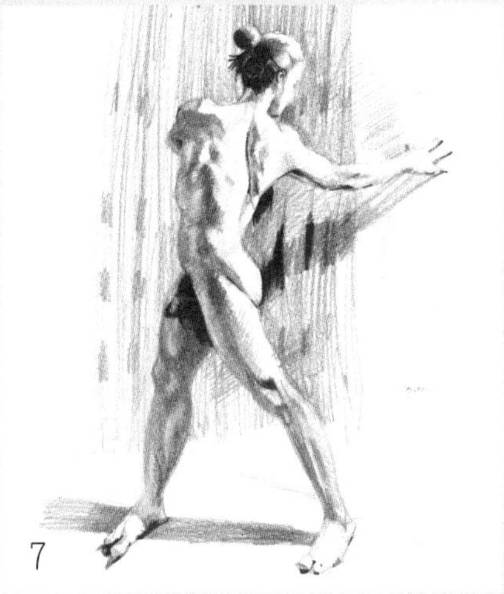

7

5. At this stage, it might be helpful to reference the background for some context and tonal reference. Include the cast shadow if it is apparent.

6. You can use a rubber to mark in some reflected light at certain points. Reflected light tends to be on the darkest of shaded areas, coming not directly from a light source, but indirectly by being scattered and bounced off walls or other nearby objects. Here, it shows most obviously down the front of the left thigh.

7. Using your darkest pencil, or even a pen, or increasing the pressure of your charcoal, add the very darkest occlusion shadows. There probably won't be too many of these, so identify them carefully.

8. Look away from your work for a minute, then return with fresh eyes. Take a step back and spend a couple of minutes looking at both the figure and your drawing. What are the discrepancies? To increase clarity and focus, emphasise some of the darker shadows, or use your rubber, chalk or white paint for clearer highlights.

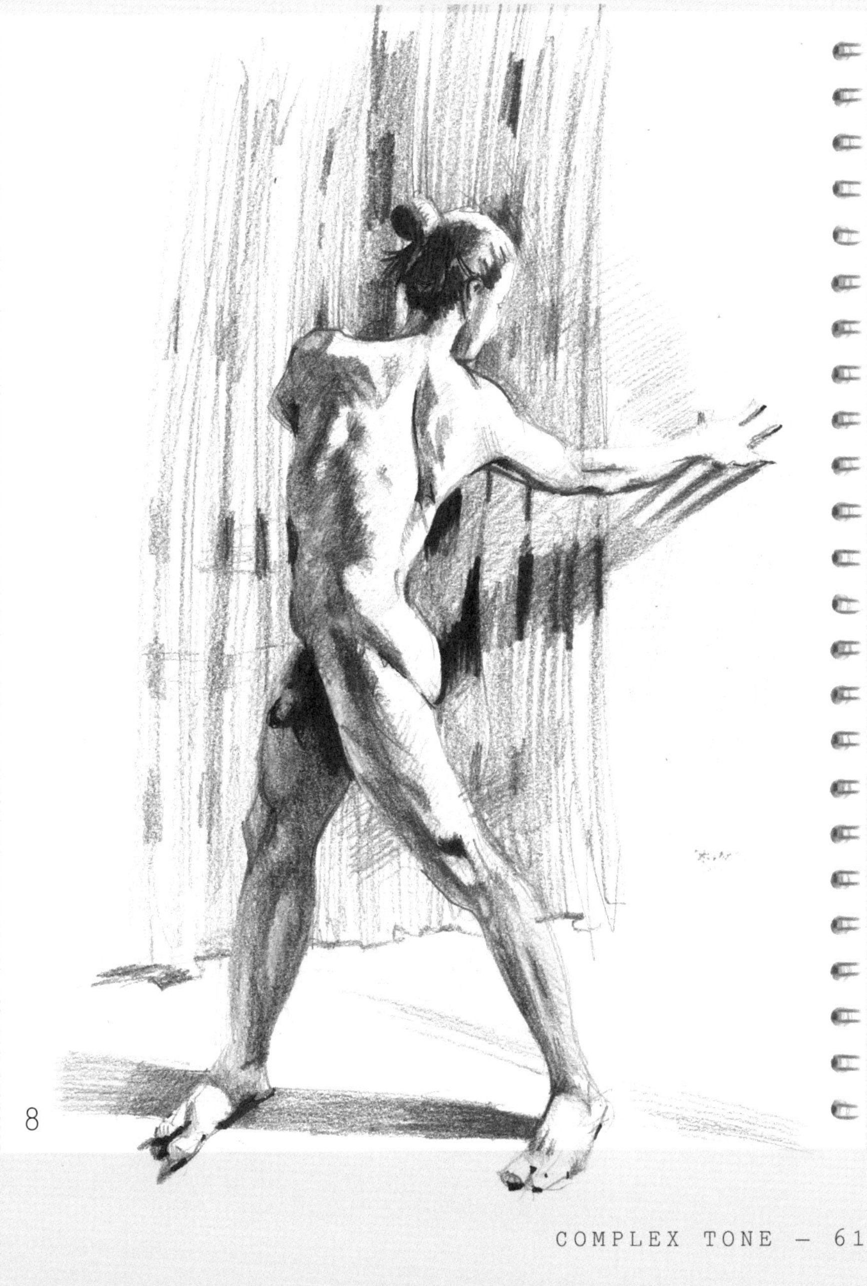

8

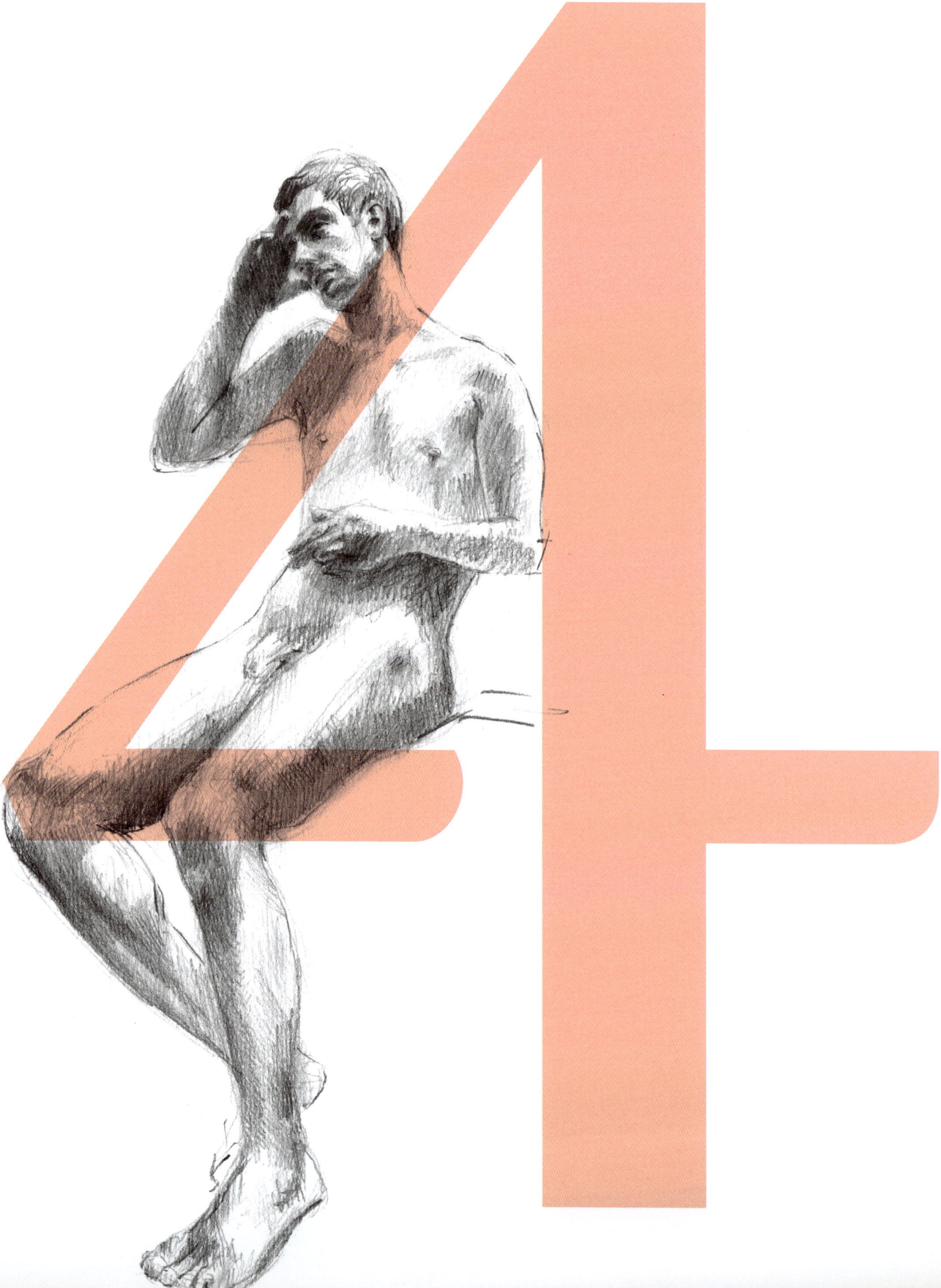
4

Anatomy

The human body is familiar to us, but its internal workings may not be. Although I emphasise the merits of looking objectively at a life model, I hope that a basic awareness of anatomy will increase the likelihood of noticing bumps and bulges under the skin. The exercises in this chapter are not all necessarily applicable to a life drawing class, but after working on them, you will remember where certain bones and muscles are located, which in turn will help you in the class setting.

I will also explore 'difficult features', i.e. the head, hands and feet. I will show you how to break them down into simple steps, which can then be used in the life drawing class for either quick sketches or longer, more detailed drawings. The last exercise pulls together everything discussed so far in a step-by-step full figure drawing.

Skeleton

Much of the skeletal system will obviously be hidden. However, some of it will be visible, more so in some models than others. Most obvious are the collar bones (clavicles), cheek and jaw bones, eye sockets, wrists and ankles. We may also see evidence of the ribs, the top of the pelvis, shoulder blades and shin bones (tibias). Although we needn't know their names and what they represent while we're drawing – in fact, I think it's useful to forget these – having an awareness of them can draw your attention to the subtleties in tone they might elicit.

In the illustration, I have exaggerated the protrusions to emphasise the skeleton. Drawing the skeleton just once or twice will mean you are always aware of its intricacies when you see it evident in a model. This awareness may help you when you come to look for landmarks in order to break the figure up into simple shapes (see page 36). Think about the shape of the ribcage – is there evidence of this form in your view of the model? The skull is also a useful building block, especially if the model has close-cropped or no hair.

The skeleton can be thought of as the armature for your drawing, aiding you when thinking about construction lines. A rough knowledge of the position of the leg and arm bones, and how they support the body, may help you decide where to position construction lines within the limbs. You can also use visible bones as construction lines, for example, the clavicle, the spine or the bottom of the ribcage.

Bony protrusions under the skin can provide landmarks when measuring. Although it's not necessary to know *what* the protrusions are when you're drawing, you will hopefully notice if they are impossibly positioned when you check your work.

Acknowledging these bones in your tonal representation of the body will show an understanding of the anatomy and/or a deep attention to detail in your observation (figs 1). They will add finesse to your work, constituting a finishing touch that can really make the difference in developing your work to a higher level of accomplishment. For example, a slight strengthening of shadow along the tibia will give the leg a lifelike quality. An insight into the position of joints can inform facets of tone on a simpler level.

The skeleton itself is a beautiful object that is complex but rewarding to draw (figs 2). Having little or no colour variation, it offers opportunities to flex your tonal dexterity. It is structurally complicated and will require you to think through the main shapes first, before refining and delineating the separate bones. The bones themselves recede and disappear behind each other – the ribcage is especially tricky, presenting layers of loops of bones, which must appear well-proportioned and correctly angled, while hiding each other at various points. The pelvis is always foreshortened in some direction, so must be looked at completely objectively – its outline as a whole being noted first, before tone is then added to illustrate its curvature and undulations.

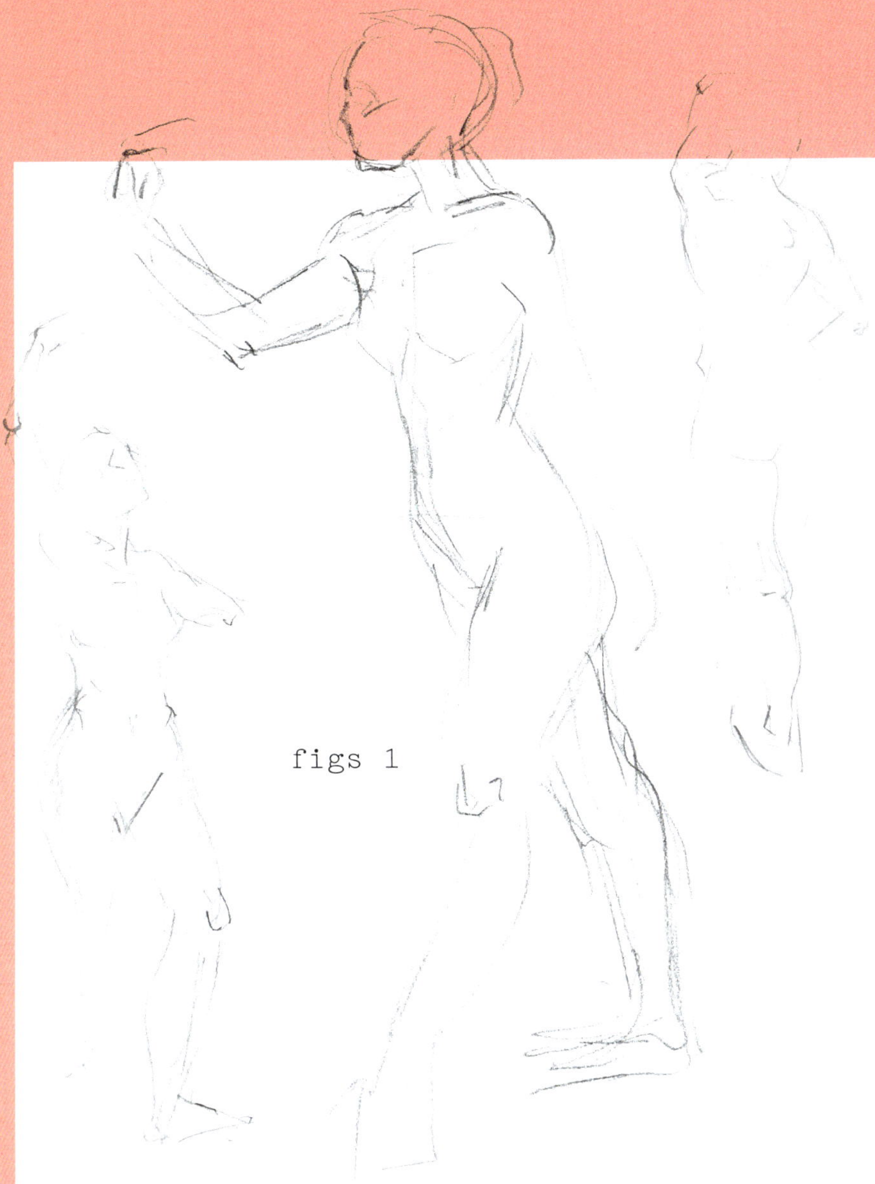

figs 1

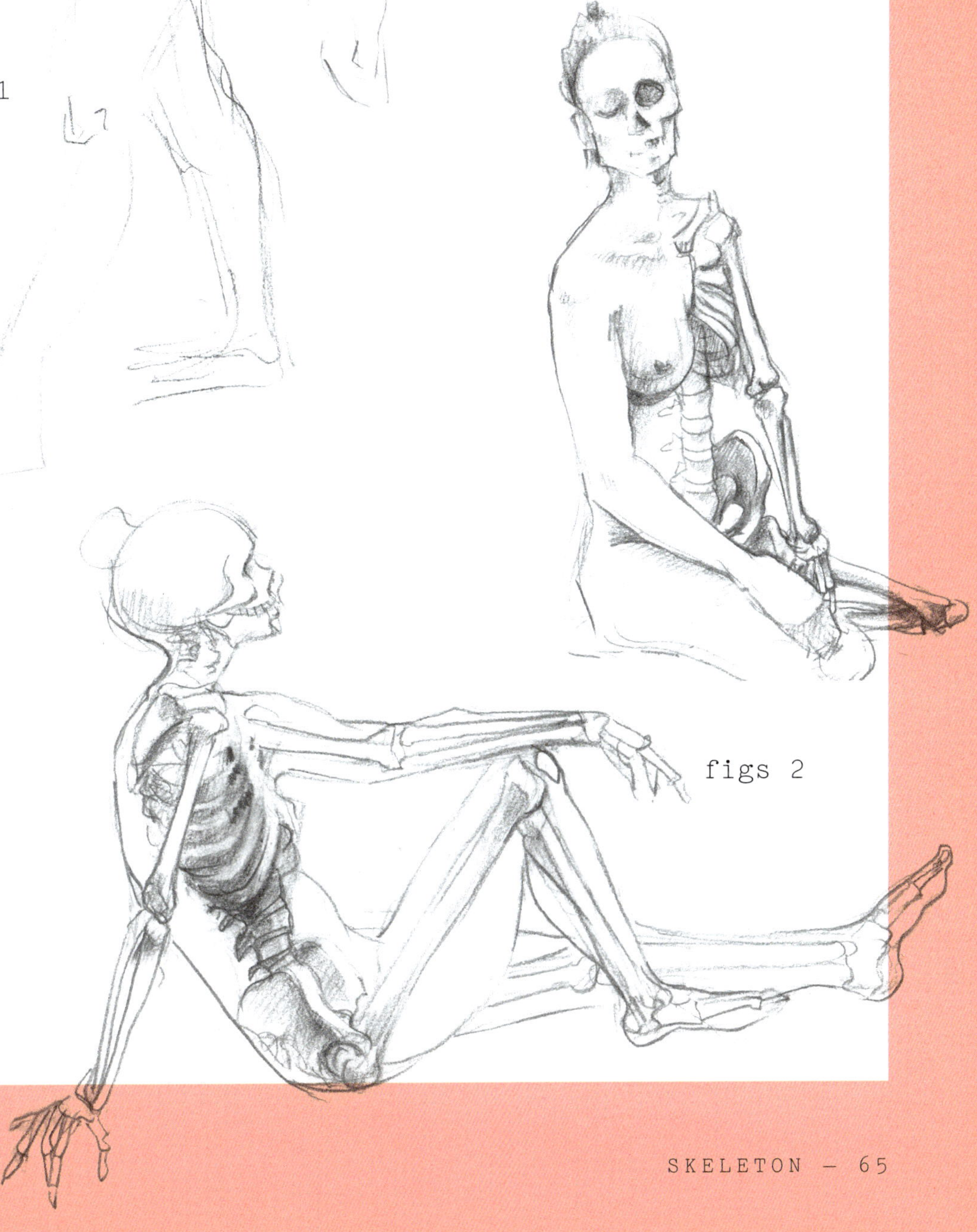

figs 2

Skeleton Exercise

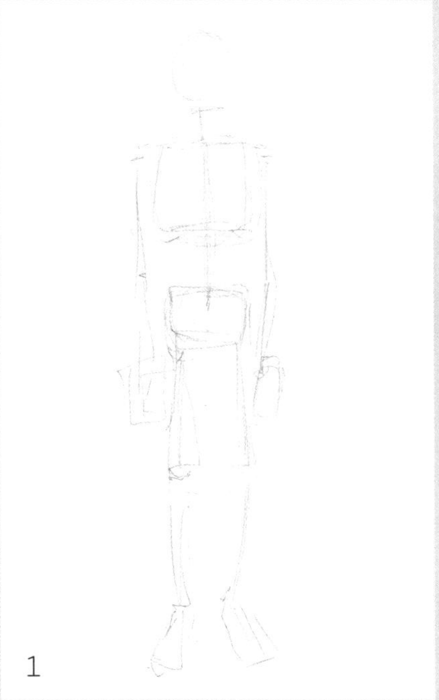

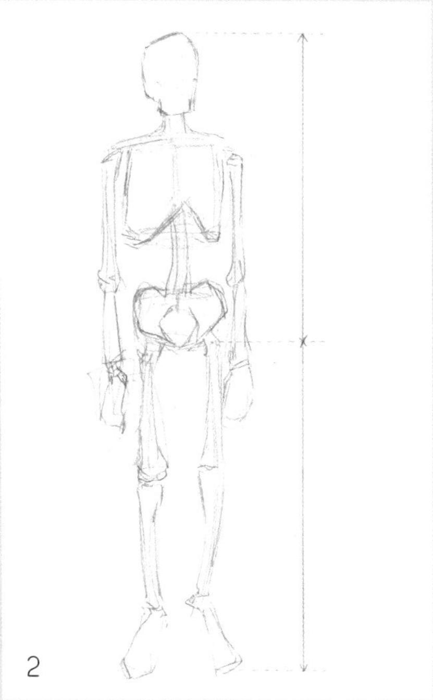

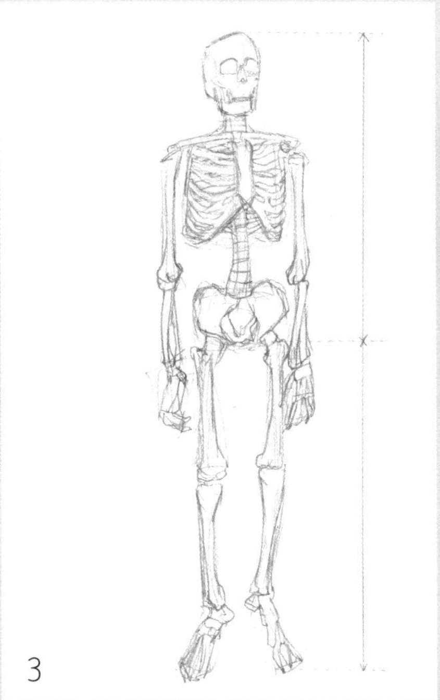

1. Choose a simple position for the skeleton – you needn't challenge yourself further with foreshortening. First draw out the main shapes in a light pencil, using longer bones to act as construction lines. For this exercise, pencil is the most sensible medium – you need to be able to erase marks, otherwise your picture will become convoluted. Begin with the skull. Add the spine as a construction line. This will inform the shape and position of the ribcage as a whole and the pelvis. The leg and arm bones can appear as construction lines. The feet and hands are best represented as simple block shapes at this point.

2. Use your pencil to check angles and distances – measuring is more important than intuition in this case, since the skeleton isn't as familiar a form as the fleshed-out human body. Check the height of the skull when compared to the height of the ribcage and pelvis. Check the gap between the ribcage and pelvis. Ensure the hands reach down to the right point on the thigh bone and that the ribcage extends to the correct width when lined up with the head and pelvis. Refine the outlines of your shapes.

3. Still using a light pencil, add finer detail. Mark out the position of the eye sockets, nasal cavity, each rib and the two separate bones in each of the lower legs and arms. Refine the bones of the hands and feet.

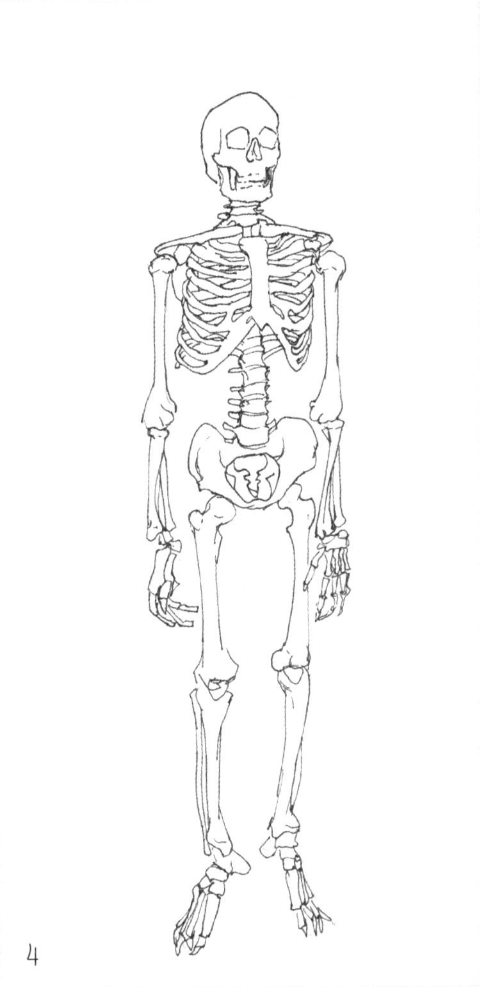

4. Once you're satisfied with the positions of all of these bones, draw in their outlines. Use a darker pencil, or even a fine liner. Pay attention to the thickness of the bones – do they taper at one end or in the middle? Take care to accurately represent the ends of the joints, in all their knobbly splendour. Lighten or erase the unresolved marks and construction lines.

5. If you wish to develop your drawing, mark in the tone. You won't need to represent extremes, as the skeleton isn't shiny and there is very little colour variation. But the tone will begin to make clearer the aspect (the position, particularly in relation to the light source) and curve of the bones.

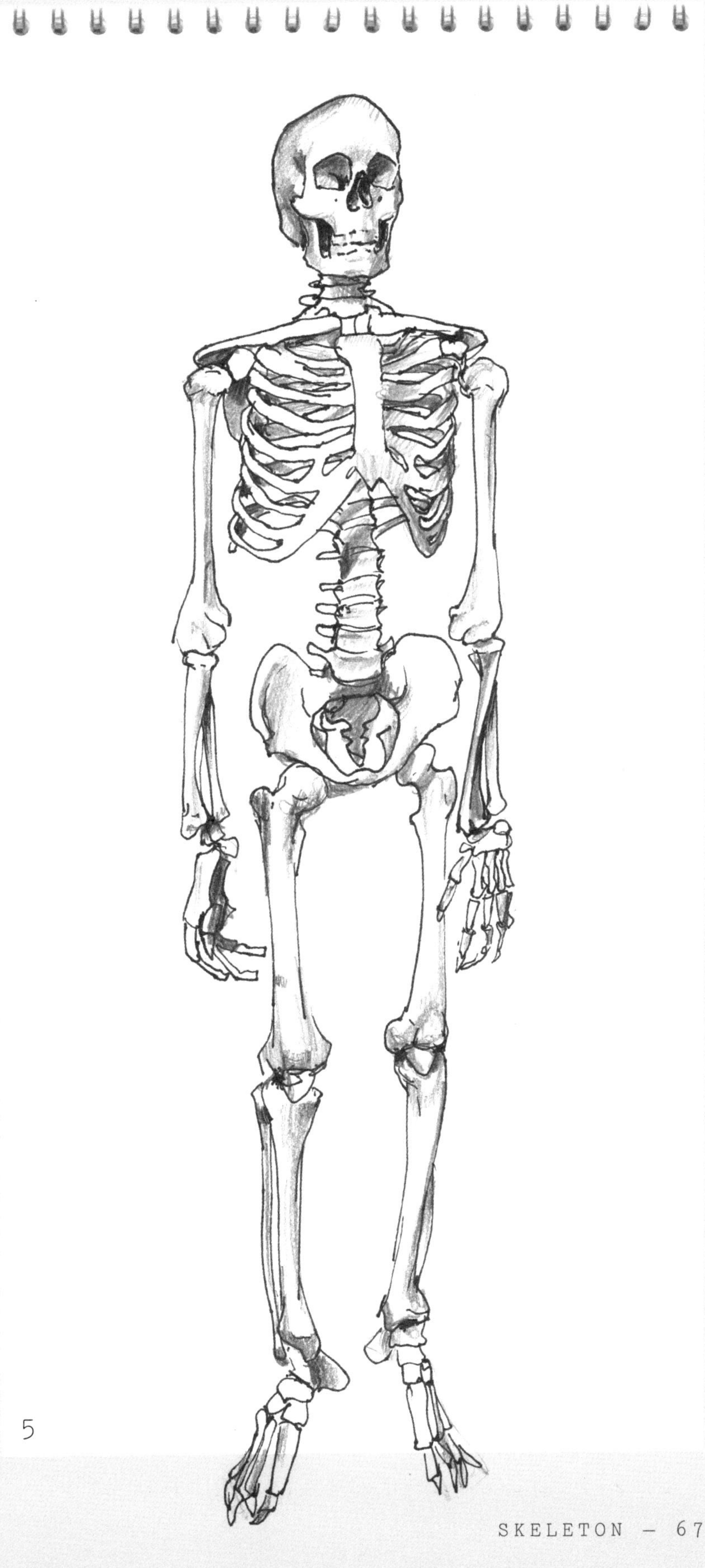

Muscles

The muscular system may be very apparent in some models, and barely at all in others. As with the skeletal system, an understanding of muscles should not be relied upon too heavily when drawing, but it is still worth knowing a little about musculature so that you are conscious of certain tonal and structural nuances.

Once you have the main shapes and structure of the figure in place, your more detailed outlines will be dictated by the shapes of the muscles under the skin. The arms will bulge and taper at various points due to the arrangement of muscles. Having a basic knowledge of which muscles are where will help you account for these shapes and note them down accurately.

Tendons (the strong bands of tissue that connect the muscles to the bones) should also be acknowledged in the exercise that follows. They are distinguishable as chord-like shapes under the skin, accompanying 'working' (or stretched) muscles around the body in such places as the neck, the backs of the legs and the inside of the arms. As mentioned on page 24, drawing standout tendons can add a sense of movement and gesture to your quick sketches – implying tension and strain in certain mobile areas. In long drawings, tendons will similarly add a sense of movement, as well as ensuring tonal variation and a more lifelike and detailed portrayal of the figure. They can be shown in quick drawings as swift, well-placed lines (appearing where they do in the model, joining muscles to bones). In longer poses, they can be described with tone, representing long shapes under the surface of the skin.

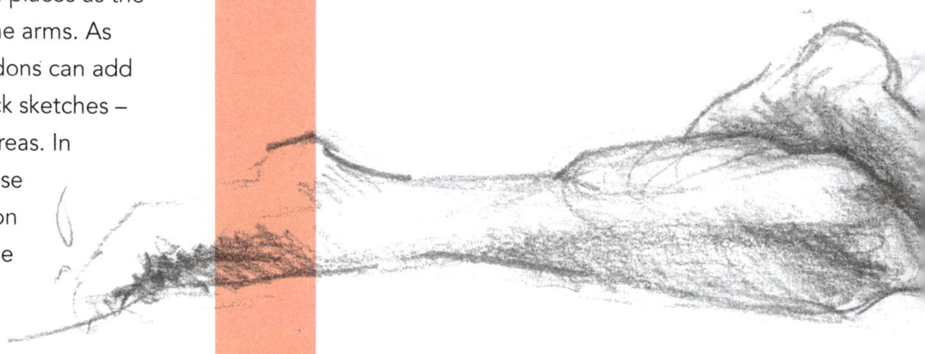

The muscles themselves will clearly provide opportunity to show movement in your drawing, tensing and relaxing as they do within various poses. Your use of tone will play a large part in the successful rendering of muscles – their dimensions, as opposed to merely their outlines, being portrayed by the shadows that wrap around them.

When you have looked in detail at the muscular system and drawn it, you will have a better insight into the shape and position of the muscles in relation to the body as a whole, and how you might approach the idea of tonal patterns across the skin. Exaggerating the tone in places will exaggerate the appearance of muscles, which will add to the dramatic effect you may wish to create in your drawing.

You will notice the muscles aren't so apparent in the face, until you begin to look at facial expressions. We will concentrate mostly on the body, paying attention to the most apparent areas such as the chest (pectoral muscles); buttocks (gluteus maximus); the trapezius muscles, which are important in connecting the head of our drawing to its body – the angle must be correct and they must join the neck at the correct place; and the deltoids (the outer curves of the shoulders), biceps, triceps and flexors (the muscles in the forearm that move the wrist), which will provide the arm with a realistic outline, as well as some tone to break up the arm. The hamstrings, quadriceps and calf muscles will similarly shape the legs.

Muscles are not pronounced in the hands and feet, but the reference to tendons in your drawing will bring definition to wrists and ankles.

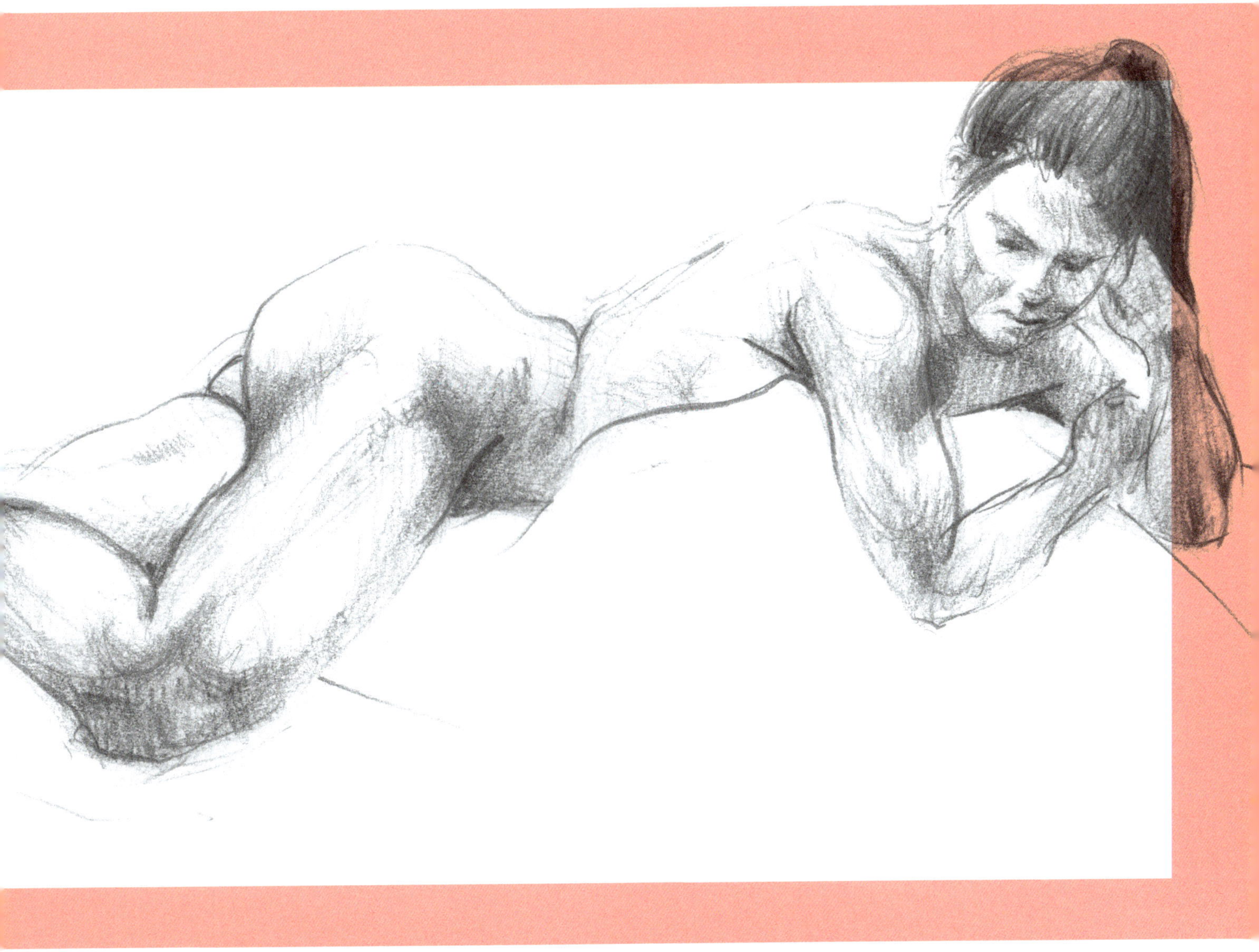

Muscles Exercise

For this exercise you will need to draw from a model who has reasonable muscle definition. We are not drawing an anatomical diagram here but a life drawing with exaggerated muscles. This is a slight departure from my normal insistence on truthful observation, but the exaggeration in your drawing will highlight the muscles for your future reference. The lighting should be quite strong so as to emphasise contrast and create strong shadows. If you can create the right conditions (good lighting and a model with clear muscle definition), you will need to exaggerate less.

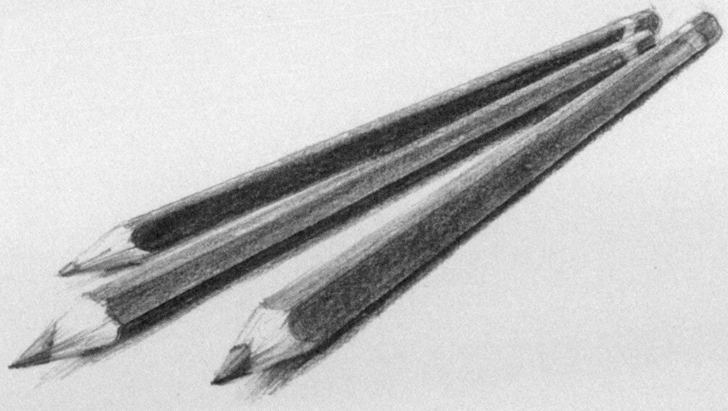

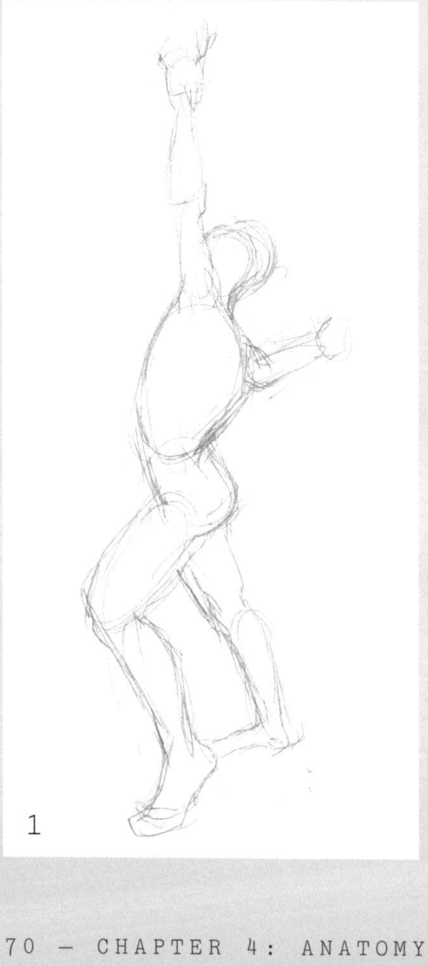

1

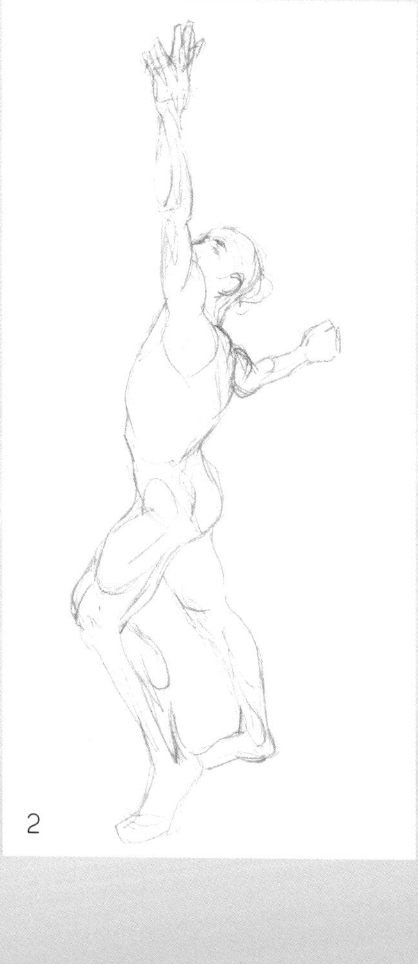

2

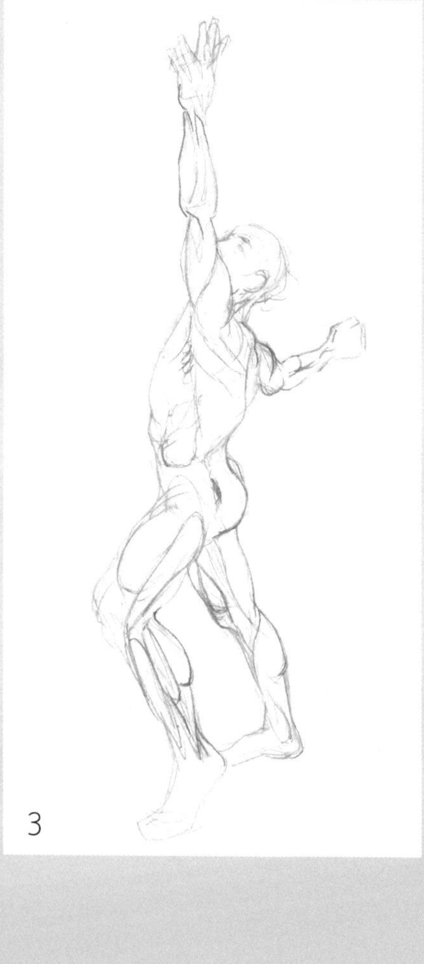

3

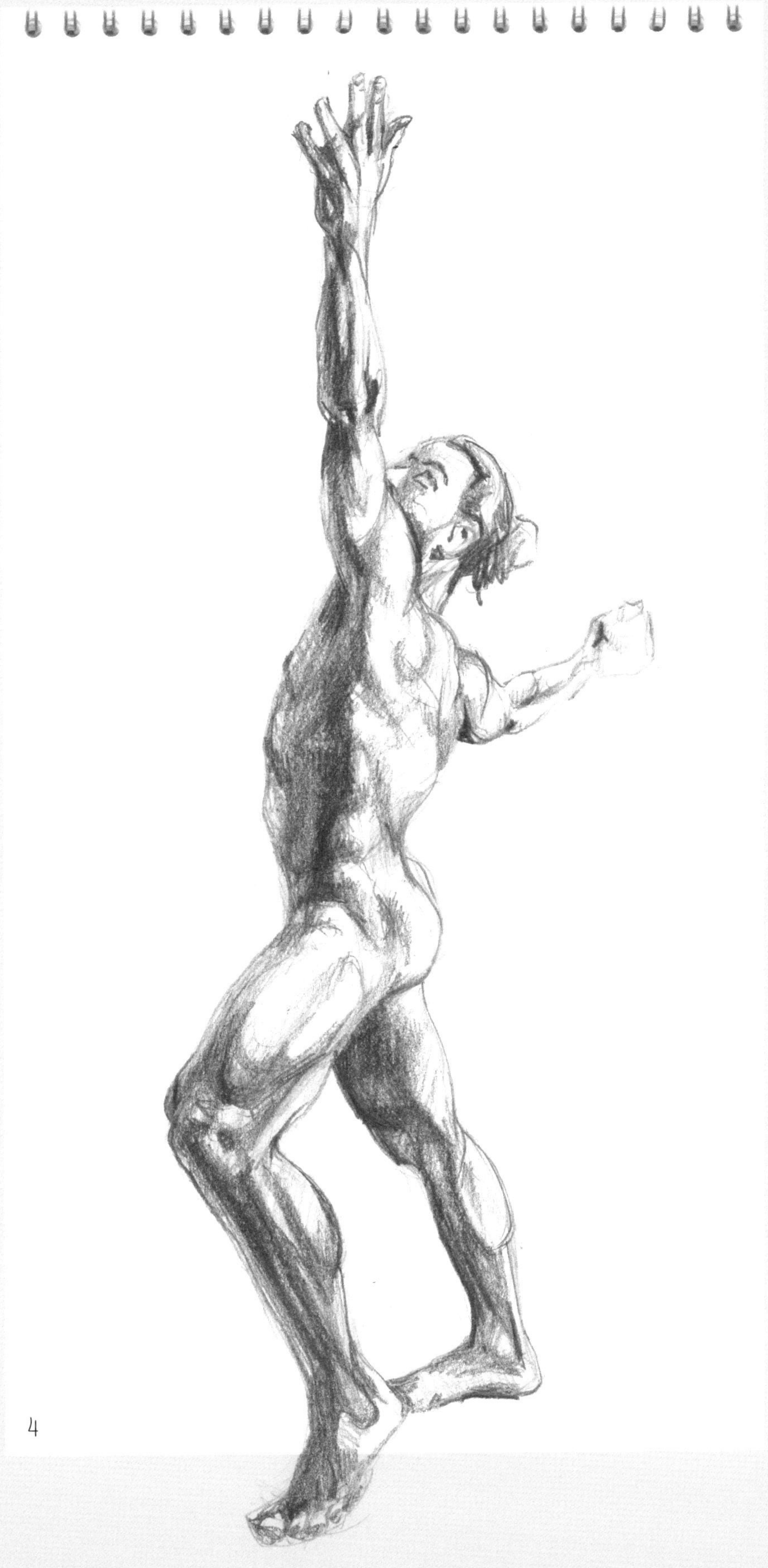

1. Sketch out the figure in large simple shapes, measuring to gain a level of accuracy in the proportions. Use a light pencil so that you can erase your shapes to provide a cleaner surface on which to concentrate on the muscles.

2. When you are satisfied, look hard at your figure and draw in the most obvious muscles and tendons as they appear. Although these shapes are represented by tone, rather than line, you may like to lightly sketch the outlines first, so you can position them all successfully. Think of the round shapes made by the muscles and the lines made by the tendons, especially around joints.

3. Refer to an anatomical diagram of the muscular system to help you make sense of the shapes and recognise the muscles apparent in your model. There are many online, and you may need a selection so you can choose the closest pose to that of your figure. Once the muscles are in the correct position, aim to emphasise them by defining and slightly enlarging them, using the anatomical diagram as a guide. You can also use the diagram to add muscles that are not visible in the model. Do not add muscles to the face, unless there are very distinct ones in your model.

4. Referring to the life model and to the anatomical diagram, add tone to your muscles and tendons. You should aim to slightly exaggerate the tone, to accentuate the shapes under the skin.

Head

The head is a daunting part of life drawing. People worry about drawing faces and often leave them out. Here I offer you a solution so that you get something convincing down, without being committed to accuracy and likeness. The key is keeping it simple. It is preferable to have a portrait with accurate but very scant detail as opposed to a very detailed portrait that is slightly out of proportion. I always include the basics: the eye sockets, the shadow under the nose and the shadow of the top lip. These features don't require detail in a short pose, but can still be effective in suggesting a likeness, representing as they do the fundamental structure of the face.

For longer drawings, the main concern is getting a likeness where your drawing truly resembles the sitter. This is the Holy Grail and comes through the strictest of observation. Stuart Pearson Wright manages to capture a convincing likeness while exaggerating and distorting various features. He shows us how important observation is, even if the later decision-making favours artistic licence over accuracy.

When drawing portraits, think of the head as a whole, rather than the face. Although the face is the most engaging part, it takes up a relatively small area, and should not be given overdue prominence. There is a lot of head behind the face. Although observation is crucial, an understanding of the skull is essential here. Students often put too much emphasis on the obvious features such as the eyes, mouth and nose, without thinking of the underlying structure, which is arguably more important.

Another factor is hair. Although I look at it in detail in the final Finishing Touches chapter (see page 90), it should still be acknowledged as an important factor in determining the shape and size of the head. It is also necessary to ascertain the position of the hairline, in order to judge the position of the rest of the features. For the same reason, always include the ears if they are visible. Bald heads are the most difficult as you cannot hide slight errors in the hair and the outline must be spot on.

As you draw more people, you will realise how unique each face is. There are some fairly reliable truths, but not as many as you might think. These truths are not to do with the tenets I mentioned earlier such as the distance between the eyes being equal to the width of an eye (see page 28), but general observations which, after drawing many different people, seem to recur. These may include the fact that there is often a shadow at the top of the nose, between the eyes; the top lip is often darker than the lower; there is normally a shadow directly under the lower lip. There is almost always light reflected up into the shadow of the chin; the whites of the eyes are normally darker than the skin around them.

Construction lines are very helpful in mapping out the structure of the face – the positions of features are more important than the features themselves. As mentioned on page 40, they show us the fundamental shape of an individual's face. With this knowledge, you can suggest a face with the fewest of marks in quick sketches, without the risk of making an unconvincing likeness. In three-minute drawings, the addition of only the eye sockets, the shadow under the nose and a smudge for the mouth are sufficient. If these marks are in the correct place, you can refine them in a longer pose. Look at Hans Holbein's portrait drawings – they are very simple but very strictly observed. This shows evidence of a very objective scrutiny of the sitter.

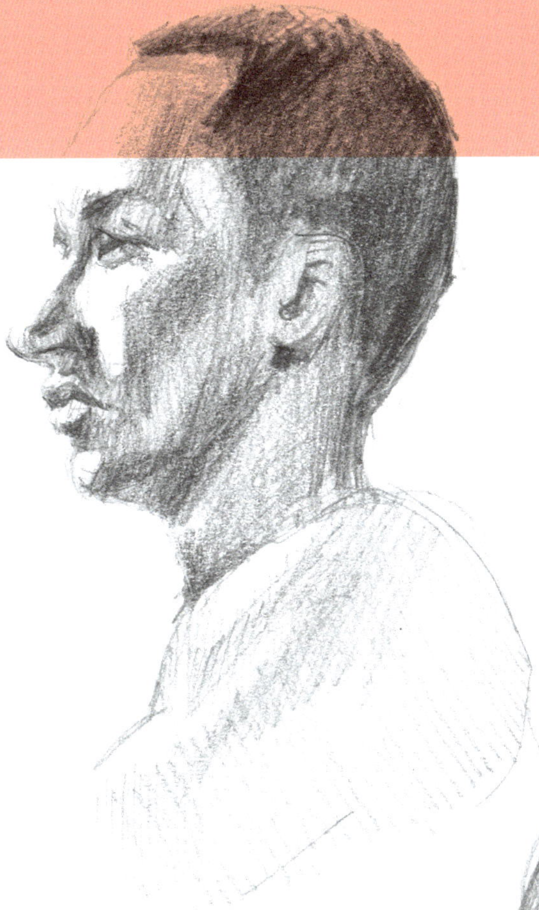

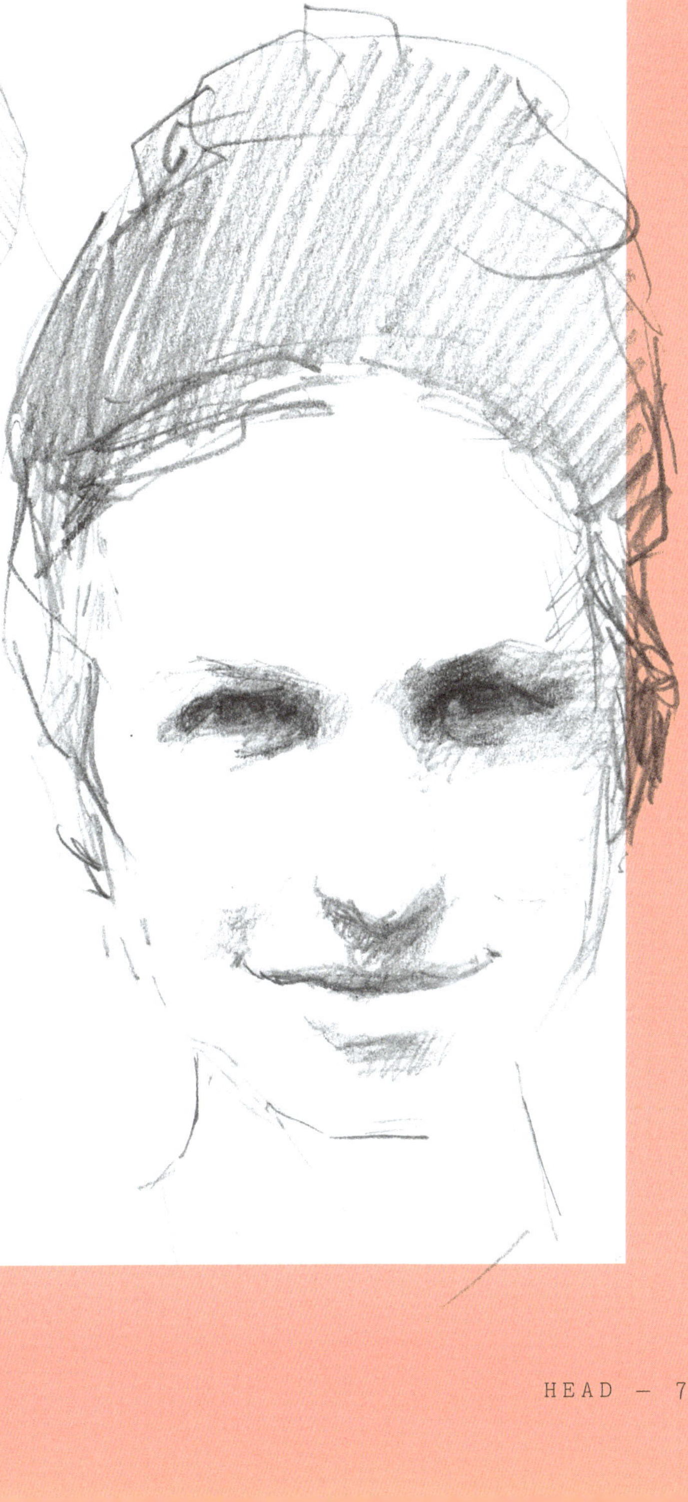

REMEMBER:

- Observation is key – you should be looking at the model 85 per cent of the time.
- Getting the correct relationships between features is important.
- Be honest – draw only what you see.

Skull Exercise

This exercise is a strict observation of the skull so that you'll have an automatic awareness of it when you draw portraits from now on. As you are looking at it, feel your own face and see how it fits under your skin, how it underpins your own features. It is useful to have the skull orientated at a slight angle, neither facing front on, nor in a full side-on profile. Anything in-between is fine; you'll be able to see the eye sockets clearly, as well as some detail behind the cheekbones.

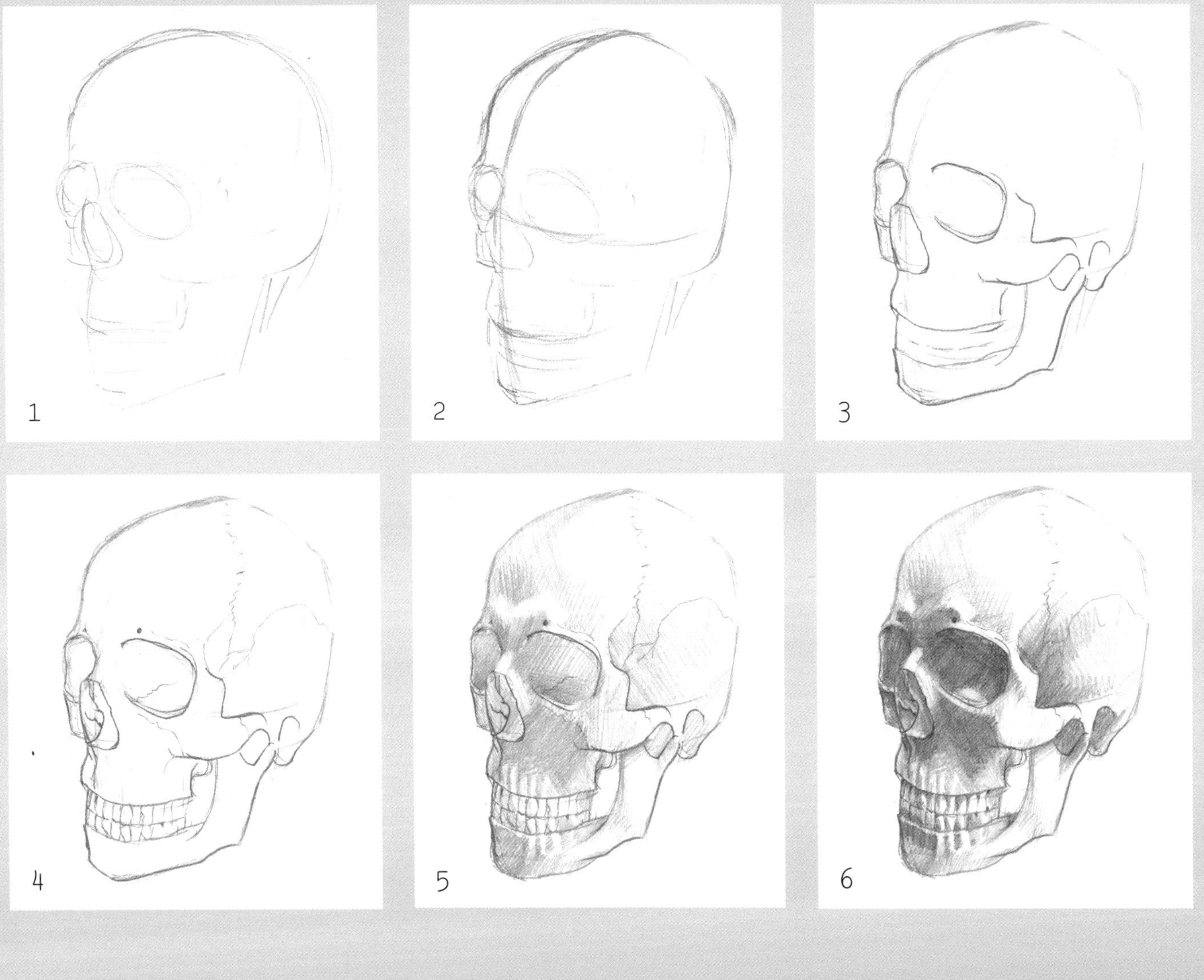

1. After a minute's careful scrutiny, sketch out the shape of the skull vaguely, including the eye sockets, the nasal cavity (pyriform aperture) and the jawline.

2. Impose some helpful construction lines. These may include the central vertical line, a horizontal line through the eyes and a horizontal line between the teeth. Alter the outlines if you need to.

3. With the aid of the construction lines and measurements, consolidate the size and shape of the eye sockets, nasal cavity and cheekbones (zygomatic arches), which start under the eye sockets and extend almost to the ear. At this stage, don't depict separate teeth, but mark out the boundaries of tooth and skull (the alveolar margins). Some of the more definite lines may be drawn with a darker pencil.

4. Now the structure is well defined, add in any other details that may be expressed with a line. These may need to be faint lines, for example, the gaps between the teeth; sutures dividing the main bulk of the skull: the parietal (crown), occipital (nape) and frontal bones; the outside edge of the eye socket closest to you, which curves around the temple; any details within the nasal aperture and the eye sockets; small holes (foramen). These lines should be faint because they might represent very fine lines – lines that don't stand out tonally or lines that fade and disappear. Weight can always be added later if necessary.

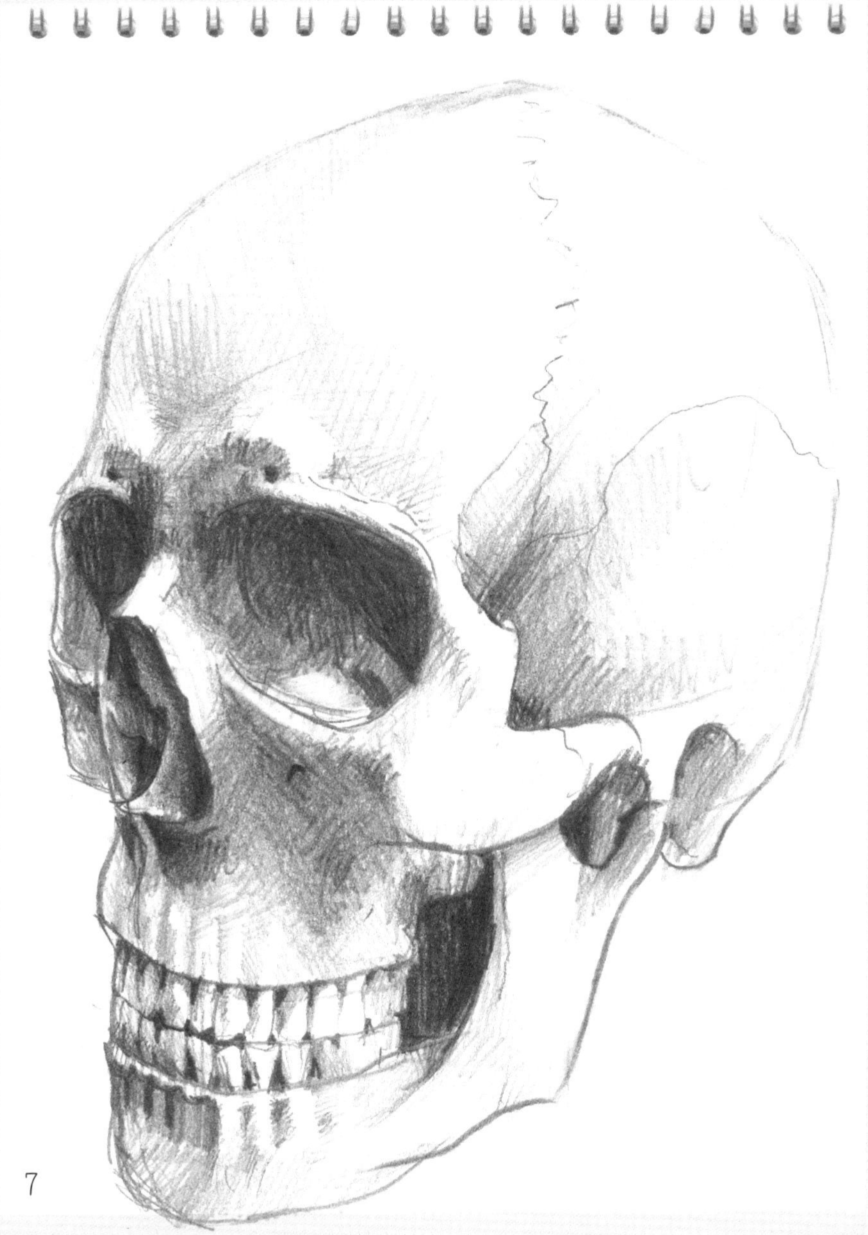

5. Next add tone (see the chapter on Tone for more guidance, pages 52–61). Start with the lightest shadows. You will be able to describe features that aren't linear such as the brow; the middle of the brow (the glabella); and the regular indentations of the alveolar margins into which the teeth are set. To ascertain these, squint at the skull.

6. Next add the darker shadows. Use a smooth gradient of tone, from mid-tones to darker tones.

7. Finally, darken any lines and occlusion shadows; add the darkest values, which may appear in the eye sockets and nasal cavity.

Head Exercise

1

2

1. Looking at the model's face, detach yourself from the familiarity of the features – see everything as a collection of shapes and shadows. Sketch the outline and the most obvious features vaguely and using a faint line. Include the neck and the shape of the hair, if there is any.

2. Add construction lines (refer to the Construction Lines Exercise on page 42). Unless the face is in profile, the vertical central line will be the most important. Next, add the horizontal line that joins the eyes and, if they are visible, the tops of the ears – does this line curve? Are the tops of the ears lower or higher than the eyes? Include any other useful construction lines such as those on which the mouth and the underside of the nose lie. You will begin to see how rules of standard proportions should be ignored since they change from pose to pose, with the heights and angles all being determined by your viewpoint of the head.

3. Make some measurements using your pencil to check the distances between the construction lines (see page 44). Also check the distances between features and outlines. Check the angles of various parts and planes of the face, outlines and features. Distances may be awkward when concentrating on the relatively small area of the head, in which case, rely mostly on angles. Think carefully about the spaces of the face just outside of the main features – between the eyes and the ears; the position of the hairline. Add and adjust according to your measurements.

4. Consolidate the lines, at the same time adding in some tone if it helps denote certain features: the eye sockets (usually a general area of shadow, perhaps with some obvious highlights such as any on the lids); the underside of the nose, including the shadow it casts (don't overstate the nostrils, heavier shadows can be added later); the lips – the bottom lip may not have any outlines but may instead be defined by the upper lip and the dent above the chin (the mentolabial sulcus). The hairline may appear as a tonal boundary, rather than a hard line. Check your measurements again – is anything out of place? Rub out any extraneous pencil marks and construction lines if you can.

5. Concentrate on tone in earnest now (refer to the Complex Tone Exercise on page 60). Include the hair: it's important to shade this correctly in relation to the skin and shadows, so that your sketch has a sense of balance. Simultaneously add in any subtler lines that may appear: under the eyes, next to the nostrils, wrinkles. Don't forget that the whites of the eyes may be darker than the lids, as they are in shadow. Look carefully at this relationship.

6. Add the darkest tones and occlusion shadows – these might include the eyelashes, the pupils, the line between the two lips, shadows in the hair. Also rub out some pencil to represent reflected light where it appears, perhaps under the chin.

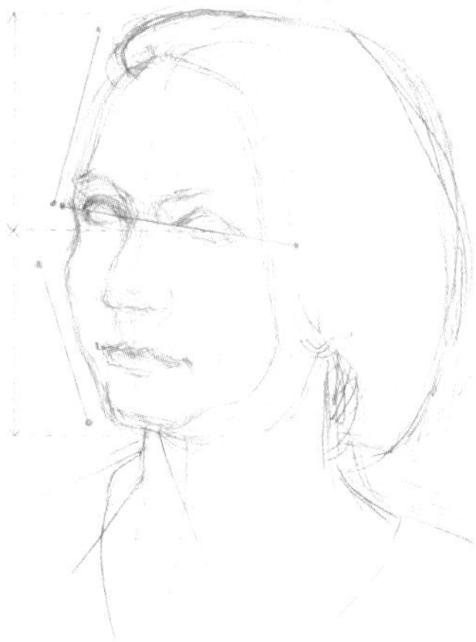

3

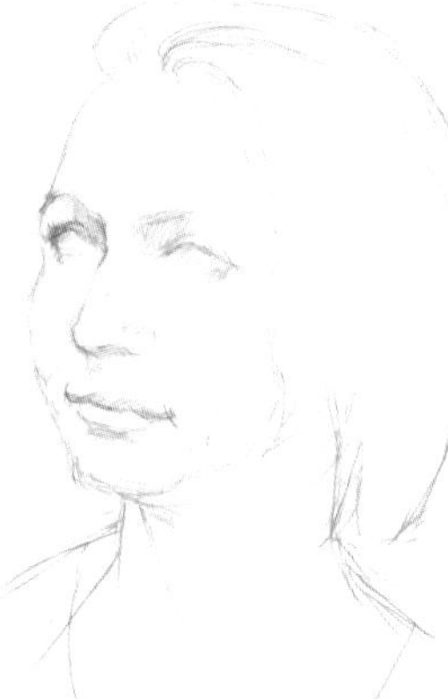

4

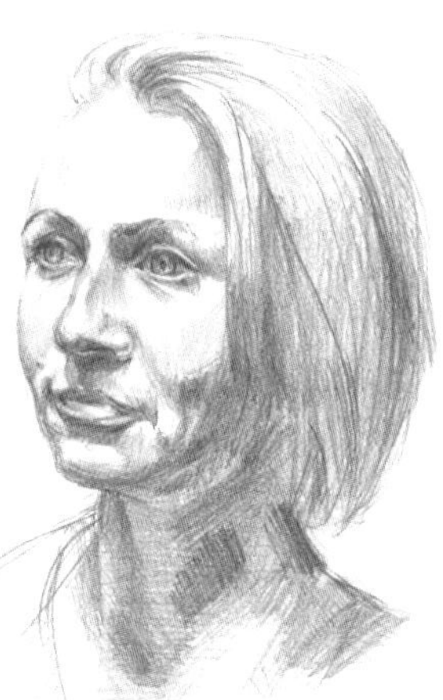

5

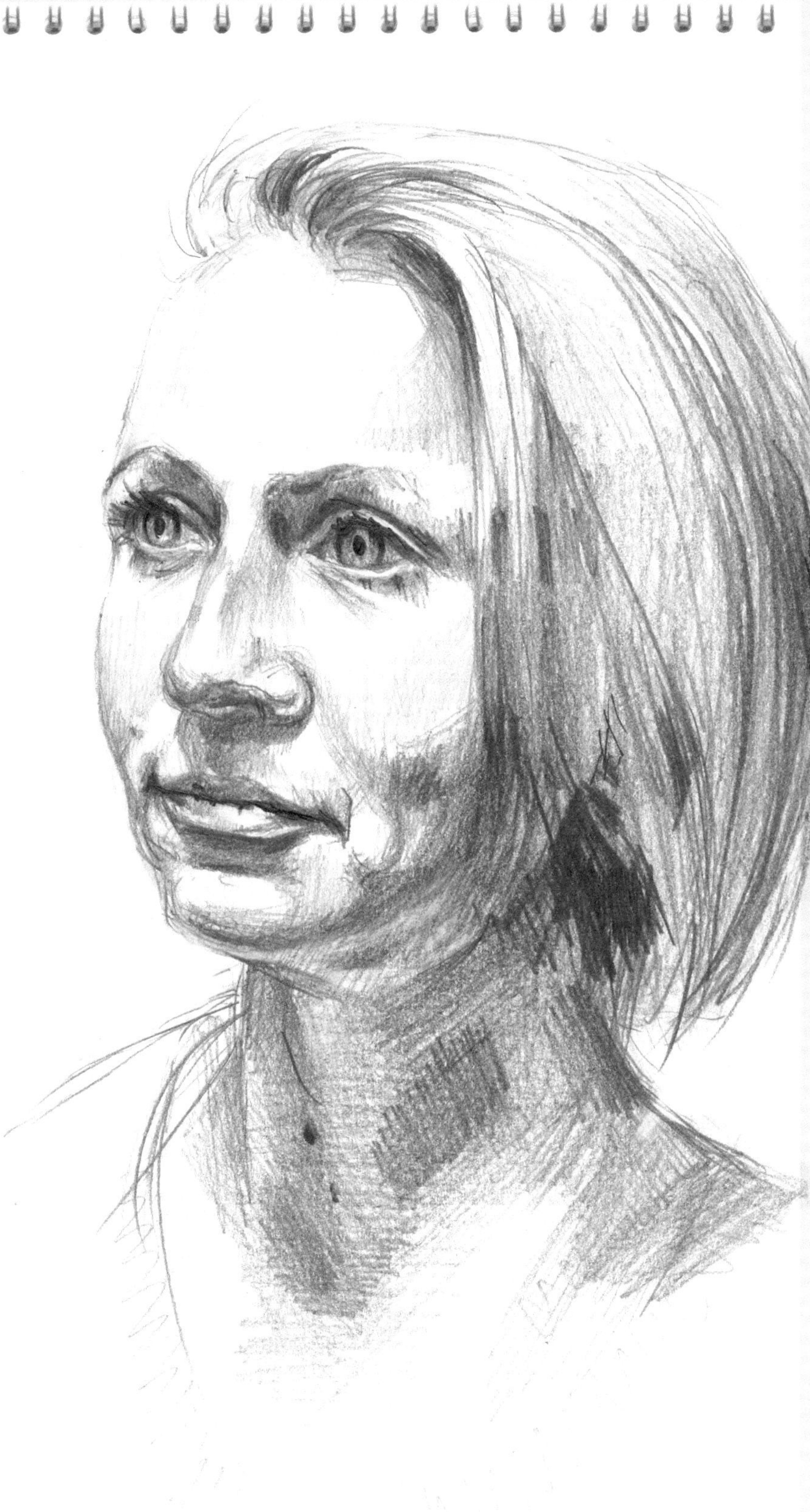

6

Hands

Hands are often thought of as even trickier to draw than faces. Learners might avoid them altogether and leave severed stumps on the arms, or else overdo them, portraying sausage-like fingers.

They are indeed complex – they contain so many variables: five independently mobile digits, all jointed in several places and at least some of which may be foreshortened. They are inconveniently arranged to break up into smaller, manageable blocks, and they are normally too small to be able to measure the distances between features successfully.

Because of the endless possibilities in arrangement of any one model's hand, it is impossible to define a standard drawing formula – the only way to tackle drawing hands is to see them objectively for the shape they happen to present in any pose.

A trick that will help enormously, however, is to draw the hand as a mitten. It is much easier to get an accurate mitten shape than an accurate hand shape (fig 1). For a very quick sketch, rather than leave out the extremities altogether, see the arrangement of the hand as a blocky shape, and even if the fingers are splayed, pretend they are in a mitten, albeit a stretched one. Depict the thumb as separate, as in a mitten. This is a perfectly adequate option for a quick pose – it is preferable to have something simple and well formed than something developed but inaccurate.

For a slightly longer pose, you still don't need to worry about the separate fingers. Separate fingers often match a level of detail that you might not even find in a twenty-minute pose.

The next step to breaking down the hand shape is to create construction lines that correspond to the joints (fig 2). This will give an indication of the position of the fingers within the mitten shape. If you have time to add some basic tone, you will create a convincing three-dimensional representation of the hand. Leonardo da Vinci's hand studies show how tone is effective in simple and detailed drawings.

Only after having done all of the above would I consider separating the fingers (fig 3), and possibly not if they are very close together, without a dark occlusion shadow to distinguish them from each other. This level of detail is only needed in longer poses, perhaps of half an hour or more. When you do divide the mitten into fingers, draw each independently, rather than split the hand into four equal parts. Now that each finger is a basic shape, it is possible to refine the outline and add tone.

In a long pose, you can think about the fingernails and the wrinkles of the knuckles. The fingernails are normally distinguished by their edges, and by a difference in tone, being shinier than the skin. Depending on the age of the model, there may also be veins and more wrinkles to consider. If you are using colour, you will notice that the hands often appear pink in comparison to the rest of the body, especially around the knuckles and the fat pads at the ends of the fingers and on the palms.

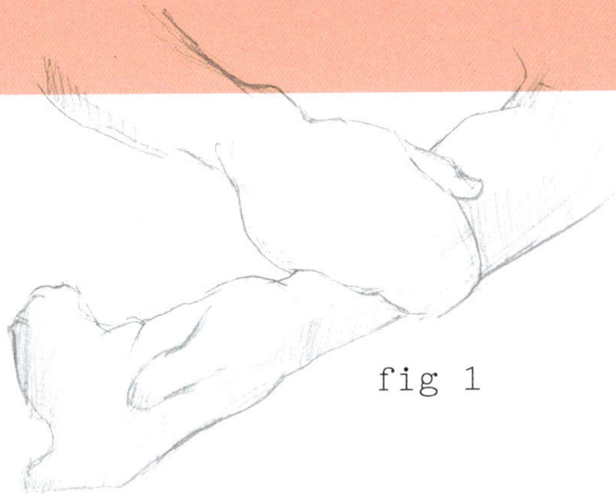

fig 1

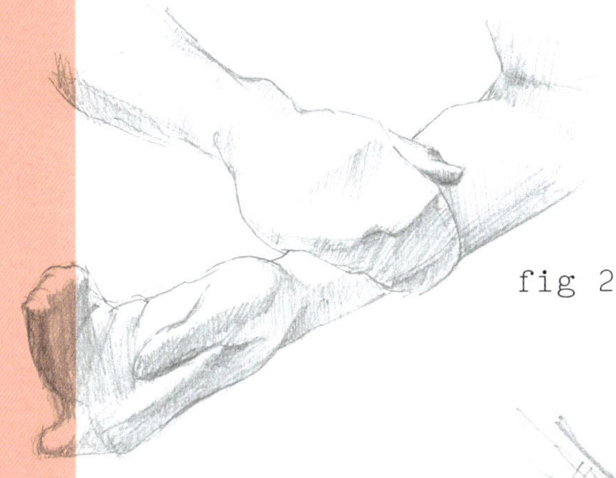

fig 2

REMEMBER:

- Think in terms of 'mittens'.
- Delay the depiction of separate fingers.
- Adding simple tone will help provide definition.
- Check angles, heights and distances if possible.

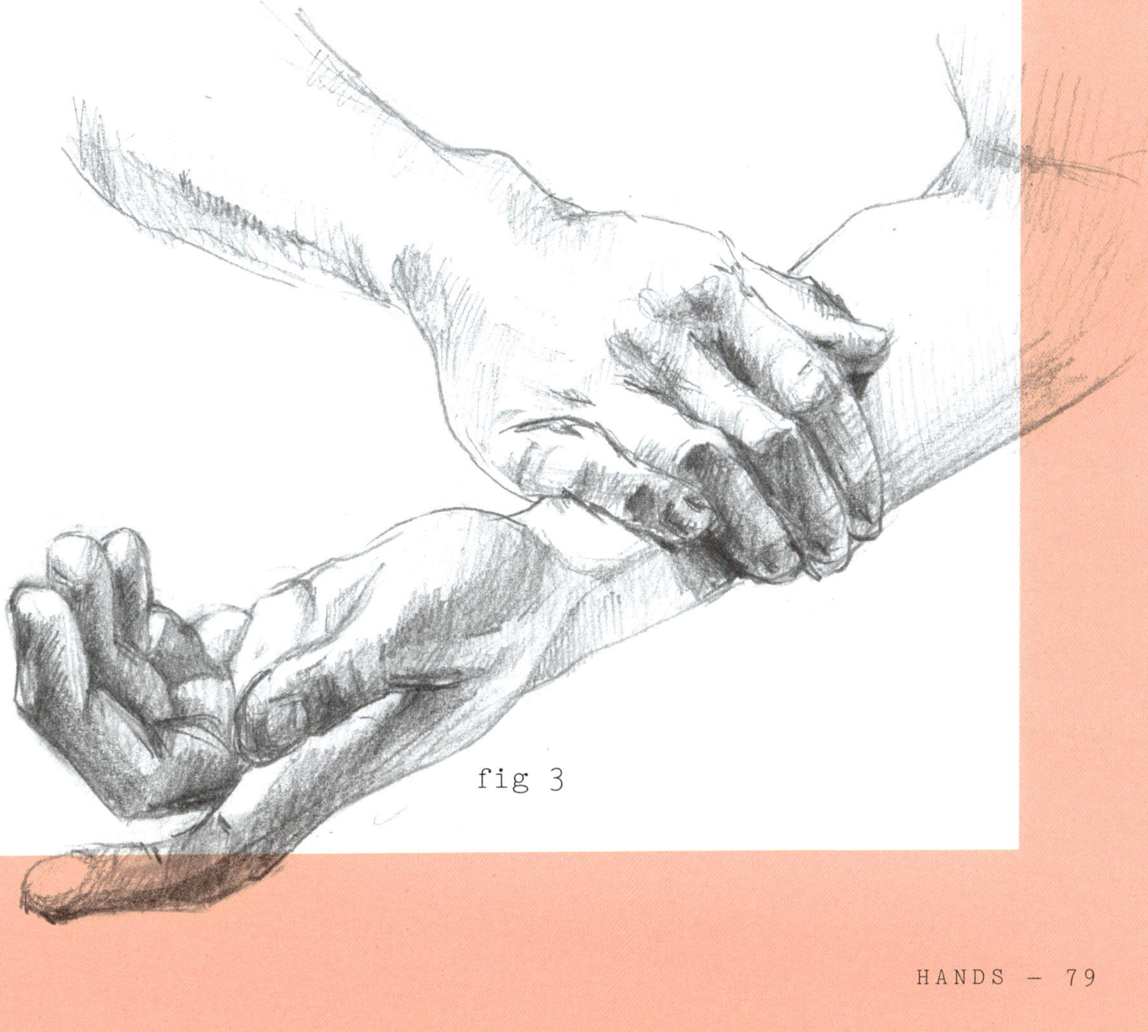

fig 3

Hands
Exercise

1. Look hard at the hand and imagine it inside a mitten. Draw the outline of this mitten, either in light pencil or lightly in charcoal, remembering to draw the thumb separately from the main block of the fingers. The wrists and their relationship to the arm are worth practising so include a reasonable chunk of forearm, about a third of the way to the elbow.

2. Sketch in construction lines that transect the hand at each set of knuckles.

3. Use a pencil to measure angles and distances. Check the angle of the forearm and its relationship to the wrist. Check the width versus the height of the hand. Adjust anything that isn't correct.

4. Let your eyes go out of focus and assess the tone across the whole shape. You don't want to add detailed tone at this stage, but instead think of sculptural planes such as the flat area of the back of the hand, the underside of the forearm and the light across the fingers before they bend at the knuckles. Add simple tone, just one shade of grey. Employ flat and uninterrupted hatching if you are using pencil and large blocks if you are using charcoal.

5. Look carefully at the basic shape of each finger and draw them in one at a time.

6. Rub out the marks that are left over in the gaps. Refine the outlines – carefully observe the shape of the lines, including the ends of the fingers. If you can see the underside of the fingers, you might need to represent the roundness of the fingertips. Add tone along the length of the fingers where it is needed. Still keep the tone basic at this stage.

7. Add lines to denote wrinkles, veins, folds in the skin and fingernails. Use a rubber to add highlights and refine the tone around these details. Think about how you might translate the colour into a tonal value (i.e. what shade of grey is most appropriate).

8. Advanced students may want to add deeper shadows and occlusion shadows to develop and refine their drawing, making the hand appear more realistic.

1

2

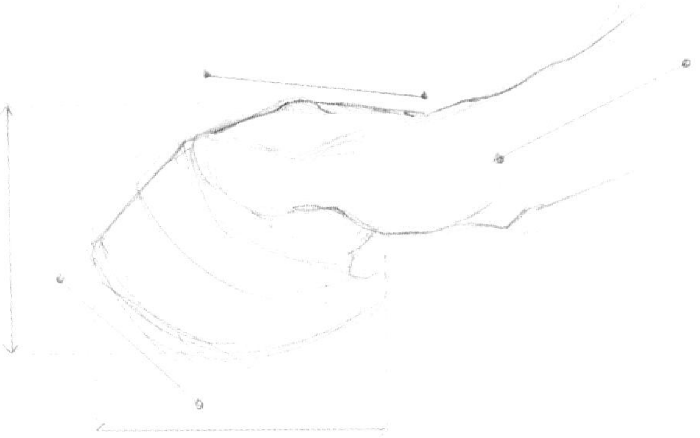
3

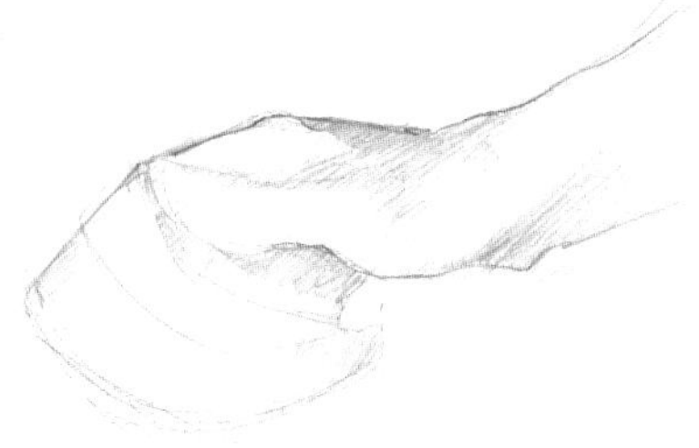
4

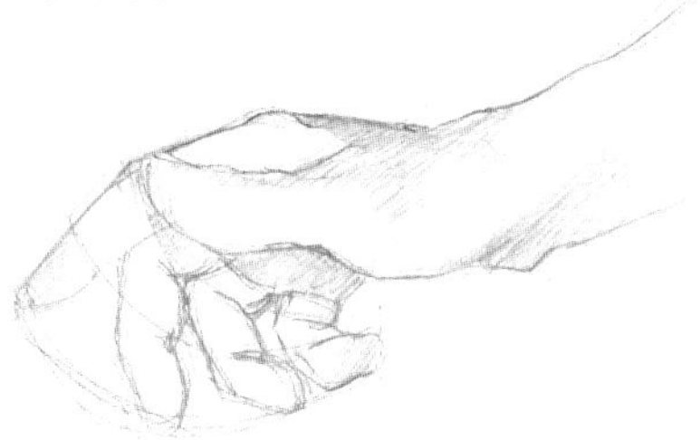
5

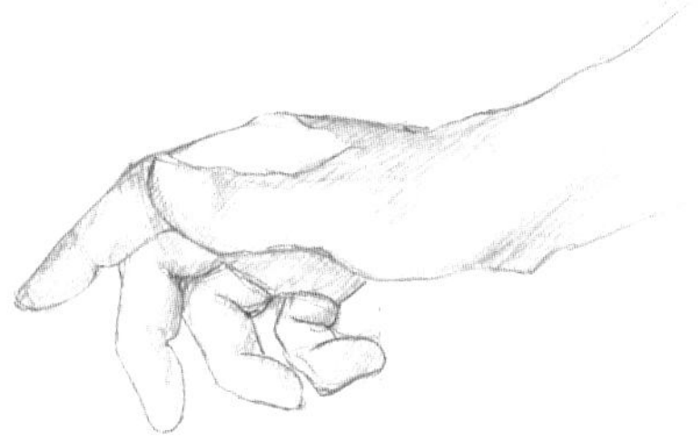
6

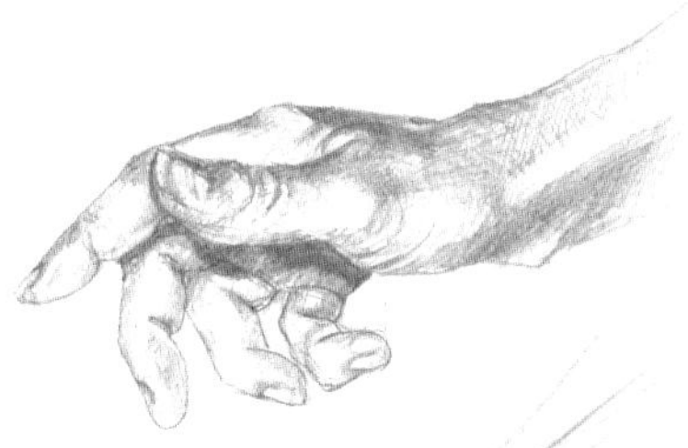
7

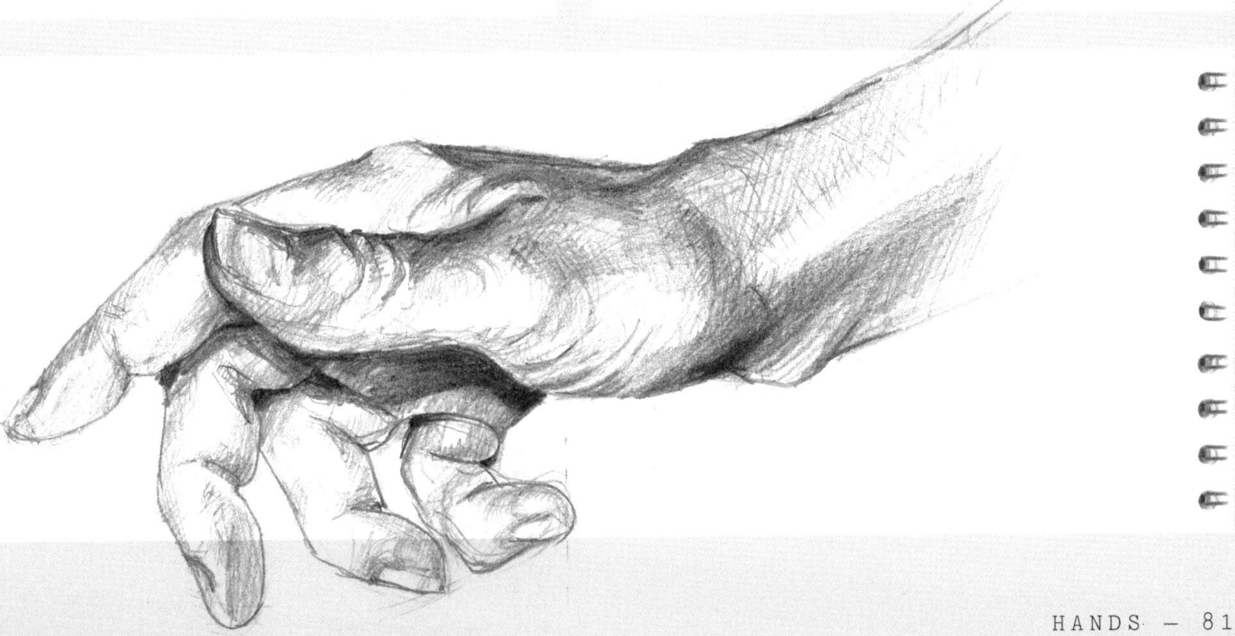
8

Feet

Feet are almost as tricky as hands, but with a slightly different set of problems. The digits are not quite so variable and independent. However, they don't have the distinguishing features that hands have, so are harder to break up into easy shapes. It is often only tone that provides sensible landmarks, so your foot outline can seem incorrectly drawn until you add some shading. Feet are wedge-shaped, so it is often possible to see both the top and the bottom at the same time – the instep and the sole of the foot can both be visible in the same view.

Feet are often foreshortened (see page 48), especially in a standing pose. It might be necessary to measure their length compared to another established length of the body. It is essential to see the whole foot as a two-dimensional shape. Imagine looking through a window and drawing round the outline of the foot, straight onto the glass. They look unconvincing without tone and detail, but it is important to get this silhouette established first. Approach drawing feet in the same way as you did the hands – draw a sock, rather than a foot (figs 1). This will suffice for a very quick sketch, and will serve as the best starting point for a longer drawing.

A couple of features that might aid you are the ankles and the toe joints. As with the fingers, don't draw distinct toes early on in a drawing, or in a very quick study. Sketch a contour line that corresponds with the beginning of the toes, and perhaps another that shows the joints. You may need to treat the big toe separately. If you are looking at the underside of the foot, there may be folds between the balls and the arches, where the fat pads are compressed.

The early addition of tone will help to highlight any problem areas (figs 2), as well as show you whether your main outline is correct. Keep this simple at first, using just two values – white and grey. Let your eyes go out of focus in order to simplify this tone. In a ten- or twenty-minute pose, this is probably enough detail and will describe the foot adequately.

When your shaded sock shape is looking structurally sound, you can separate the toes (figs 3). As with the fingers, do each toe one at a time. Feet are quite characterful and peculiar to the model and the toes can point in slightly different directions, so each must be observed carefully and individually. You may find that one partially blocks its neighbour, or ends pointing upwards – do draw this, don't try to play it down. Feet always look more realistic when you include their personal idiosyncrasies.

To develop your drawing further, you can add complex tone: erase shadows to pick out highlights; observe the undulations of the ankle bone; deepen shadows where veins and bones appear; add occlusion shadows under and between the toes, perhaps in the creases of the underside of the foot too. You can include wrinkles and toenails, but make sure they are not too heavy-handed: weigh them in relation to the rest of the lines and tone of the foot.

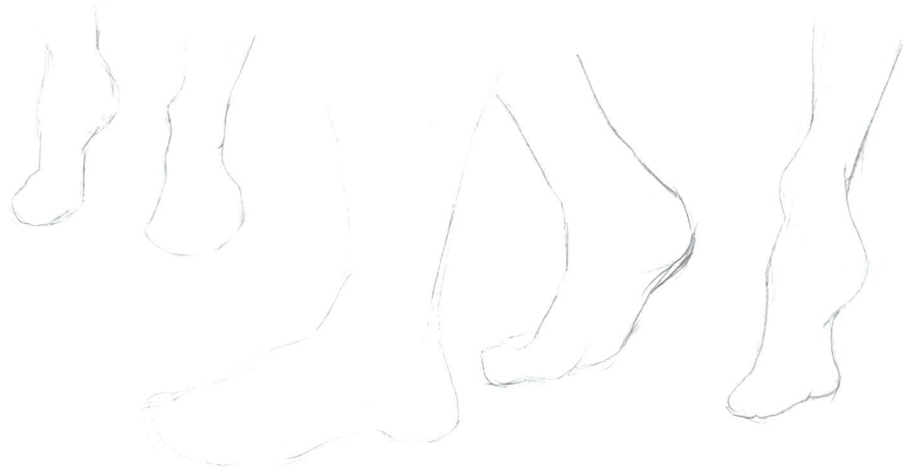

figs 1

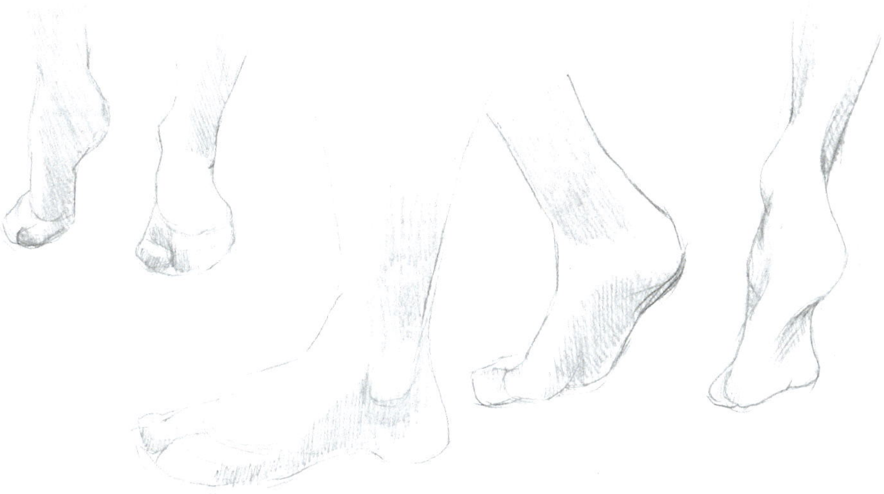

figs 2

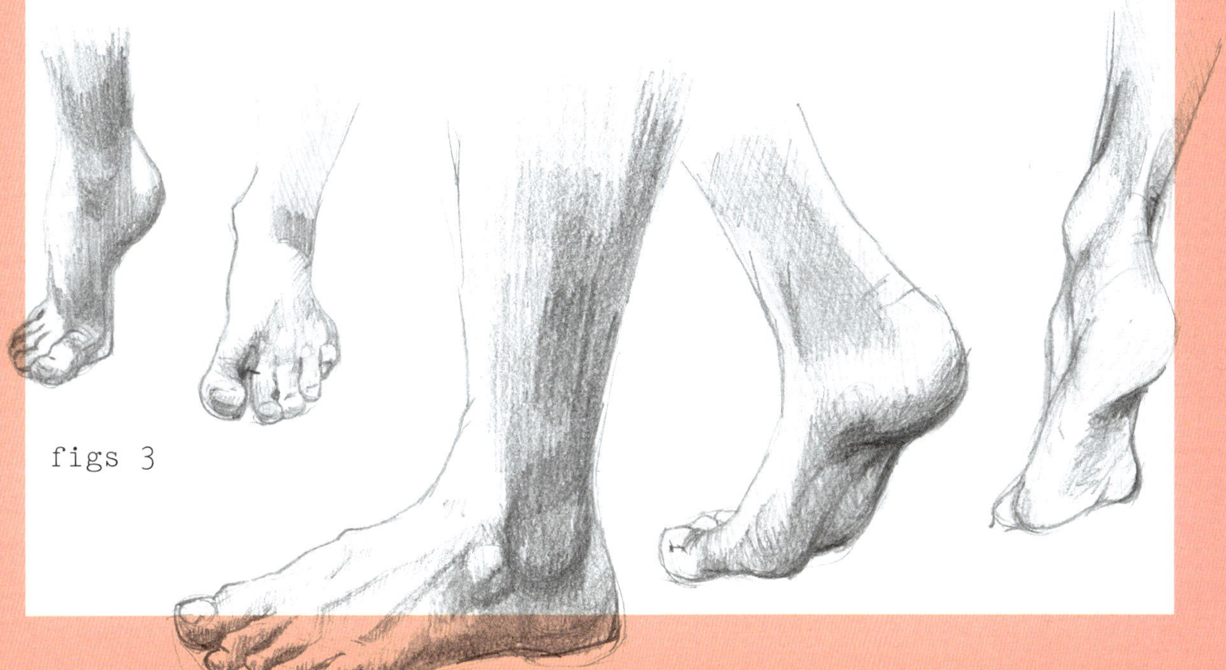

figs 3

Feet Exercise

1. Draw your foot outline as if the model was wearing a sock. Include part of the leg to about halfway up the shin bone. You can use charcoal or pencil, but begin with faint lines.

2. Carefully check the angles: the angle between the foot and the leg; the top, bottom and front of the foot. It is important to get the sock silhouette as accurate as possible at this stage.

3. Establish the positions of the toes and the joints by using construction lines. These may arch and appear like straps of a sandal. If you are viewing the underside of the foot, you may not see any joints, but will see a line between the toes and the ball of the foot.

4. Let your eyes go out of focus to distinguish the most obvious areas of shadow. Mark these in using even pencil hatching, or blocks of charcoal. Don't make the shadows too dark, they are just there to distinguish the different facets of the foot.

5. Carefully separate the toes, beginning with the big toe and concentrating on the shape of each toe one at a time. Add any other obvious lines and wrinkles.

6. Advanced drawers could develop tone, using a rubber to regain the white of the paper where you need highlights to appear. Darken some areas with cross-hatching or another layer of charcoal, perhaps at the ends of the toes, under the ankle bone, around the fat pads and arches. Use darker lines cautiously to depict any visible veins and the shadows on the top of the foot: the knobbly navicular and cuneiform bones (these are small bones which form the instep), and the long metatarsals which run down the length of the foot to the toes. Include the toenails if they are obvious. These may all be different shapes and sizes, and may need highlights of their own.

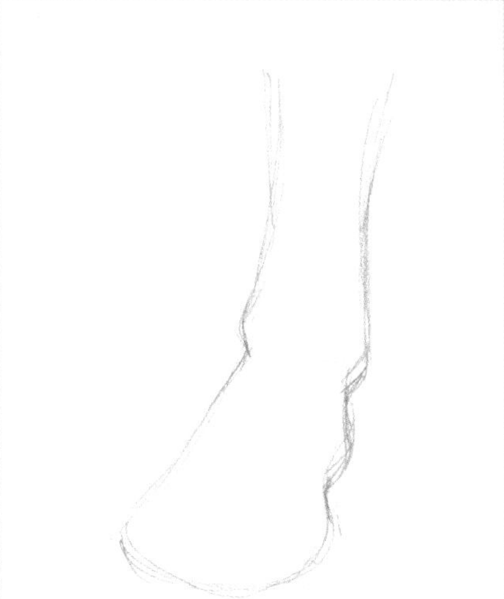

1

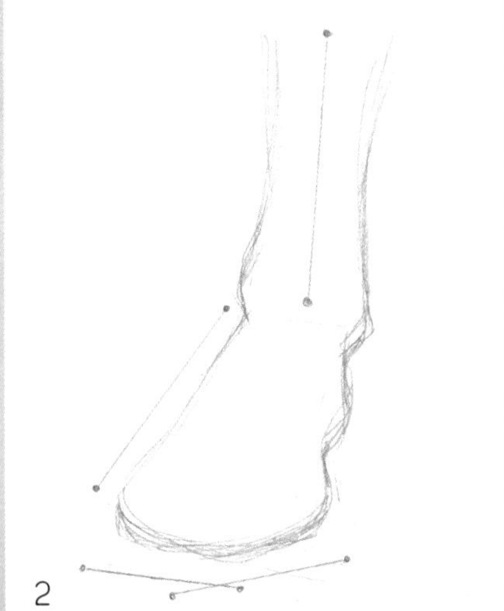

2

3

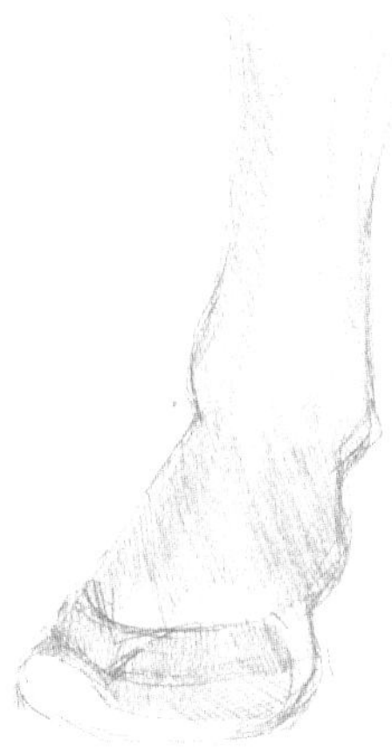

4

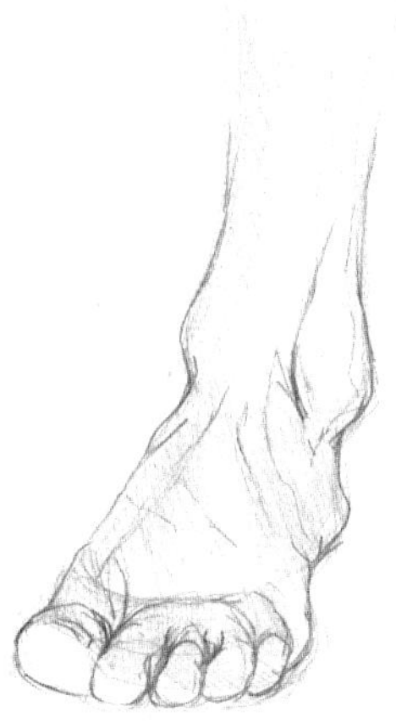

5

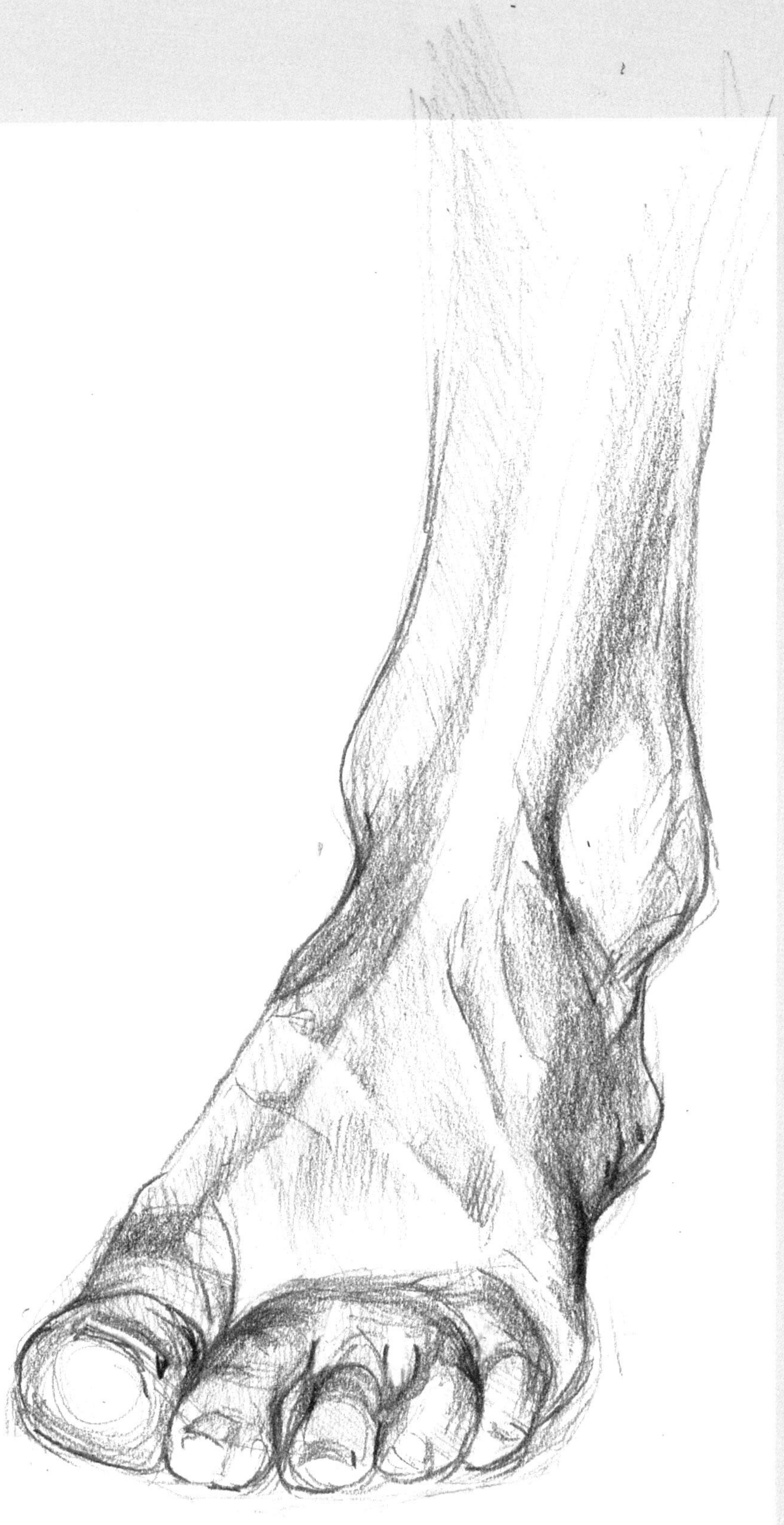

6

Final Full Figure Drawing

We have looked at how to build up a figure drawing from the beginning, using simple shapes and faint lines. We have seen how to develop and measure a simple drawing to a level of convincing accuracy and how to use tone. We have also found ways to approach challenging parts of the body, as well as acknowledging the muscles and skeleton underneath. In this exercise I will show you how to gather all of these methods together to compose a full figure drawing.

---

1. Spend a minute looking objectively at the model, with slightly unfocused eyes. Detach yourself from the familiarity of the human body and see a collection of shapes. Think about the overall height compared to the width. Draw the whole figure, broken into manageable shapes (see the Shape Exercise, page 38). Press lightly with pencil, charcoal or ballpoint pen, or use a light grey pen. If you wish to use paint, you can start with a light pencil for steps 1–4, or if you are brave, use a very dilute grey and a thin paint brush.

2. Check distances and angles, adjusting as necessary (see Measuring, page 44). Think of the angle of the central line of the head, compared to the angle of the central line of the torso. Check the length of the limbs and the distances between both feet. Depending on the pose, there may be other helpful measurements – perhaps the slope of the shoulders or a shin, maybe even some distances that show foreshortening at work (see page 48). Faintly add any useful construction lines (see the Construction Lines Exercise, page 42).

3. Using the construction lines as a guide, add landmarks such as the genitalia, navel, breasts, eye sockets, ears, nose, mouth and jawline. Sketch the outline of the hair. Check the positions of these features using your pen or pencil as a plumb line, or by checking their distance and angle in relation to other landmarks (see the Measuring Exercise, page 46).

4. Erase any extraneous marks such as sketchy lines, mistakes and construction lines, and consolidate your correct lines. Think about the shapes of the muscles and the skeleton in the arms, legs and torso (see the Muscles Exercise, page 70, and the Skeleton Exercise, page 66). Don't exaggerate them, but be aware that they may affect the detailed outline of the figure. Don't make the lines too

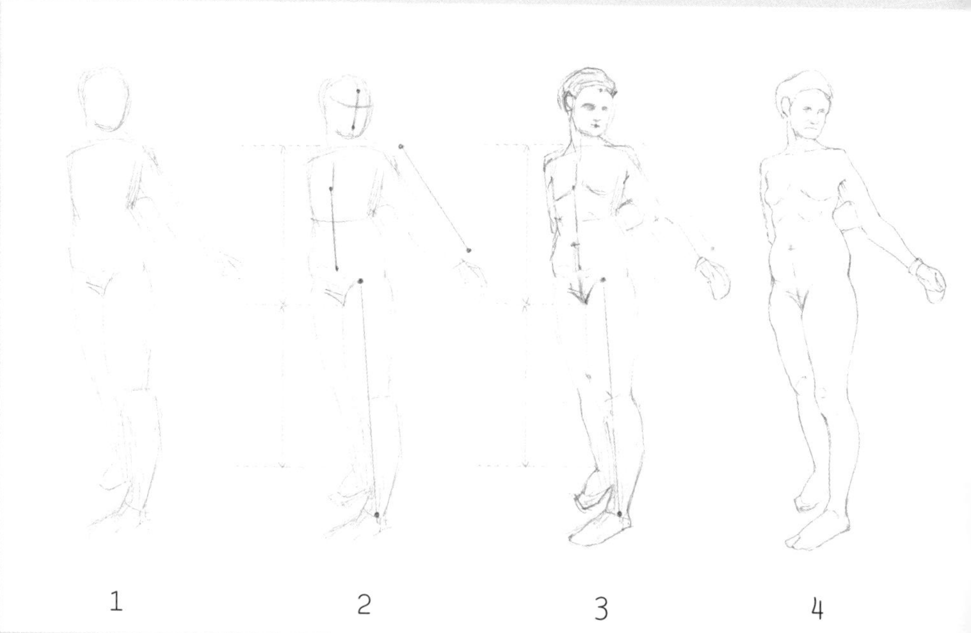

dark, as most of the definition will come from the application of tone. If you have been using paint, you could use a very slightly darker grey to show the correct lines; the earlier paler marks will become less noticeable by contrast.

5. Use your lightest pencil, pen, the softest pressure of charcoal, or a very dilute ink/paint to cover the whole of the figure, excluding highlights, as described in Complex Tone on page 58. Allow for colour variation: tanned skin, rosy cheeks, hands, knees, chest, feet, hair, areolae. Remember, you should be looking at the model 85 per cent of the time throughout this drawing.

6. Using slightly more pressure, add the core shadows (everything that could be called 'a shadow'). Get some distance from your work and assess the tonal balance so far.

7. Using a darker pen or pencil, darker grey paint, or a harder pressure of charcoal, add in further detail – for example, the eyes, nostrils, wrinkles and nipples. Separate fingers and toes if the boundaries are distinct. Develop the tone, noticing how the skeleton causes darker shadows and highlights, especially around the collar bone, ribcage, jaw, cheeks and eye sockets.

8. Add a simple tonal representation of the background, including the cast shadow. Assess the figure as a whole and check for errors. Include any jewellery or tattoos. Add the occlusion shadows and lighten any areas where light is reflected into the core shadow. If you were using pencil, you may like to add occlusion shadows in ink to broaden your tonal range.

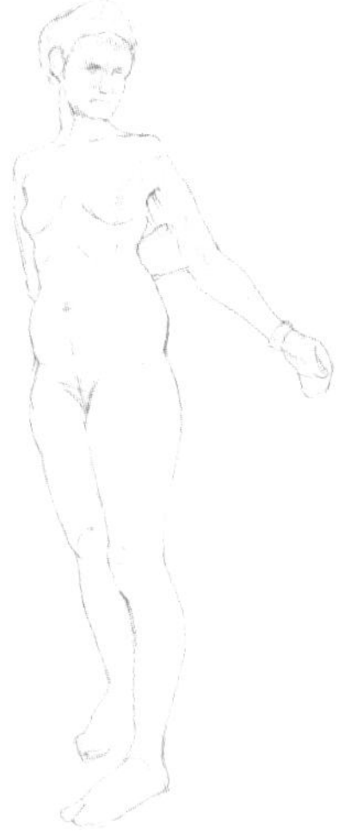

5

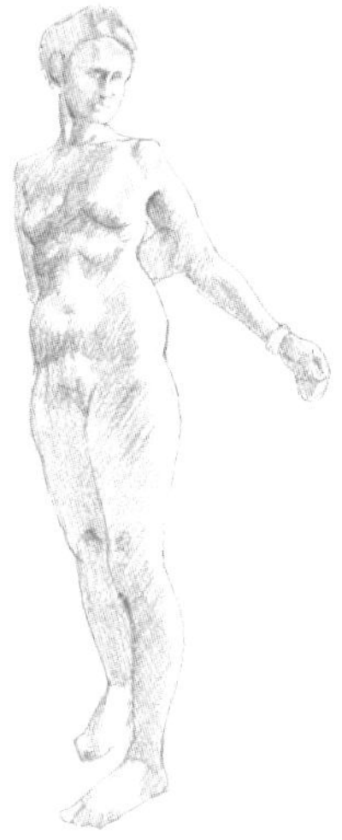

6

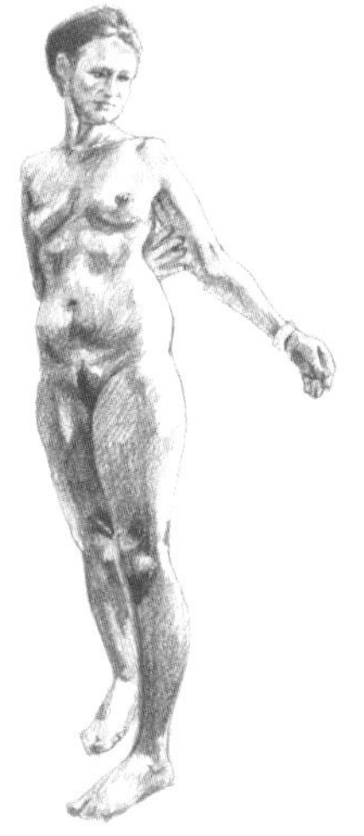

7

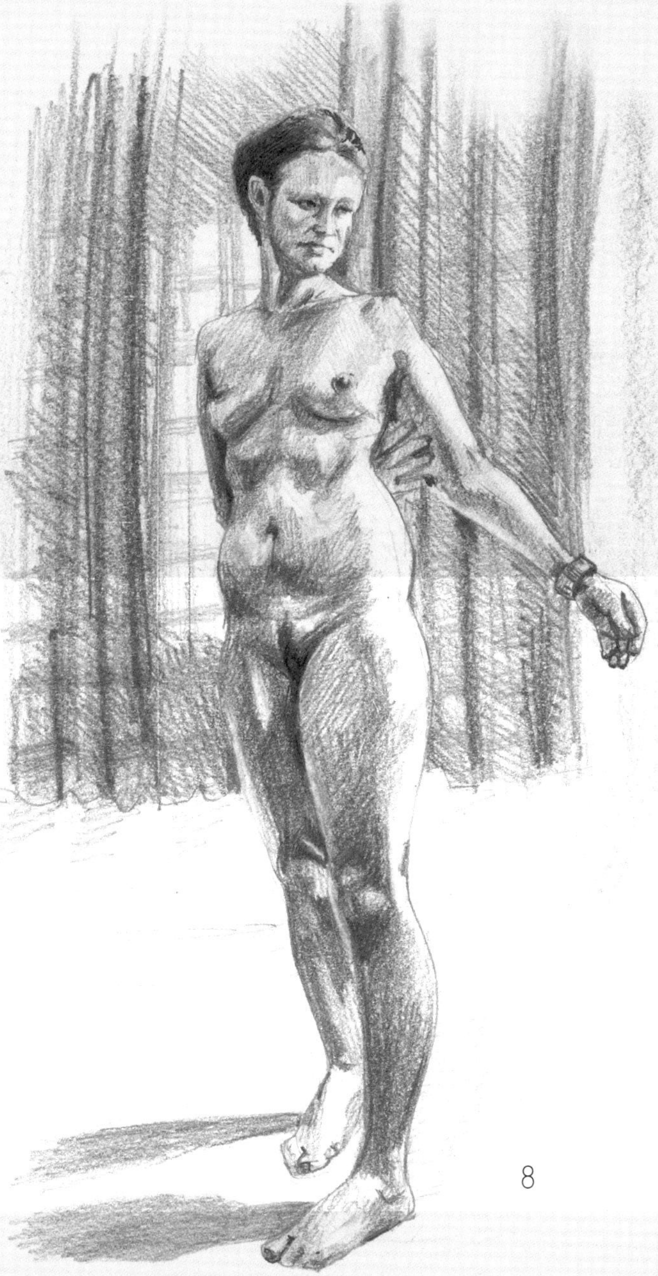

8

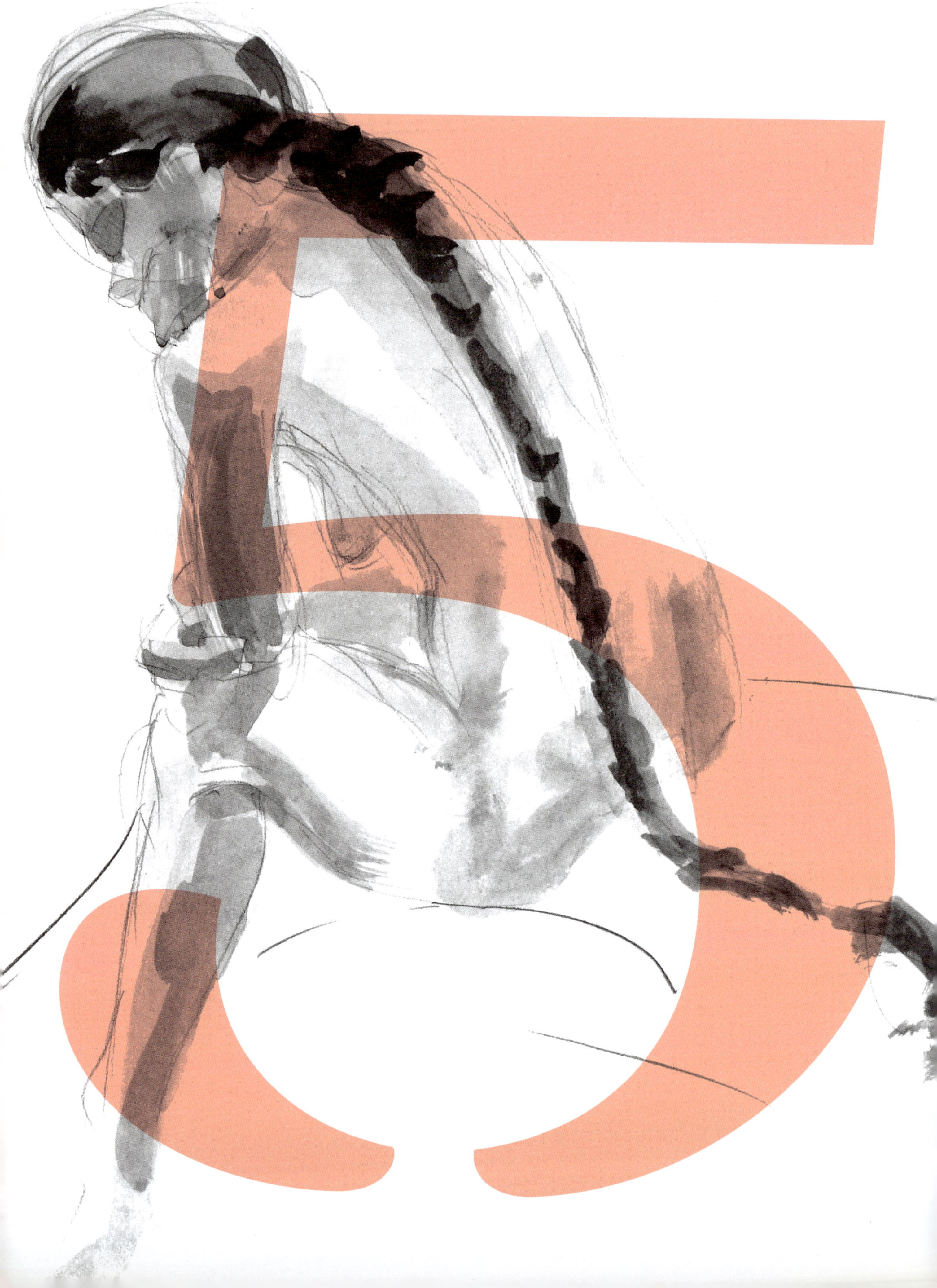
5

Finishing Touches

We have looked at all of the fundamental building blocks of life drawing: how to intimate movement and to sketch rapidly; how to construct and measure the figure accurately; how to use tone; and basic anatomy and how it affects the way we see the figure and difficult body parts. This final chapter explains how to add finishing touches to your drawing, concentrating on features such as hair, skin and clothes that are occasionally overlooked. These elements are important to acknowledge, and a reasonable competence in handling them can add refinement to a piece of work. As with everything else covered, the emphasis will be on observing these details objectively and representing them honestly. Tone is often the most important factor in these final touches, so I'll frequently encourage you to look hard at light and dark.

Finally, to really develop your work, it is important to know how to check for errors and remedy them. This chapter explores negative space and its importance in discovering mistakes, as well as other devices that should help you make the best drawing you can and, crucially, know when to stop.

Hair

Often an afterthought, hair is actually very important in a figure drawing. It serves as a definite upper limit and should be considered among the constituent shapes and overall height of the model. There are many varying hair types and, in the same way you have learnt to view the figure, the hair of each model should be looked at objectively and treated as an arrangement of shapes and tone. Because of the diversity, it is impossible to present different formulae for approaching different hairstyles and types, but here are some tips.

Your use of tone and tonal contrast will suggest colour, style and sleekness. As we get older, our hair may become less shiny, and this can be represented with competent use of tone.

Adding tone, hatching in the same direction as the flow of the hair, will give the appearance of detail.

Bald heads are the most difficult heads to draw – you must observe the curve of the skull very accurately and draw it exactly. Any discrepancy will stand out, so use construction lines and check the height and angles carefully. If the hair is very closely cropped, it should be drawn in as an area of tone.

Long hair may obscure the shoulders and when this is this case, the shape of the shoulders and neck shouldn't be guessed at – they should be represented as seen.

Wavy and straight hair, especially if it is very glossy, may have much tonal variation – from very dark occlusion shadows to very bright highlights. Make full use of your materials to represent this large range.

Strands. It isn't necessary to try to draw in every hair, but if a few strands are obvious, whether on top of the main body of the hair or sticking out from the outline, do depict them.

Outline. Wavy hair may have a wavy outline, and will also have a more complicated pattern of light and dark – tone will show the undulating shape, with sequences of highlights and shadows describing the vicissitudes.

Curly hair may appear to be of mainly one tonal value, or there may be very small areas of light and dark, depending on how tight the coils of the hair are. You can simplify your view of the tone by letting your eyes go out of focus.

The hair may not have a defined outline. You may need to phase it out tonally, rather than draw all the separate strands visible at the margins. For longer poses, look at Leonardo da Vinci's painstaking drawings, especially those of curly hair. His drawing *Study of a Child's Head* shows many simplified ringlets, with highlights and shadows on each. Similarly, his painting *Ginevra de' Benci* makes use of fine highlights to show curls and ringlets.

The hairline may also require a soft tonal gradient to transition into the skin of the face, unless the model has a clear fringe or loose hair either side of the face.

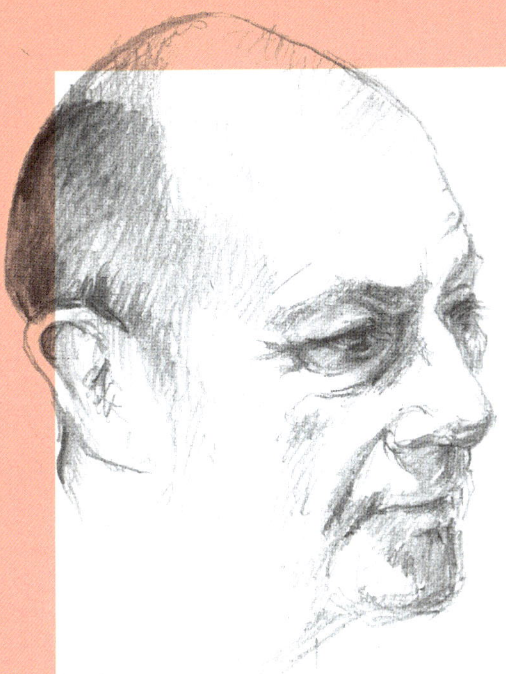

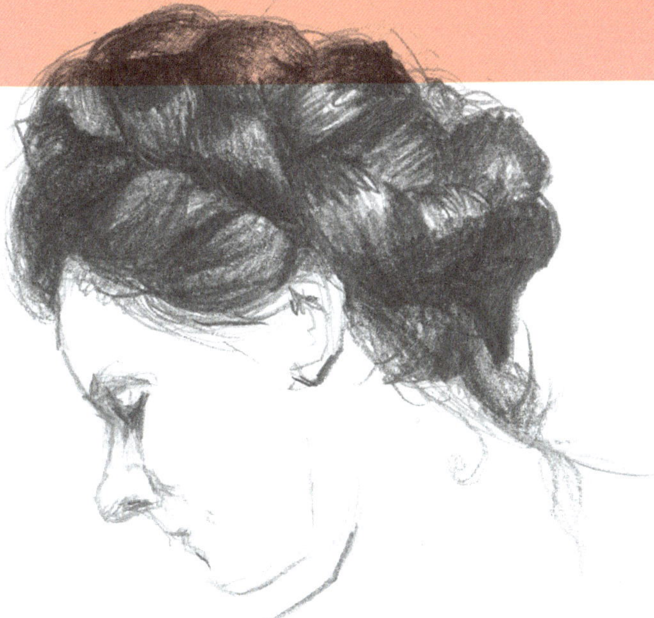

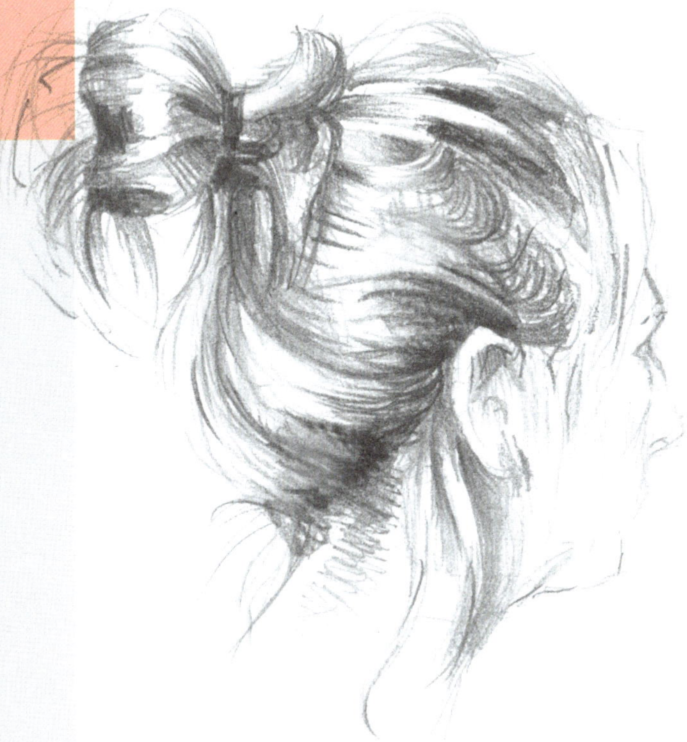

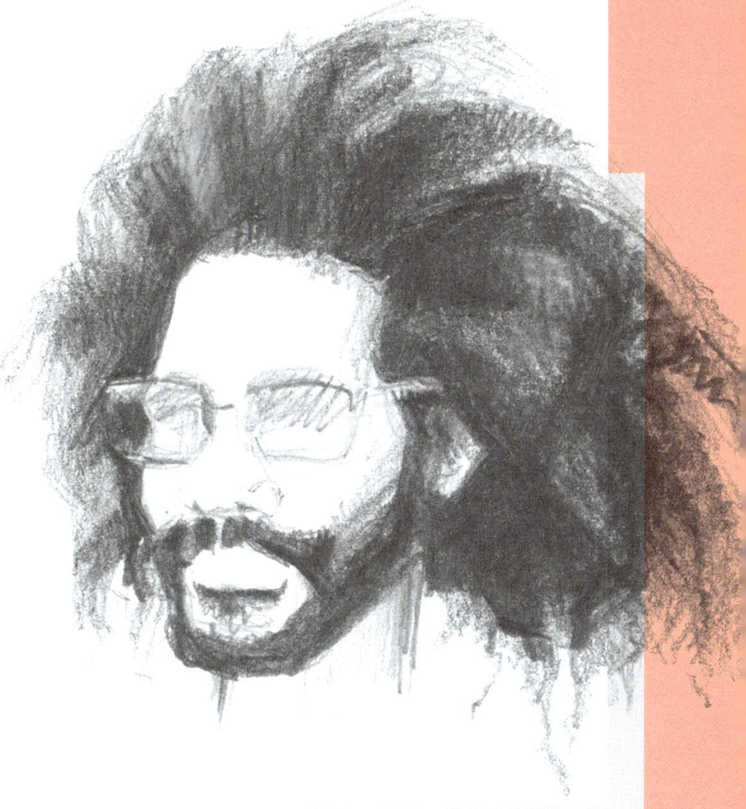

Ponytails and topknots. Hair that has been put up into a ponytail, topknot, or other 'up' styles can be broken down into separate shapes, then approached tonally as with any other hairstyle or type.

Braids, ringlets or dreadlocks should be approached objectively – if they can be broken down into large, simple, manageable shapes, do so. If not, let your eyes go out of focus to simplify further, then judge where the tone and lines will fall.

Facial, pubic and body hair can be approached in the same way: observe very objectively, draw the outline (which may need to be gradual, or depicted tonally rather than in a linear way) and then shade it as it appears when simplified through unfocused eyes.

Hair Exercise

Because of the variety of hair types you may come across, it is well worth trying this exercise a few times on different models, using the same approach for each. You don't need to add the detail of the facial features for this exercise, but vague landmarks may provide a sound structure to aid you when drawing the hair.

1. Break the head, hair and shoulders into simple shapes. This is possible even if the outline of the shoulders and face are obscured. Just let your eyes go out of focus and draw what you see. You may notice distinct areas within the hair, such as the fringe, or layers.

2. Measure the angles of the outlines of the hair and the shapes within the hair that you might have drawn in the previous step. Check the size of the 'hair shape'. Try to be as accurate as possible; however, there may be room for error with this, unlike with the dimensions of the body, as hair has less of a familiar anatomical structure. Rub out any extraneous lines and consolidate the outline. This should be very faint, especially if the outline is not a sharp, distinguishable line. As mentioned previously, include details like ringlets or stray curls and shapes within the main shape, such as layers or a fringe.

3. Identify any highlights. In some hair colours, these won't be white, they may be slightly darker, represented by a light grey – this highlight, whether white or grey, will be your starting point, your lightest value. Let your eyes go out of focus and identify the mid-tones – this is likely to be the main colour of the hair. Don't include shadows yet. If the hair is black, you may already need to use a very dark value by this stage. If the outline is unclear, your shading will need to be phased out in a steep gradient at the margins of the hair shape.

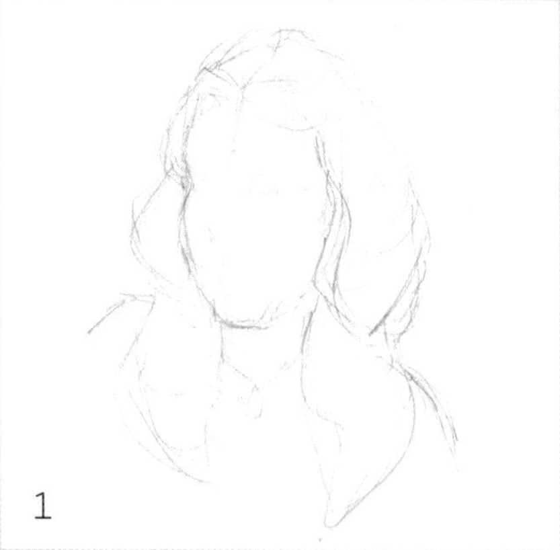
1

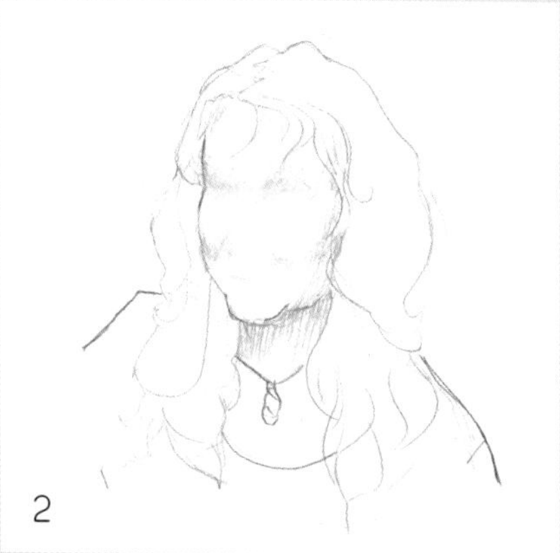
2

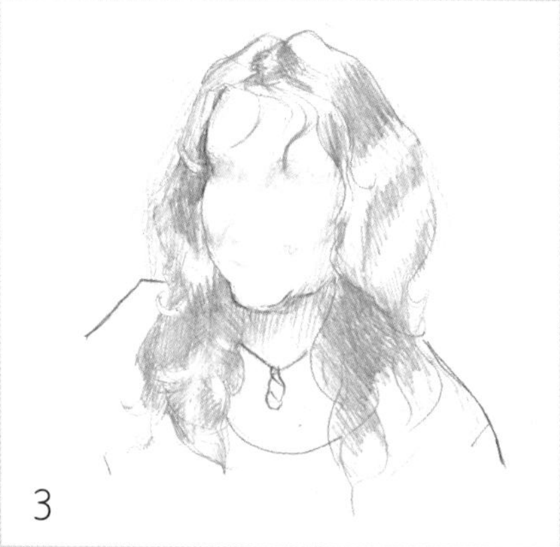
3

4. Draw in the darker tonal areas. These normally appear towards the bottom of the hair shape, often around the ears and the side of the face, and sometimes around the parting. In curly hair, shadows fall on the side of curves that face away from the light. You could apply this tone in hatching that corresponds to the flow of the hair. Some skeins and ringlets may stand out from their neighbours, and you may find these features need to be distinguished in more detail.

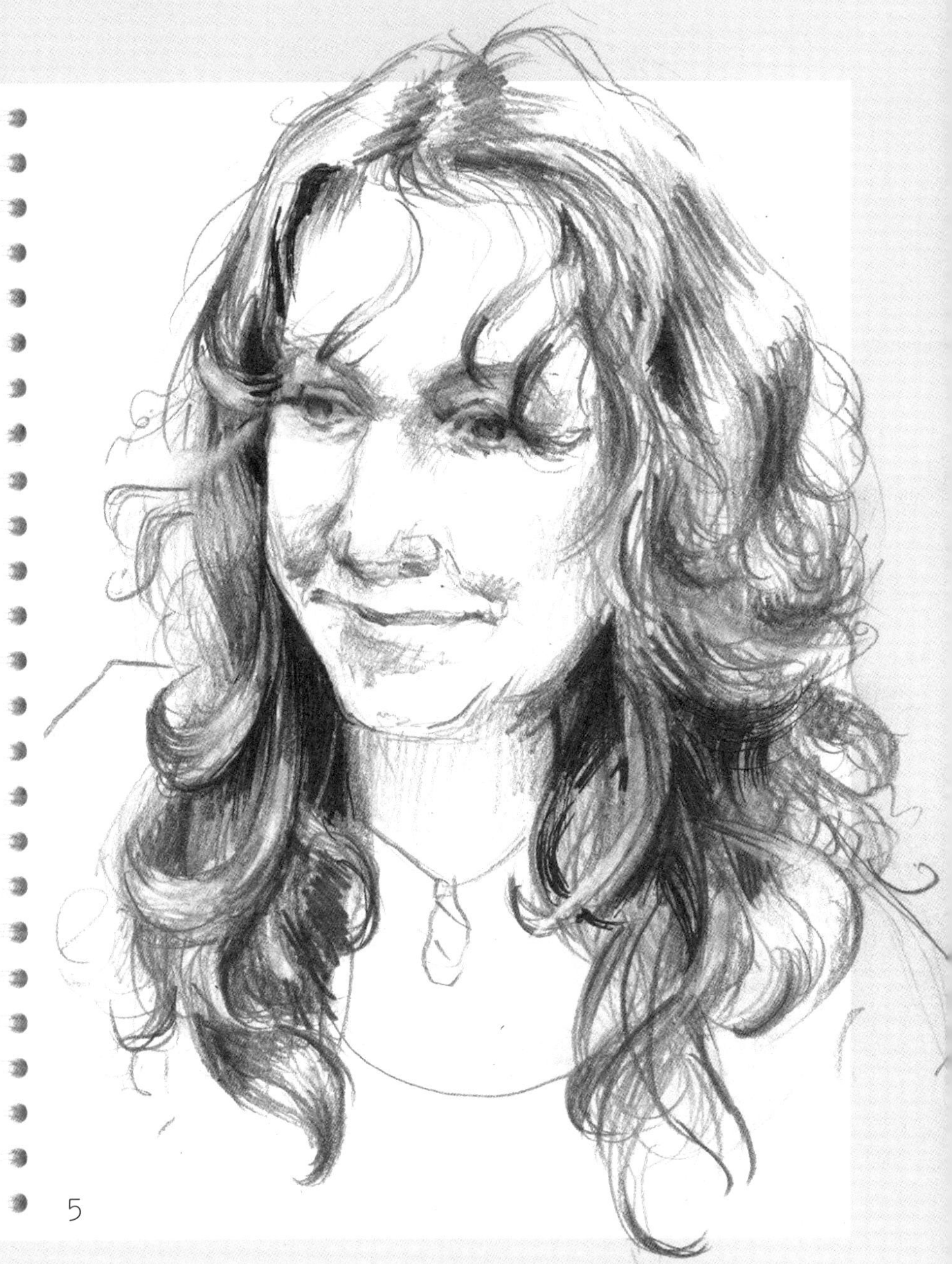

5

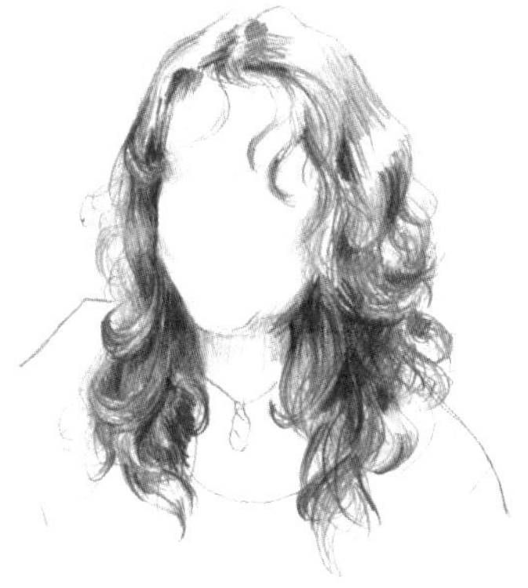

4

5. For longer poses, you may like to add more detail: stray strands breaking away from the main outline, additional tone for a more detailed depiction of curls and ringlets. Some details may be drawn with a rubber, some very dark shadows could be added with a black pen.

Skin

Skin varies from person to person, age to age. If you look very objectively and draw exactly what you see, any effects of age, sunlight, injury or other features will come across to the viewer in your drawing, without you aiming to explicitly portray them. It is interesting to look at Henry Tonks's drawings of wounded soldiers – it was necessary for him to look at his sitters very objectively, the structure and skin of their faces being less familiar because of extensive disfigurement.

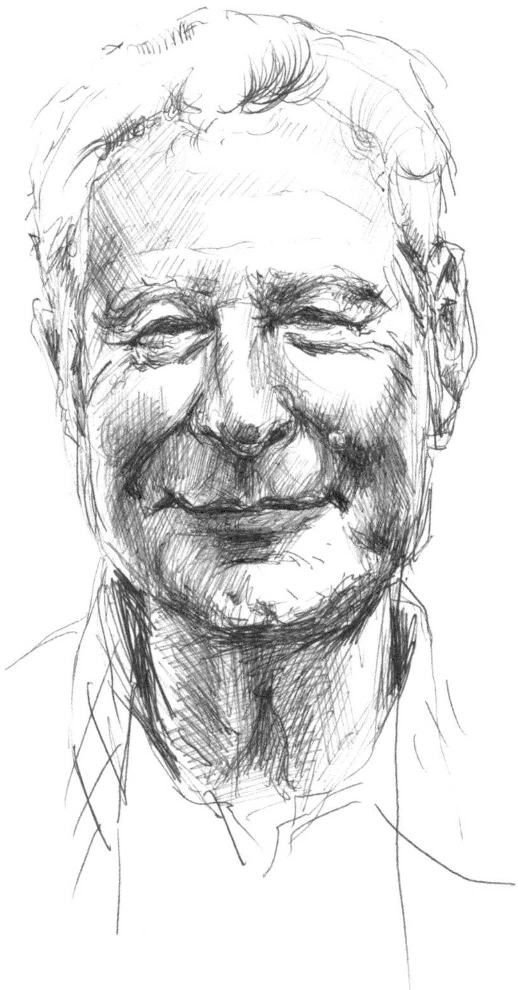

Below, I outline some of the features and effects on the skin, and how your choice of mark-making might be affected. Don't, however, seek to create these effects to suit your model – be led by objective observation.

Young skin is often plumper and provides fewer landmarks, having fewer lines, veins and scars.

Skin colouration will appear as slightly different tonal values. Look for: redness in hands, cheeks, buttocks, feet and knees; tanning on arms, chest and legs; and the blueish hue of veins under the skin.

Wrinkly skin will provide lines for you to use as landmarks and may also provide opportunity for texture. Often these lines aren't very dark, so you might only need a light pencil. Look out for highlights and shadows around prominent wrinkles. Albrecht Dürer's drawings illustrate how tone can emphasise smoothness and wrinkles in the skin.

Dark skin may require an adjusted tonal range, but as always it should be balanced in relation to the hair, the background and any shadows or highlights on the body. The form colour (that is, the skin colour not within shadow) may be a dark tone, so mid-tones and shadows may be only slightly darker in comparison. There is obviously much variation in possible skin tones, so each scenario should be taken case by case, with astute observation to tone. Don't forget to squint at the model in order to simplify tone and to better judge the tonal relationships.

Scars, moles, birthmarks or blemishes. You shouldn't worry about offending your model in your drawing, just try to draw honestly and objectively. Some marks may be a subtle change in colour, some may require more complex tone in order to show their relief on the skin. Either way, draw what you see.

Tattoos mustn't be omitted. You would be assuming the appearance of the skin underneath if you didn't include them. They may appear distorted as they wrap around the body, so look objectively. Overall they will be darker in tone, although they will follow a similar tonal pattern to the adjacent skin, being subject to the same light source.

Age

The effects of age will be apparent in your drawing if you observe your subject strictly and draw honestly, adhering religiously to the shapes, lines and tone as you see them.

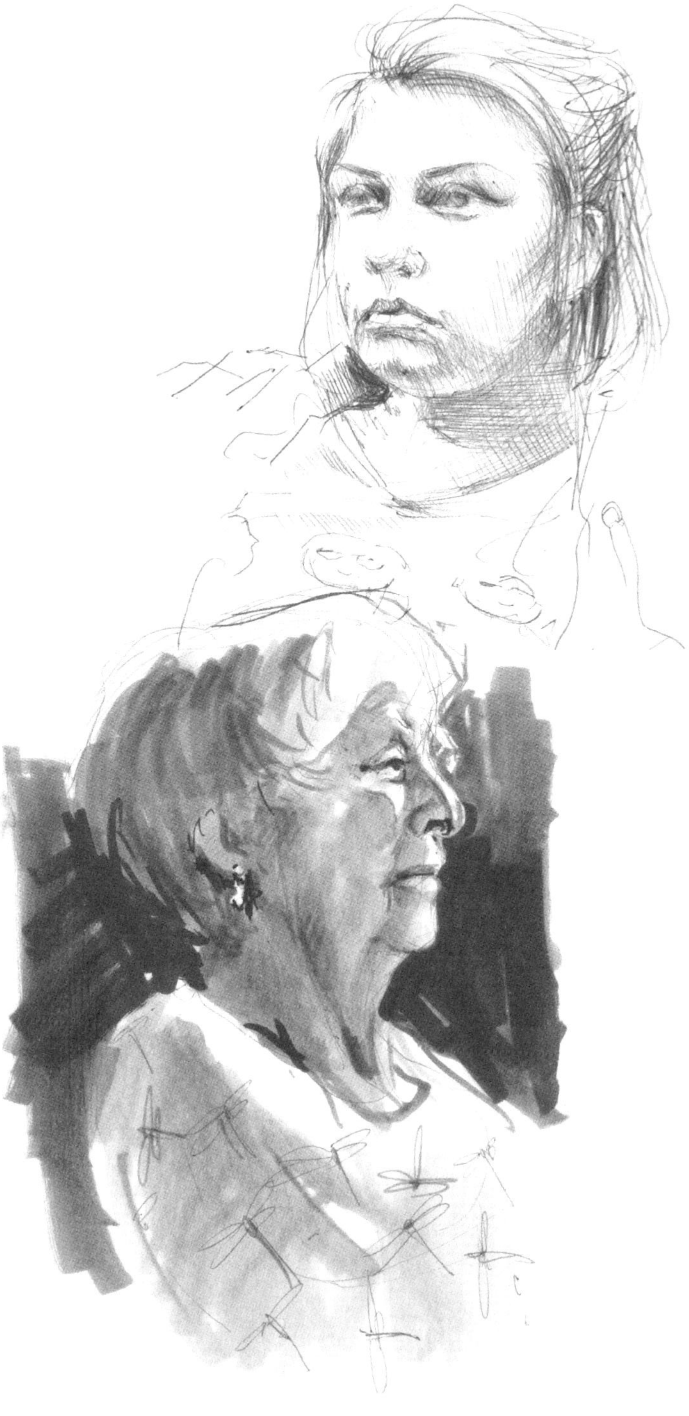

I note here some of the observations you may make, and how these may affect your technique and methods. However, as with the previous section on skin, don't seek to implement them doggedly, just draw what you see and they will come across as a result.

Eyes are often comparatively large in children and young people. They may also require less tone and line to embellish them.

Young children don't have such an obvious jawline, and their cheeks can be rounder, their cheek bones less obvious than in older children and adults.

The skin of children and young adults is plumper and less lined than that of older people. This can be problematic, presenting fewer details and tonal variation to work with. It will be necessary for you to rely even more on measurements.

Lines will appear on models in their twenties, but may need to be depicted only lightly, not being too pronounced. Lines in older adults may need more tonal definition, perhaps including shadows and highlights for each line.

Ageing skin loses its elasticity – it may droop slightly, obscuring cheekbones and the jawline. This sagging effect can be shown by observation of outlines and tone – there may be less tonal variation to distinguish the skull underneath.

Lines. There will be more lines around the eyes and lips in older subjects, although there is so much variation from person to person; detailed observation is necessary.

Lips. The colour in the lips tends to diminish with age, so definition may also diminish.

Bone structure. Some models will lose the appearance of bone structure as they age, but some may gain it, especially around the brow and eye sockets. An accurate use of tone will show this.

Skin and Age Exercise

1. Sketch the head and shoulders, starting as usual with the main shapes, including construction lines. Use charcoal, pencil or ballpoint pen – but start off very lightly. Use your pencil to take measurements and ensure that all the features are in the correct place.

2. Consolidate your lines: rub out any incorrect lines and confirm the position of correct ones. Referring often to the model, make sure the lines follow all the nuances and changes of direction they should.

3. Add in the form colour (colour represented in black and white) i.e. the very lightest value excluding the highlights. This may include an extremely light grey for a peachy skin colour, darkening slightly where the skin appears redder. The brown of tan lines will also be a slightly darker value, although it isn't shadow. Include the hair as you build up the tone.

4. Add in any deeper wrinkles, especially those which will require both highlights and shade around them. While the tone and detail are simple, you can still make adjustments to shapes if needs be – wrinkles act as landmarks so they can make structural mistakes clearer.

5. Build up the shadows, as well as the appearance of any veins or other blemishes.

6. Using a rubber that has been diagonally sliced to provide a clean, sharp point, remove some pencil or charcoal where the relief of the skin causes thin lines of lighter value. If you are using pen or paint, you may not be able to erase thin lines but could use a compass or other sharp implement to scratch the surface of the paper to reveal white. With watercolour and some inks, it might be possible to lift the pigment, using clean water, a very fine brush and a tissue for blotting. With all of these methods, you may then need to build up the shadows on the other sides of these lines – be led by your observations.

7. The darkness of the lines and wrinkles should have the correct tonal relationship to the larger shadows on the face. If they are too dark, they will look exaggerated and too deep. Check the balance is correct. Add any extra details and occlusion shadows you might require.

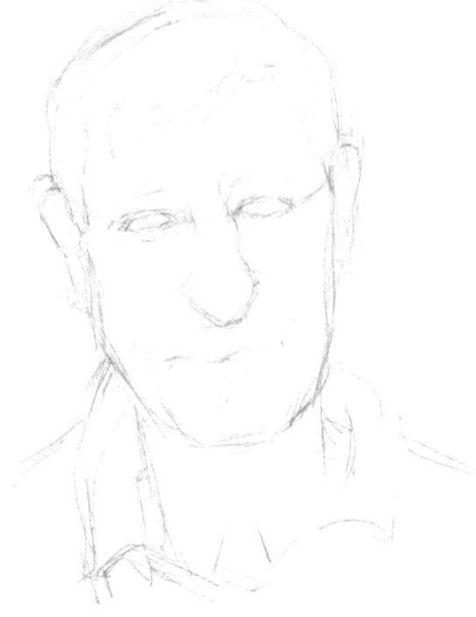

1

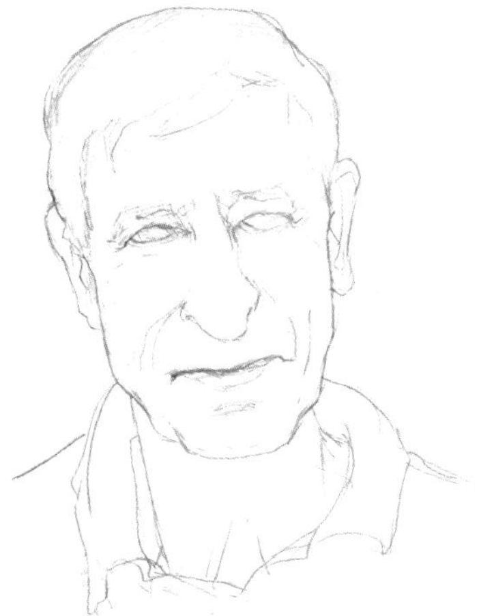

2

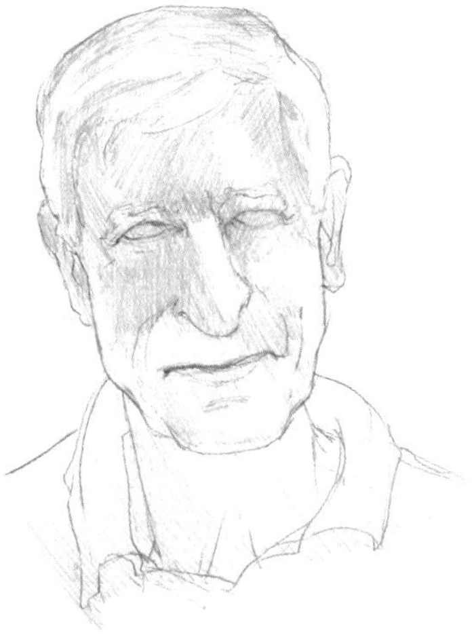

3

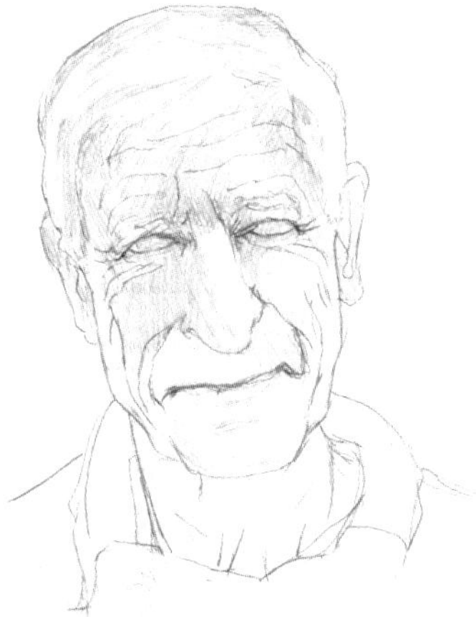

4

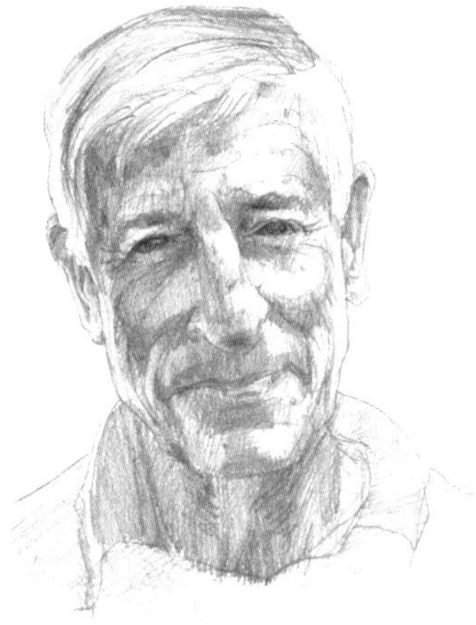

5

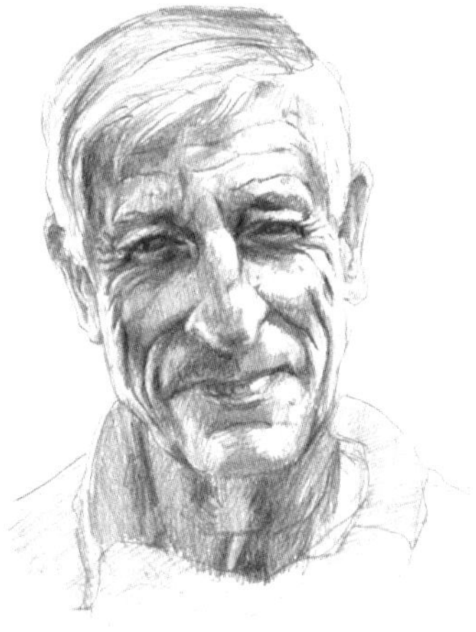

6

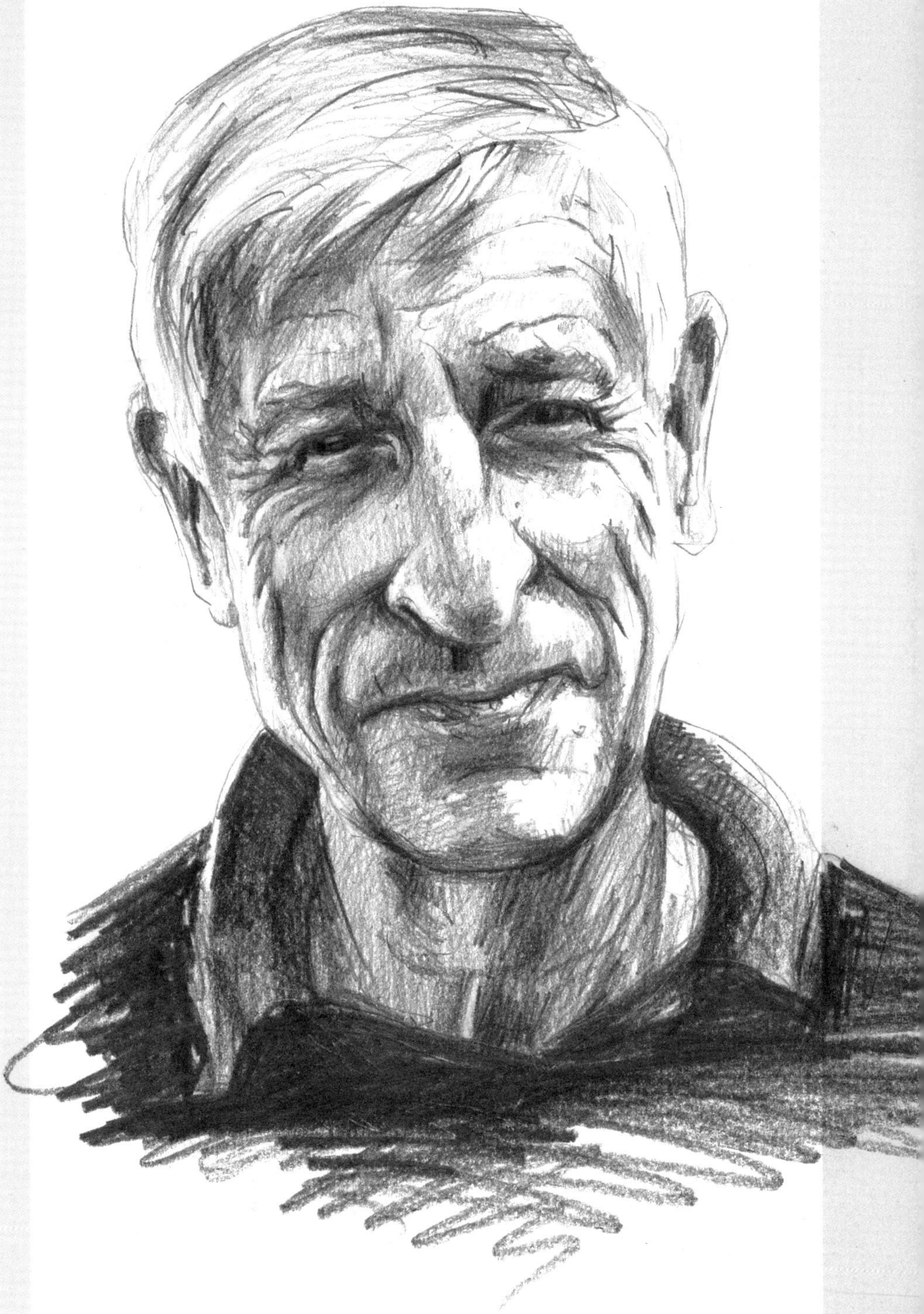

7

Clothing

Clothing should be approached in the same way as the figure – look objectively and begin with simple shapes. It may correspond in large part with the shape of the figure, especially with tight-fitting clothes, so it is important to get it correct. Checking angles is perhaps more important than distances, as this will show the fall and weight of the material. Seams and folds provide helpful landmarks and often signal a change in tonal value.

Whatever the sitter is wearing, a successful representation can be achieved through careful and objective observation.

Tone should be added before patterns and images. Shadows can give a very good impression of creases and folds, and you can make sure your patterns conform with the shadows to give an effective feeling of reality to the clothes. Tone will tell you a little about the colour, as well as the type of material (fig 1). Silk or leather may have a large tonal range. You will have to use a good range of grades of pencil, or make full use of the tonal range possible from charcoal or ink in order to successfully portray the effect of light on black leather. Johannes Vermeer illustrates how important tone is in his drawings and paintings – he used shadows to show the folds in the clothes of his models.

Conversely, the seams and details of black cotton or wool may disappear within shadows and the general darkness of the non-reflective fabric (fig 2). It is worth bearing in mind that if there are few distinguishing features in black clothes, they may just appear as a flat shape with no tonal variation. You may not even be able to distinguish the boundary between torso and arm – it is fine to draw them exactly how they appear: you can't invent details where there aren't any. White fabric might require only simple shadows, none of them reaching a very dark value.

When you have completed the tone, think about any pattern on the fabric. You may just like to sketch this in loosely, as it won't have a huge impact on the figure, but it will provide a satisfying range of marks within the drawing. Text, bold images and clear patterns can really add something to your drawing (fig 3). You have quite a margin for error, as the images will probably be distorted, falling into folds and creases. Try to see any recognisable motifs purely as shapes, letting them disappear behind a fold and reappear disconnected on the other side. Make sure your lines (of imagery and simple patterns alike) correspond with the folds denoted by your use of tone. Let straight lines curve loosely around wide folds of gradual tone, and disappear abruptly behind sharp folds and tonal changes.

Notice buttons, zips and jewellery. They may require strong highlights for which the paper will need to be left blank, and will probably need some darker shadows around them.

Make sure you don't put too much emphasis on the imagery of the clothing so that it overshadows the features of the actual model. Ensure that the tonal relationship between figure and fabric is correctly balanced.

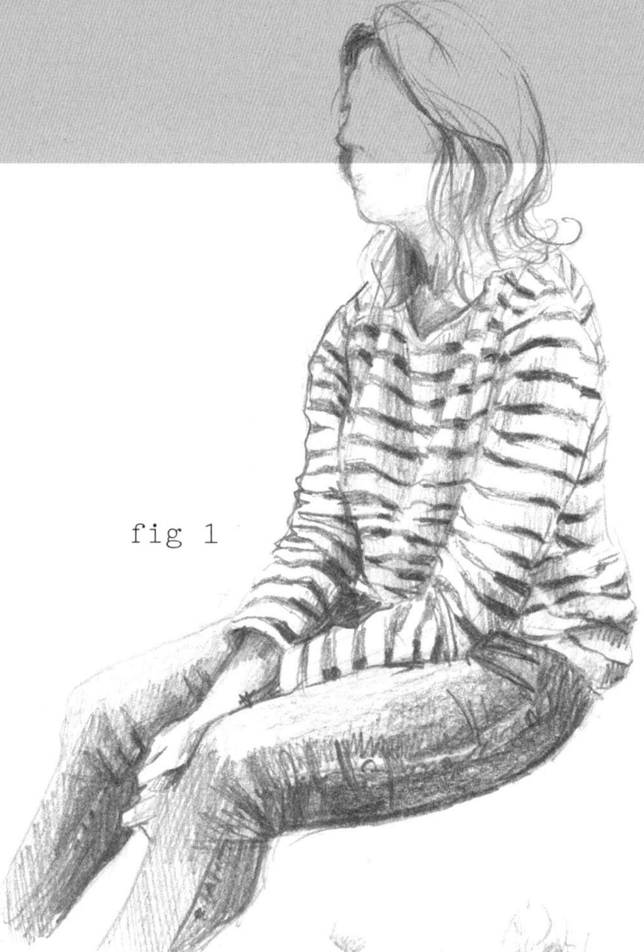

fig 1

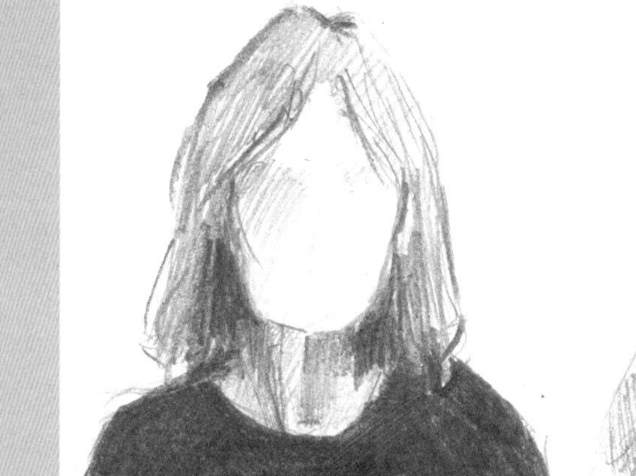

fig 2

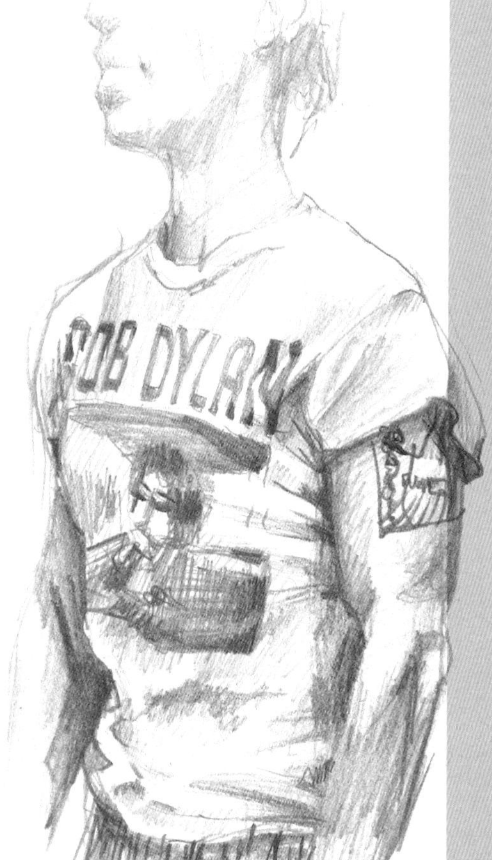

fig 3

Clothing Exercise

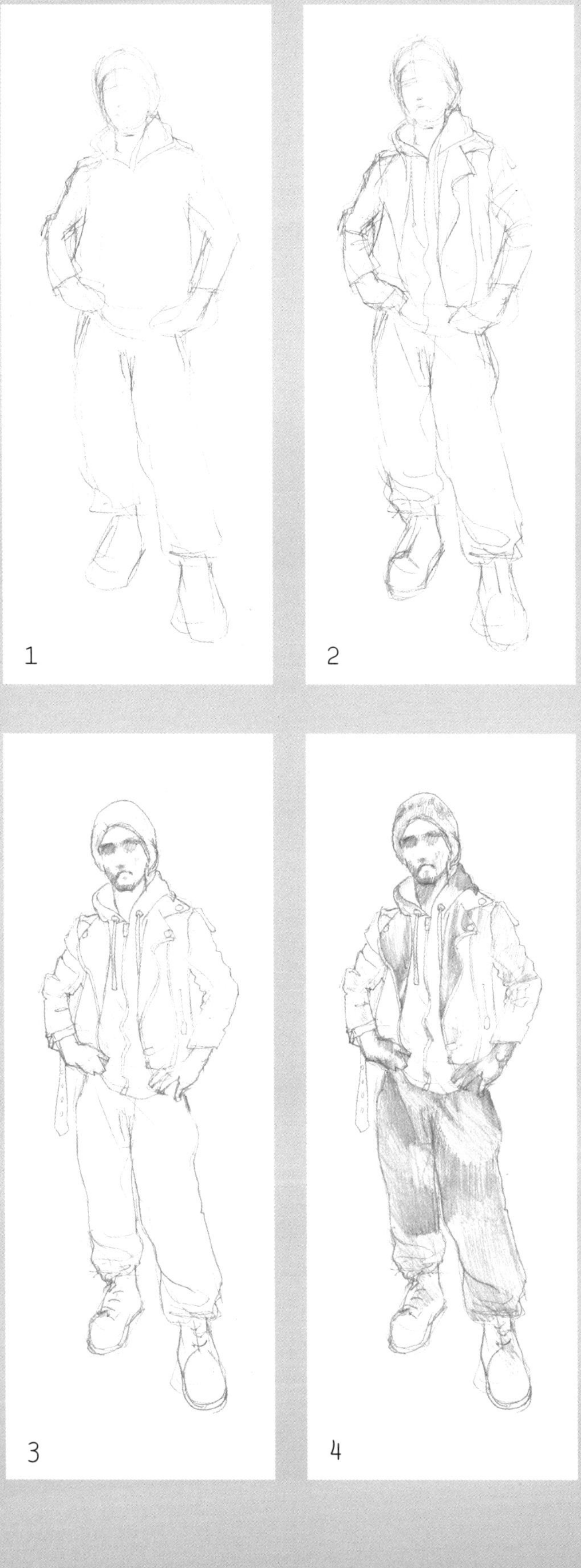

1. Sketch out the clothed model, seeing and representing the clothes as you would objectively see and represent other parts of the body. Aim to start with the largest, simplest shapes.

2. Don't worry about detail in the figure, we will concentrate on just the clothes for this exercise. Add any creases or seams in the material. To do this, look for shapes within the larger shapes of the clothing. Treat any lines in the fabric as you might treat lines in the skin – begin with the largest and most obvious lines, using these as landmarks for smaller ones. Just be concerned with the positions of seams – details within them such as tone or threads can come in a later step.

3. Check the important angles and make any pertinent adjustments. Important angles might include the point at the top of the head to the outside of the clothed shoulder, or a long line of trouser material from knee to ankle. Check the angles that make up the outline of the shoes, in case they are foreshortened. Rub out any erroneous lines and consolidate the correct ones. Draw in any buttons, buttonholes, studs, zips or other embellishments.

4. Add tone – first ring mark any highlights or areas of unshaded white fabric. Use smooth pencil hatching, faint charcoal or diluted paint to represent the colour. If this colour is navy or black, your first shade will obviously be quite a dark one, with less difference between it and the deepest shadows (i.e. a smaller tonal range).

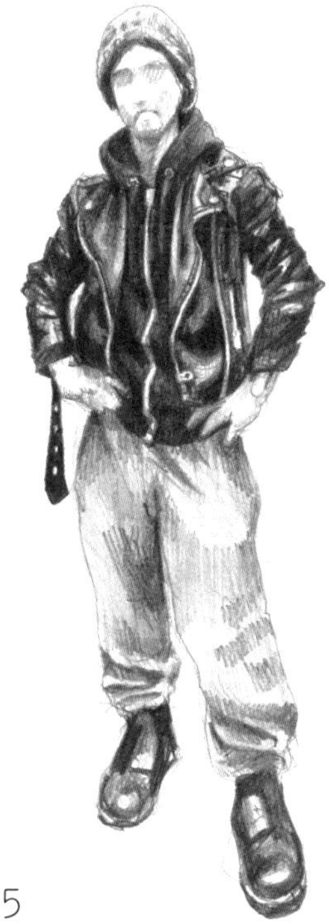

5

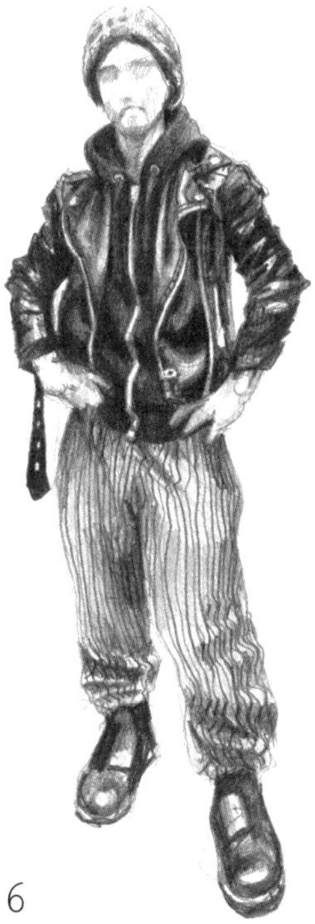

6

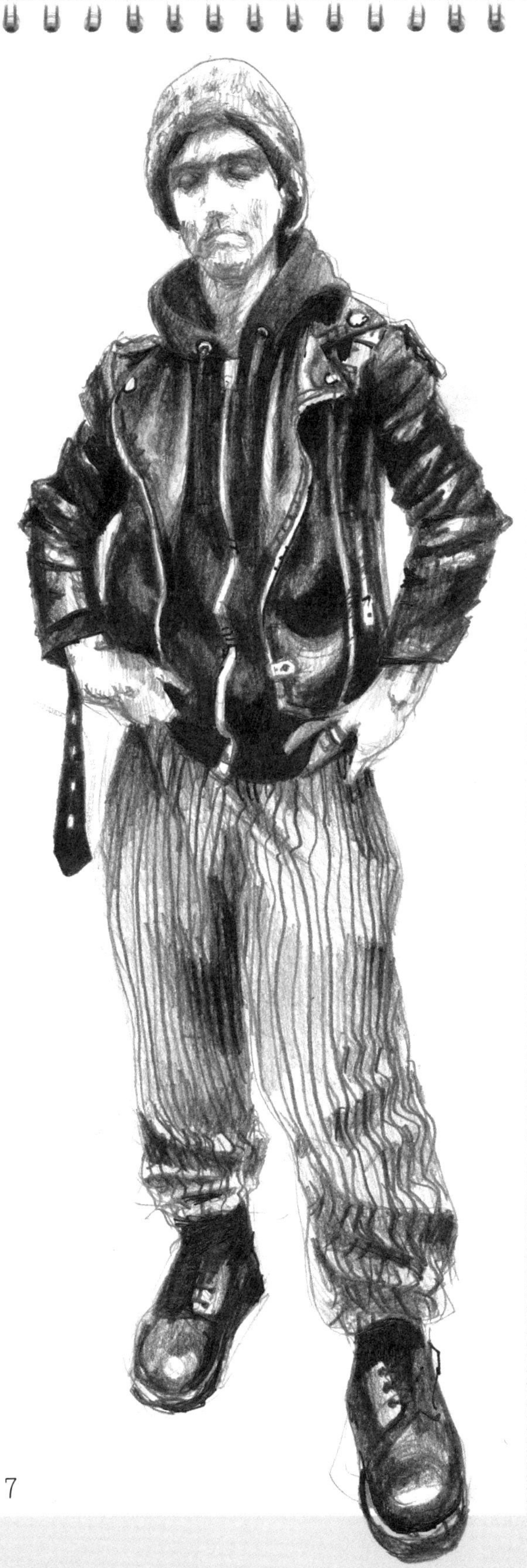

7

5. Use a darker value to portray the shadows. If there are patterns on the material, try to see through them for the time being – just concentrate on the tone. There may be some deeper shadows or reflected light in and around some folds – include them at this stage. Have you represented the right level of tonal contrast to suggest the type of material? Silk and leather might have quite a high contrast, with white highlights and deep shadows, whereas cotton, velvet or wool may have much less distinction, with little tonal variation from the lightest tones to the shadows.

6. Add any patterns on top – use a darker pencil or a pen. If you are using paint, you will need to wait until your first layer is dry in order to achieve crisp detail. Make sure that your patterns follow the creases, distorting where they need to and ending at the seams and folds.

7. Add any occlusion shadows and add some extra weight to the patterns where they appear in areas of shadow. Add detail, shade and highlights to buttons, zips and jewellery.

Checking Your Work

It is best to start a sketch carefully and continue in a circumspect way, frequently checking for errors. This is to guard against large structural changes at a late stage, which can destroy beautiful detail and careful shading. I have seen too many students draw beautiful eyes and beautiful mouths, only to realise that they are too far apart from each other. It is essential to check the structure before you add detail and complicated tone. Don't keep too close to your work. Look away from time to time and step back from it – it will quickly become clear to you when something isn't working.

You may be able to discern exactly what is wrong, and know what you need to do to fix it. However, sometimes you may see that there is an error but be unclear as to exactly where it is. In this instance, there are several things you can try:

- Walk away from your work for a minute or two, get a drink or go into a different room. Return and look at your drawing with fresh eyes.

- Keep your eyes off your work for a while as above. This time, return to the model rather than your drawing. Spend a minute or so re-familiarising yourself with the subject, then return to your drawing and see if the mistakes become clearer.

- Take a clean sheet of paper and cover areas of your drawing, one at a time. When you cover the problem area, your drawing will seem to improve – this shows you which parts you need to attend to.

- In some cases, for example with foreshortened, upside-down or otherwise awkward poses, it can help to turn your paper around and see if a different angle makes the figure seem more familiar, allowing problem areas to stand out. Artists also use mirrors or black mirrors to get a different perspective by looking at the reflection, rather than the actual model. A black mirror – a piece of dark glass – compresses the tonal values and simplifies the image, a similar result to simply squinting.

- Measure distances using your pencil and the methods outlined in the 'Measuring' section on pages 44–47. This is very important for foreshortened poses, but it will help with straightforward ones too. Check distances and angles; use your pencil as a spirit level and a plumb line to check things are aligned as they should be.

- Check negative space (refer to pages 104–107). The figure itself may look alright, but the spaces in between the arms, legs and torso could be completely wrong. This signals that there must be errors somewhere. See the exercise on negative space for more help with this.

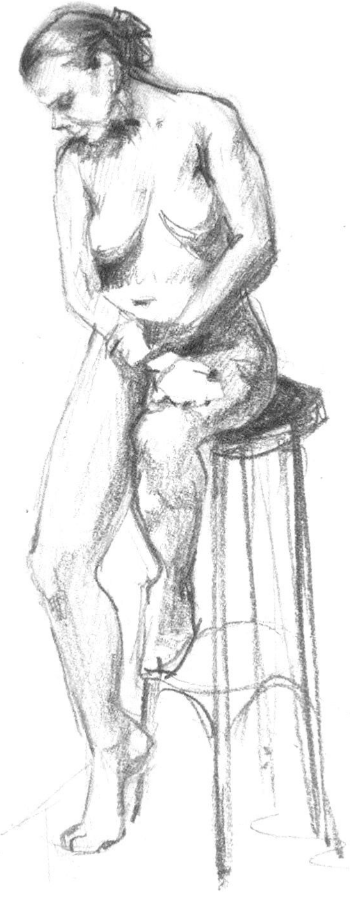

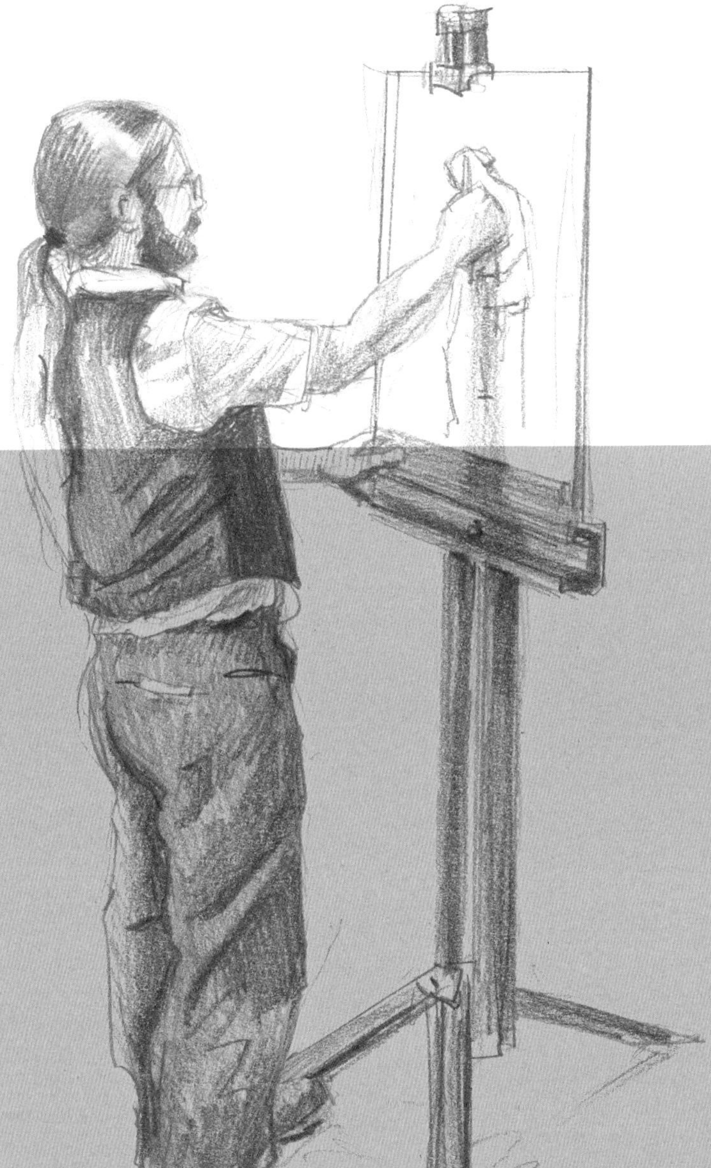

It might be that a very small miscalculation in angle or distance has a cumulative effect and causes large discrepancies elsewhere. It may be that two different lines are ever so slightly out of place, adding up to a more blatant problem in between. This is why it is important to address small mistakes. Check angles, distances and the negative shapes very scrupulously. Check small distances that make up larger ones, for example, don't just check the length of the torso, also check the distance from the collar bone to the nipples, then the nipples to the navel, then the navel to the top of the pubic hair, and then the top of the pubic hair to the lower limit of the genitalia.

- Misjudged tonal value can also have a knock-on effect – if something is too dark, it could cause the adjacent shape to be darker, and the next, until your drawing is too heavy and dark overall. Keep squinting at the model as a whole, or letting your eyes go out of focus, in order to perceive the tonal balance across your subject.

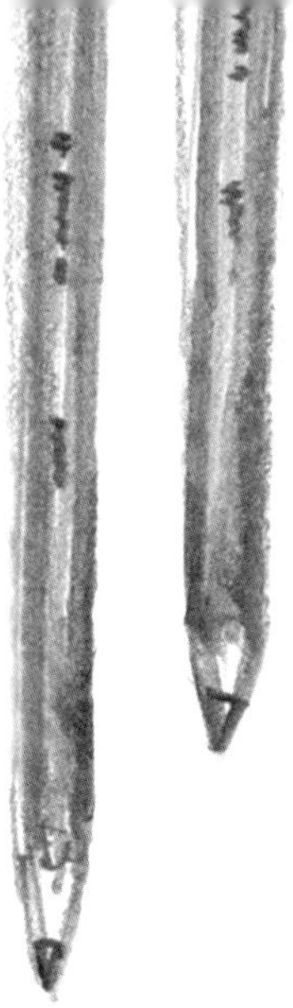

Negative Space

What is negative space? The figure in your drawing is the positive space, and anything on the other side of the figure's outline is negative space. Negative space is everything outside, in between and around the subject matter.

If your figure drawing is completely accurate, the negative spaces will be too. It is prudent to consider your negative spaces at the same time as you draw your positive spaces, rather than only thinking of them afterwards. However, looking at the negative spaces afterwards is also a good way to check for errors.

The internal angles of the body (A) may be hard to judge by eye, for example the reflex angle formed by the torso above and below the waistline – it may be easier to judge the smaller explementary angle (B) formed in the convex negative space. The same may be true for the gap between the legs and the angle formed by the arm and torso. You will be drawing the same lines but looking at the space between the features instead of the features themselves.

If negative space doesn't line up, it can throw out the whole composition – the two arms may look out of proportion, one may look thicker or farther away, or the legs may look dislocated. It is good practice to observe the shapes created by negative space with the same objective eye used for gauging positive space.

Negative space can have many layers. If the arms are folded across the body, the negative space around them will consist of the torso, rather than empty space. The figure may create negative space on furniture, which in turn creates negative space out of whatever is behind it. In each scenario, all shapes must be viewed in a detached way and rendered as accurately as possible.

If you are using watercolours, a competent rendering of negative space is even more important – you can't use a white opaque paint to draw lines over a dark area. Instead you must paint the dark negative spaces, leaving accurate gaps in the paint to portray the foreground.

Negative space can consist of beautiful shapes and add to the balance of a composition. It can provide a rest for the eye, an interval, rather than an inert gap left by the absence of the figure. The contrast between negative and positive space may be a feature in itself, each accentuating the other – a darkened negative space making the lightness of the figure pop out of the paper at the viewer. A deeply shadowed figure against a white negative space may create drama. In cases where there is high contrast, it is important to draw the negative space accurately, and it may be appropriate to accentuate the beauty of the space itself.

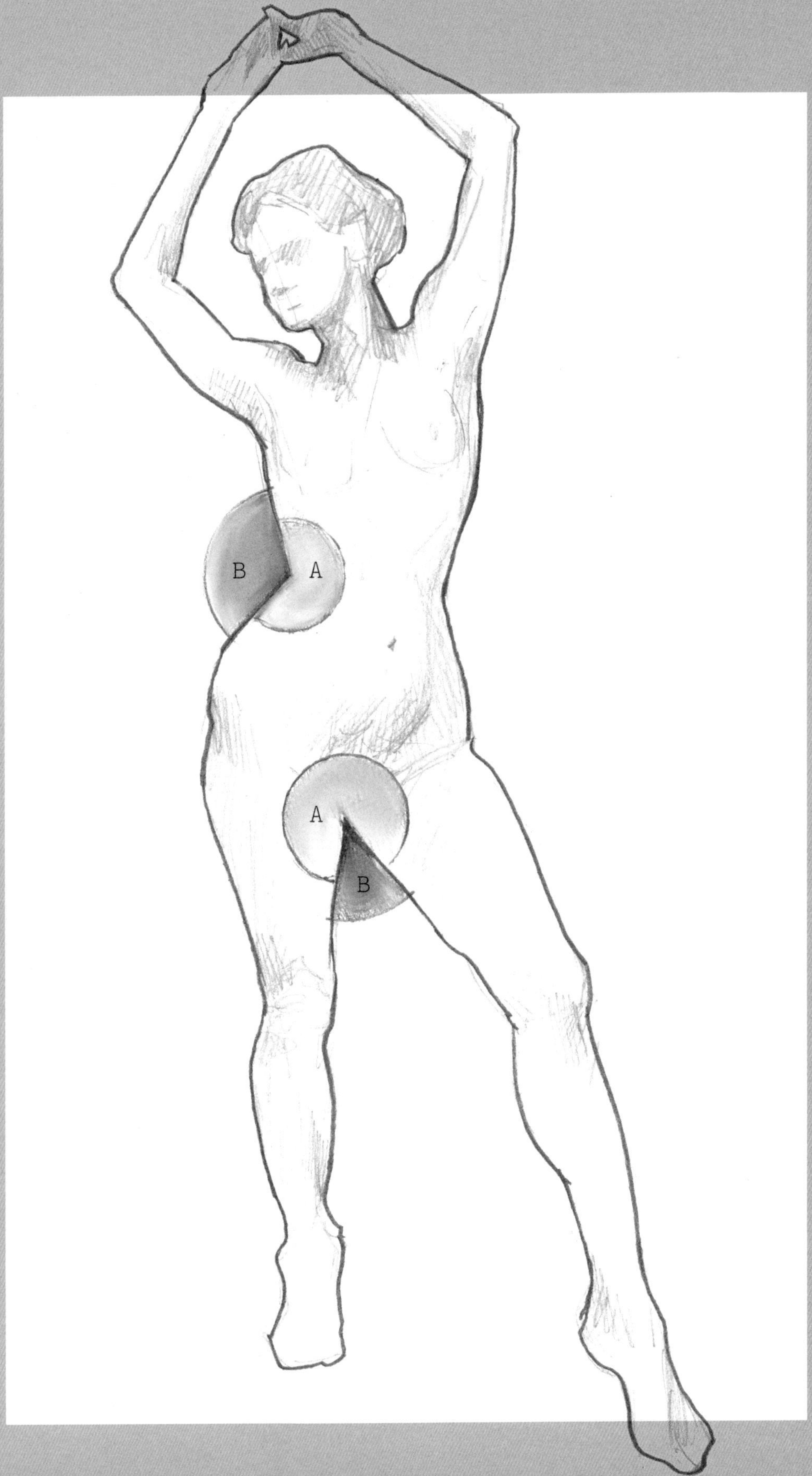
B
A
A
B

Negative Space Exercise

1. Using the same detached mode of observation you have used in all of the previous exercises when looking at the model, force yourself to look at the shapes created by the negative spaces. Map out the shapes vaguely using charcoal or light pencil. Avoid pen or paint, as you will want to alter the shapes. The space outside of the figure is unlimited – in my illustration I have broken down this space and closed the shapes to make them more manageable.

2. Check the angles of your shapes by holding up a pencil, as described in the 'Measuring' section on pages 44–47. Look at the distances between these shapes, take measurements and amend them accordingly, not so that the figure is in proportion but so that the gaps between your negative spaces are in proportion. This might be hard to do if you have invented some of the boundaries of the shapes of negative space, so you could add in some construction lines as shown in the illustration.

3. Refine and consolidate your marks, erasing any unnecessary lines. Look at the sharp points and graceful curves of the figure created by the outlines of these spaces. Letting your hand follow these abstract contours as closely as possible, trace them out on your paper.

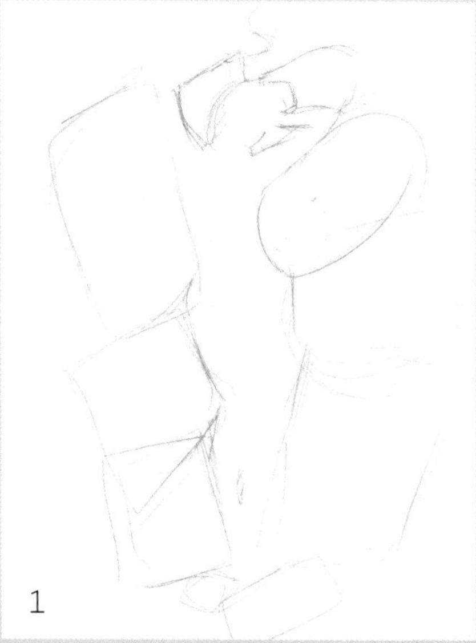

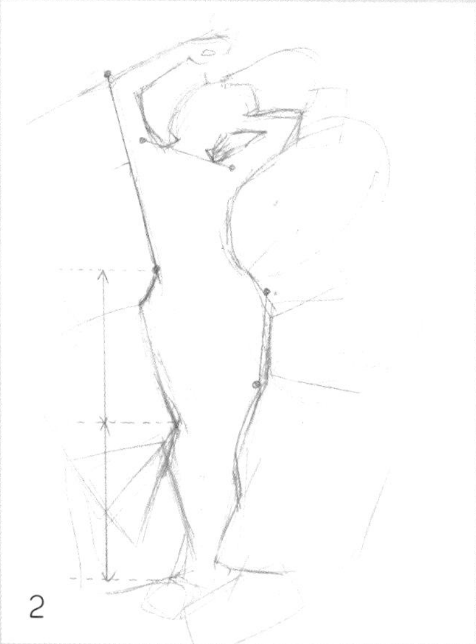

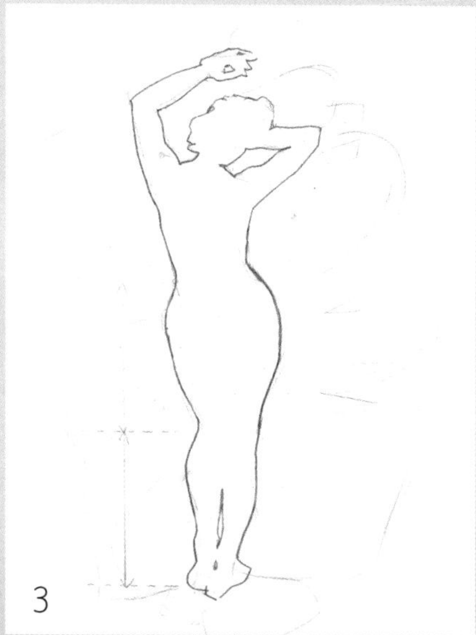

4. Add some of the tone and detail that you find in these negative spaces in order to make them stand out more. Hopefully your spaces are so well planned and measured that the figure in the centre now looks accurately proportioned, like a white silhouette. If not, check your negative spaces again – try to make your negative spaces work, rather than improving your figure. Double-check your angles and your measurements. In this exercise, it is more important that your negative spaces appear as they should, than your figure does. However, if your figure is wrong, it indicates that something is amiss with your negative spaces. By the same logic, we can see how valuable negative space is when checking a figure drawing for accuracy.

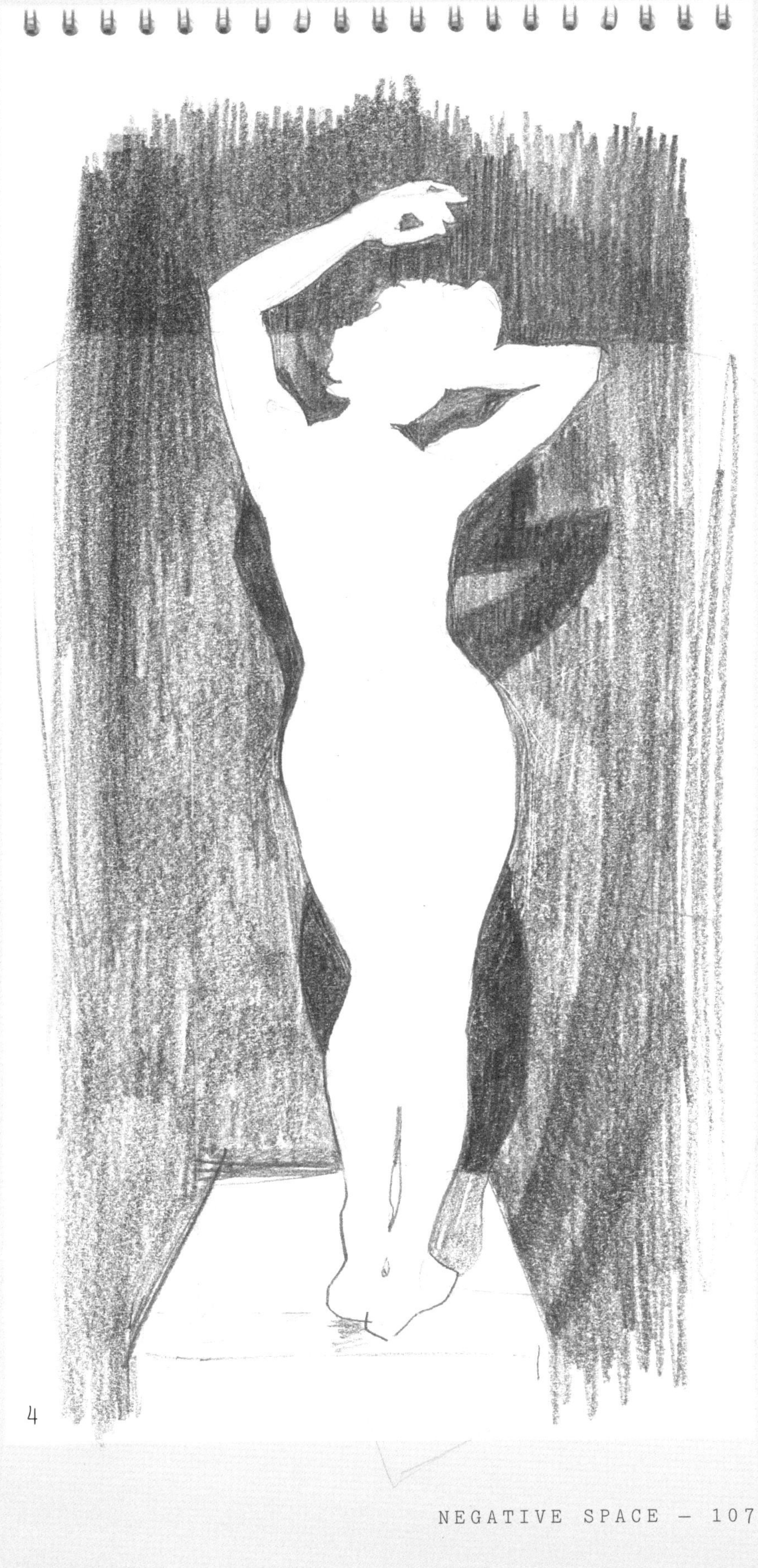

Classic Mistakes and Simple Solutions

The first structural 'workings out' should always be faintly rendered. Dark pencil lines are harder to rub out. Inaccurate marks made in light ink or paint can be overlooked once the stronger outlines and tone are added later.

If you do need to rub out any marks, make sure that your rubber is kept clean. It is helpful to have a scrap of paper next to you to clean your rubber on after two or three strokes. You can also slice the end off to regain clean, sharp corners and edges. A diagonal cut will give you a fine point for precise lines.

If you are using charcoal, you can soften and lighten lines dramatically just using your fingers, but you can also achieve lovely white marks with a rubber. Just make sure you clean it often.

There is little you can do to correct pen, so try to be confident in your estimations before you put pen to paper.

Watercolours can be blotted when still wet, or lifted with a little clean water. Agitate dry paint gently with a clean, wet brush. Don't scuff the paper, just press lightly on the surface. Then immediately blot the lifted pigment with a clean tissue.

Build up tone gradually, as it is easier to add it than it is to remove it, especially when using ink or paint. Don't press too hard with a light pencil, but move up to the next grade before you dent the paper. Ingrained marks are much more difficult to erase, and the residual scores will affect any later shading. By building tone up slowly you can balance the values across your work.

Common mistakes that people make in the life drawing class are:

Perspective
This is undeniably tricky, so make sure you measure and trust those measurements. Try rotating your page to see if problems become clearer.

Shoulders
Check the height of the shoulders – they may be surprisingly high up. In a sitting pose, the tops of the shoulders may be higher than the chin (fig 1).

Neck
Make sure the neck is the correct width (fig 2). Check where the left and right boundaries line up with the face and body. If, after measuring, it still looks wrong, add tone to see if this gives it more grace and definition.

Lips
Don't shade the lips too darkly without seeing them in relation to the skin of the face. Before you draw them in, ask yourself, 'Can I see an outline for the top and the bottom lips?' The answer is often 'No'. If you include outlines when you can't really see them, your drawing may look oversimplified (see fig 3A) .The top lip may in

fig 1

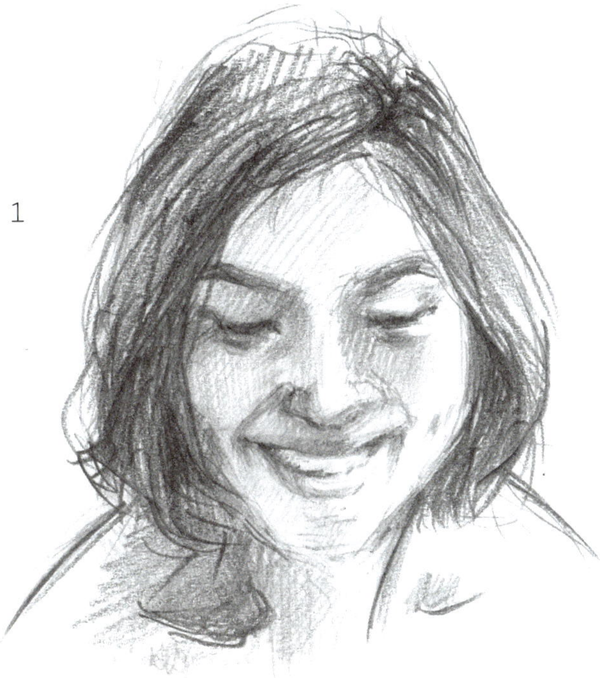

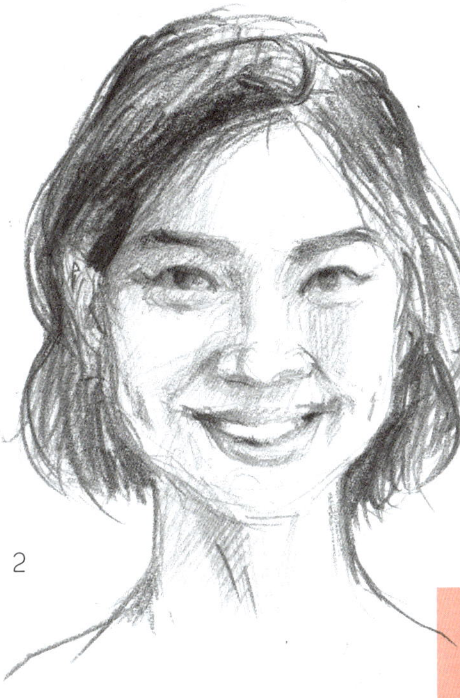

fig 2

reality be more distinguishable because of the shadow on it. The bottom lip may only be distinguished by the shadows around it (fig 3B; see also Head Exercise, step 4, on page 76).

Eyes

Don't make too much of the eyes (figs 4). They often require much less detail than you imagine. A lot of detail may be lost in the shadow of the eye sockets. Remember that the whites of the eyes hardly ever appear white – they are shaded and can look darker than the surrounding skin (fig 4A). If you leave them white after adding tone to the eye socket, they will look like headlamps (fig 4B). As with the lips, ask yourself if you can really see the outlines. There will be other lines that you should notice such as the crease of the eyelids and the lines in the corners of the eyes.

Detail

It is better to be simple and correct, than complex and wrong, or too heavy-handed in a small space (as with the fingers and toes). Sometimes things are best expressed simply.

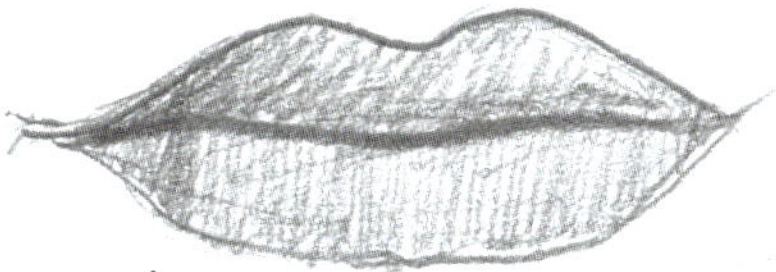

figs 3

A

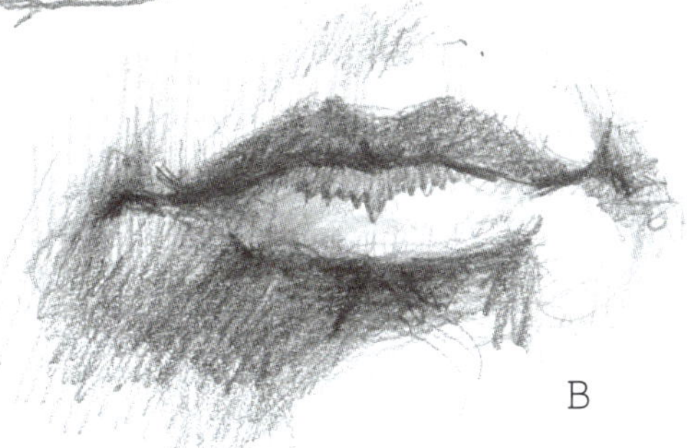

B

figs 4

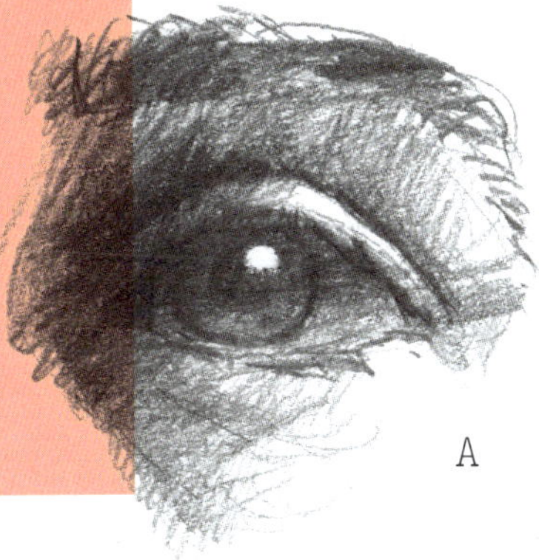

A

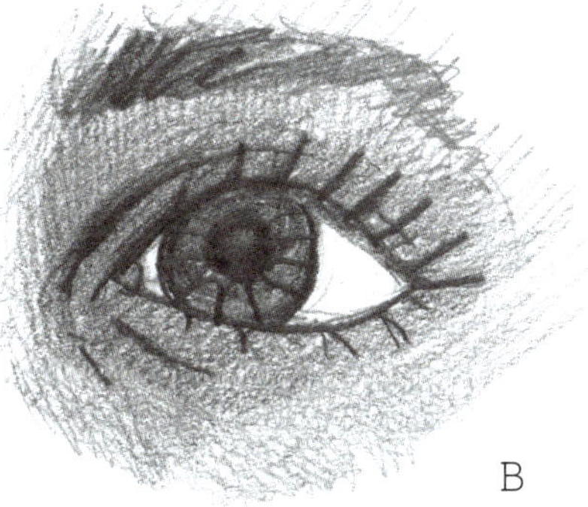

B

When to Stop

A common complaint of artists is overworking a piece that should have ended earlier. It is very difficult to know when to stop.

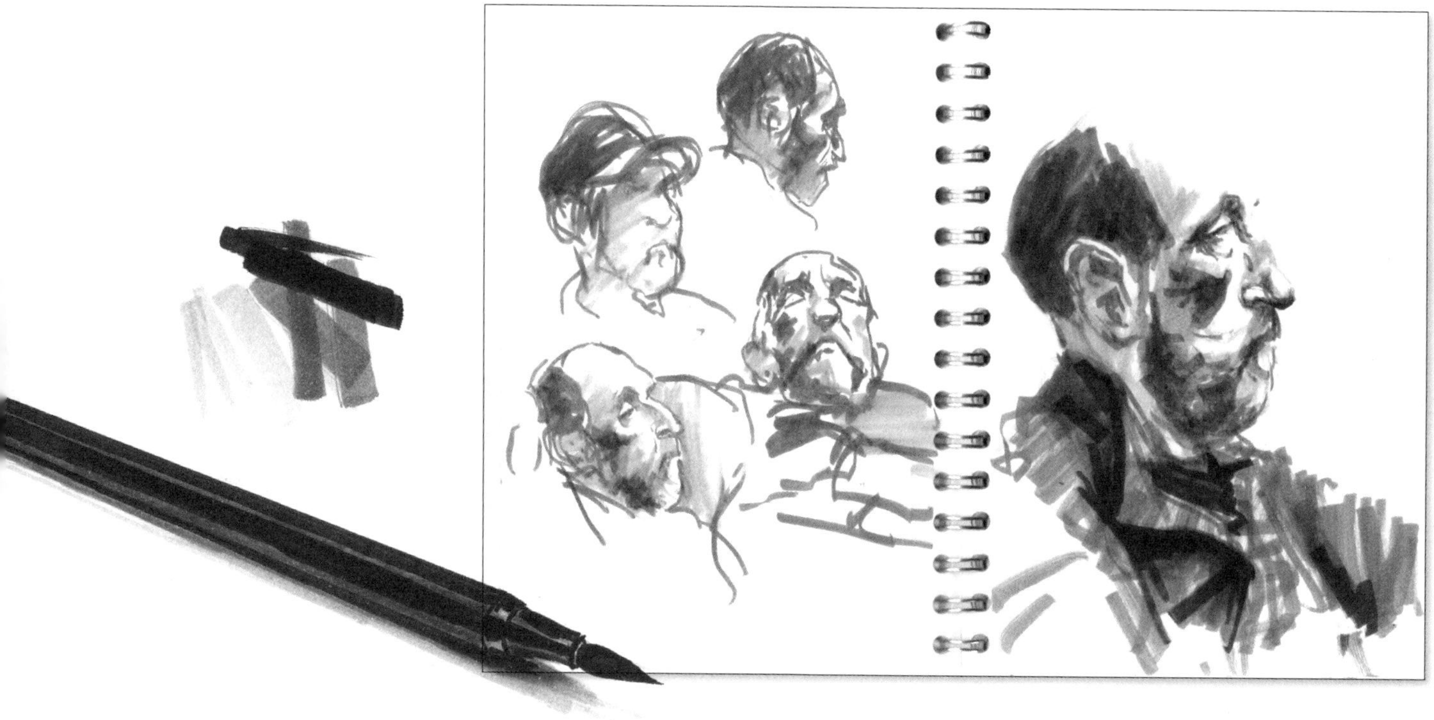

Here are some ways to avoid going too far:

- As you near the end of your drawing, slow down. Think for longer about every single addition.
- When you feel you have gone too far, don't try to carry on to redress the issues, just stop!
- Take a break near the end. Do something else for ten minutes or, if possible, longer, even overnight. Keep in mind that when you return, if you still see things that could be added, you can do it then.
- An enforced time limit is sometimes helpful. Whether due to the length of a pose, or because life requires you to stop your drawing at a certain point, these forced endings can prevent you from overworking your drawings, and they will also train you to manage your time – economising with your marks and omitting superfluous detail.
- Remember, imperfect and unfinished sketches are valuable. You will gain experience from the process, not from the finished piece. Photography is a medium that can provide perfect, finished representations – pencil, charcoal, pens and paint are for expression.

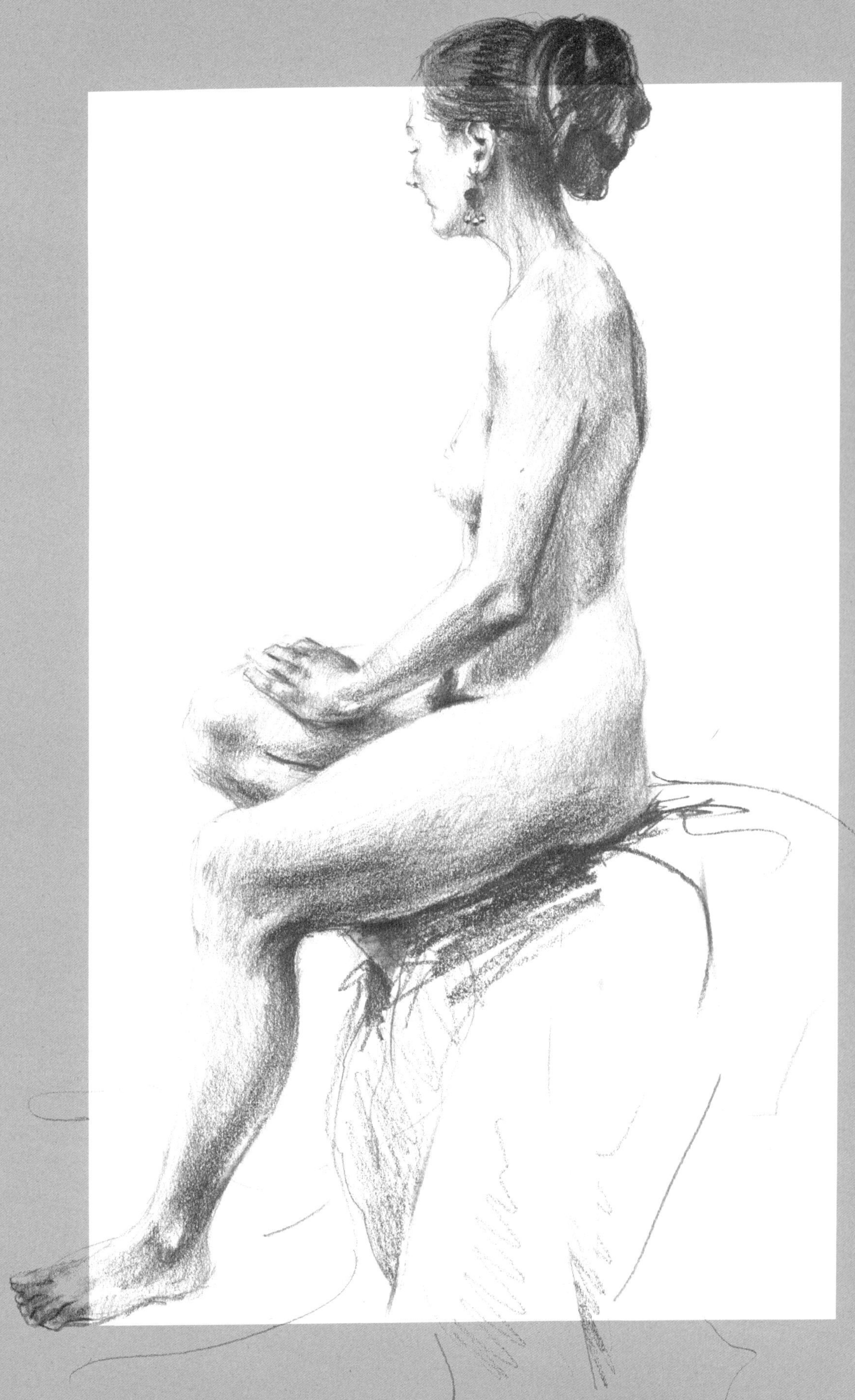

Acknowledgements

I couldn't have written this book without the encouragement, love and support of my husband David Smale and my son Zebedee. Thanks also to my youngest son, Yo-Yo, for hanging on until the deadline, which was just before his due date! Enormous thanks to Jake Spicer of Draw Brighton for advice, support and practical help. I'm very grateful to my mum, Helen Berry, for proofreading the entire book for me.

Thank you to my models: David Smale, Amanda Wright, Stuart, Zebedee Smale, Elaine Spencer, Karin Smale, Chris Hatton, Wendy Chiles, Judith Sharp, Naomi Berry, Jill, Neil Coulthard, Kathryn Potter, Francesca Cluney, Boris, Mike Woollacott, Richard Harding, Maggie Coulthard, Dee Jackson, Sashsa, Hattie, Ian Shepherd of Brighton Draws Men, John Andow, Naomi Berry, Lewis, Anne Crumpton, Paul Berry, Sue, Moses, and Felix Clement.

Thank you also to Jose Walker for photography, and the White Moose Gallery for encouragement and for bringing together many of the models.

Thank you to the Ilex publishing team, especially Zara Anvari and Ellie Wilson for their support and wise editing, also Ben Gardiner (art director), Ellie Corbett (editor) and Caroline Alberti (production).

The publisher would like to thank the following agencies for permission to use their images as reference: MangoStar_Studio/iStock; WarrenGoldswain/iStock

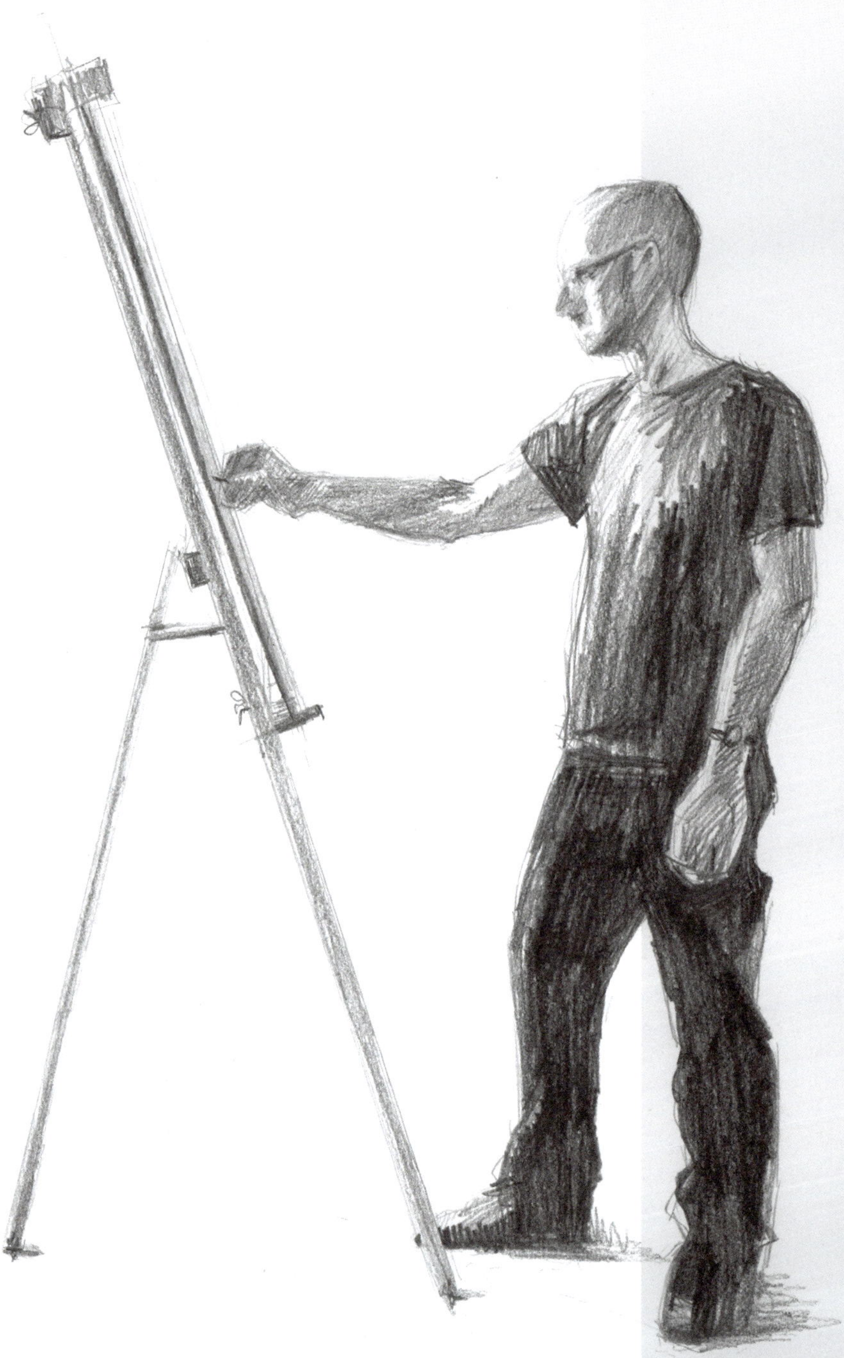